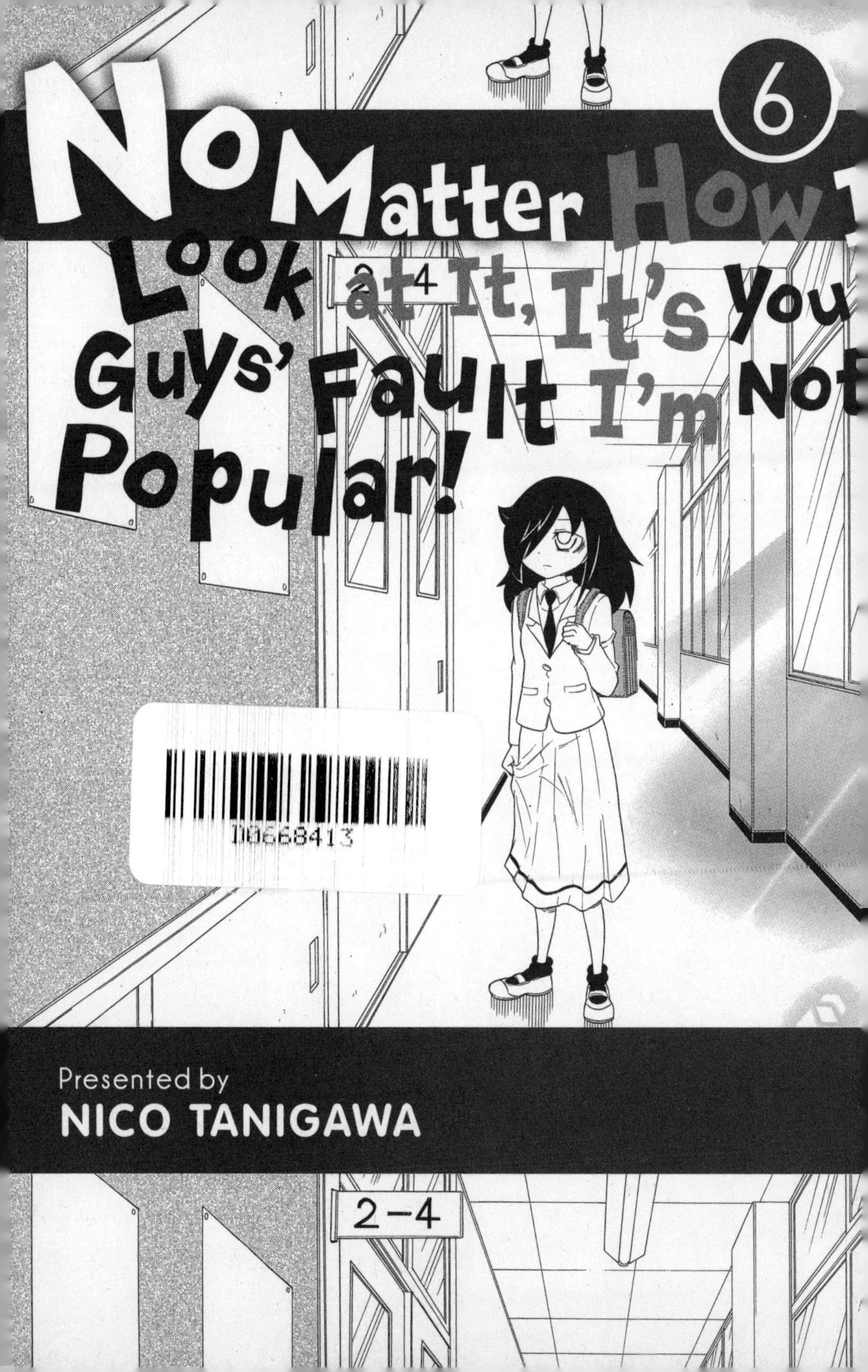
6
No Matter How I Look at It, It's You Guys' Fault I'm Not Popular!
2-4
Presented by
NICO TANIGAWA
2-4

FAIL 47 I'M NOT POPULAR, SO ▶ I'LL REMEMBER AN OLD ACQUAINTANCE. 003

FAIL 48 I'M NOT POPULAR, SO ▶ I'LL FIGHT LOW-KEY. 017

FAIL 49 I'M NOT POPULAR, SO ▶ I'LL DECIDE WHERE TO GO. 027

FAIL 50 I'M NOT POPULAR, SO ▶ I'LL HANG OUT BY MYSELF IN A TWILIT CLASSROOM. 037

FAIL 51 I'M NOT POPULAR, SO ▶ I'LL TAKE NOTICE OF THE SAME SEX. 053

FAIL 52 I'M NOT POPULAR, SO ▶ I'LL WRITE A SONG. 061

FAIL 53 I'M NOT POPULAR, SO ▶ SOMETHING GOOD WILL HAPPEN. 069

FAIL 54 I'M NOT POPULAR, SO ▶ I WON'T CHANGE. 081

FAIL 55 I'M NOT POPULAR, SO ▶ IT'S TANABATA. 099

SPECIAL CHAPTER 3 111

...AWW, IF I'D BEEN A WORM, I WOULD'VE HAD A MAN FROM THE GET-GO AND DEFINITELY HAVE HAD SEX, NOT TO MENTION KIDS...

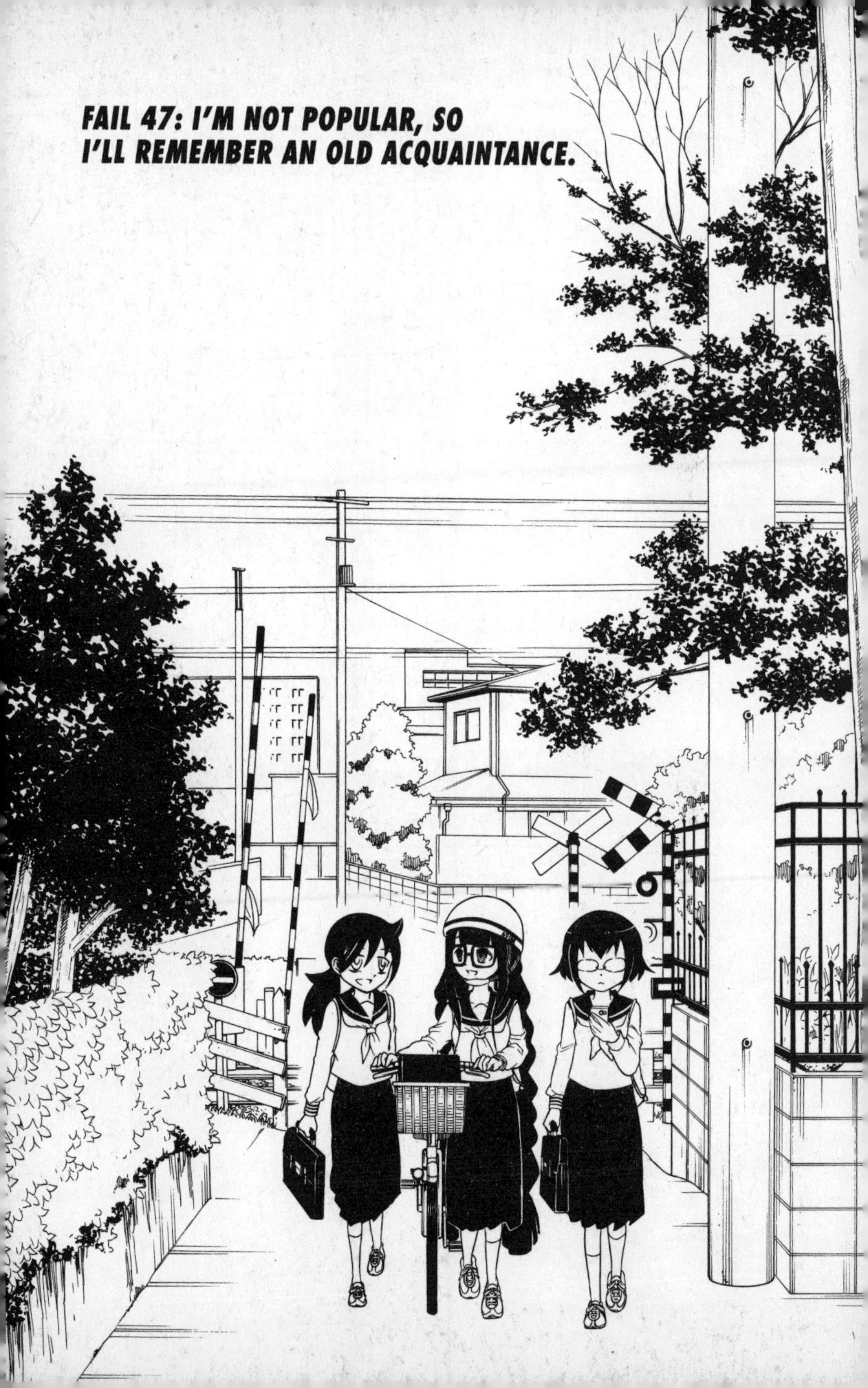
FAIL 47: I'M NOT POPULAR, SO
I'LL REMEMBER AN OLD ACQUAINTANCE.

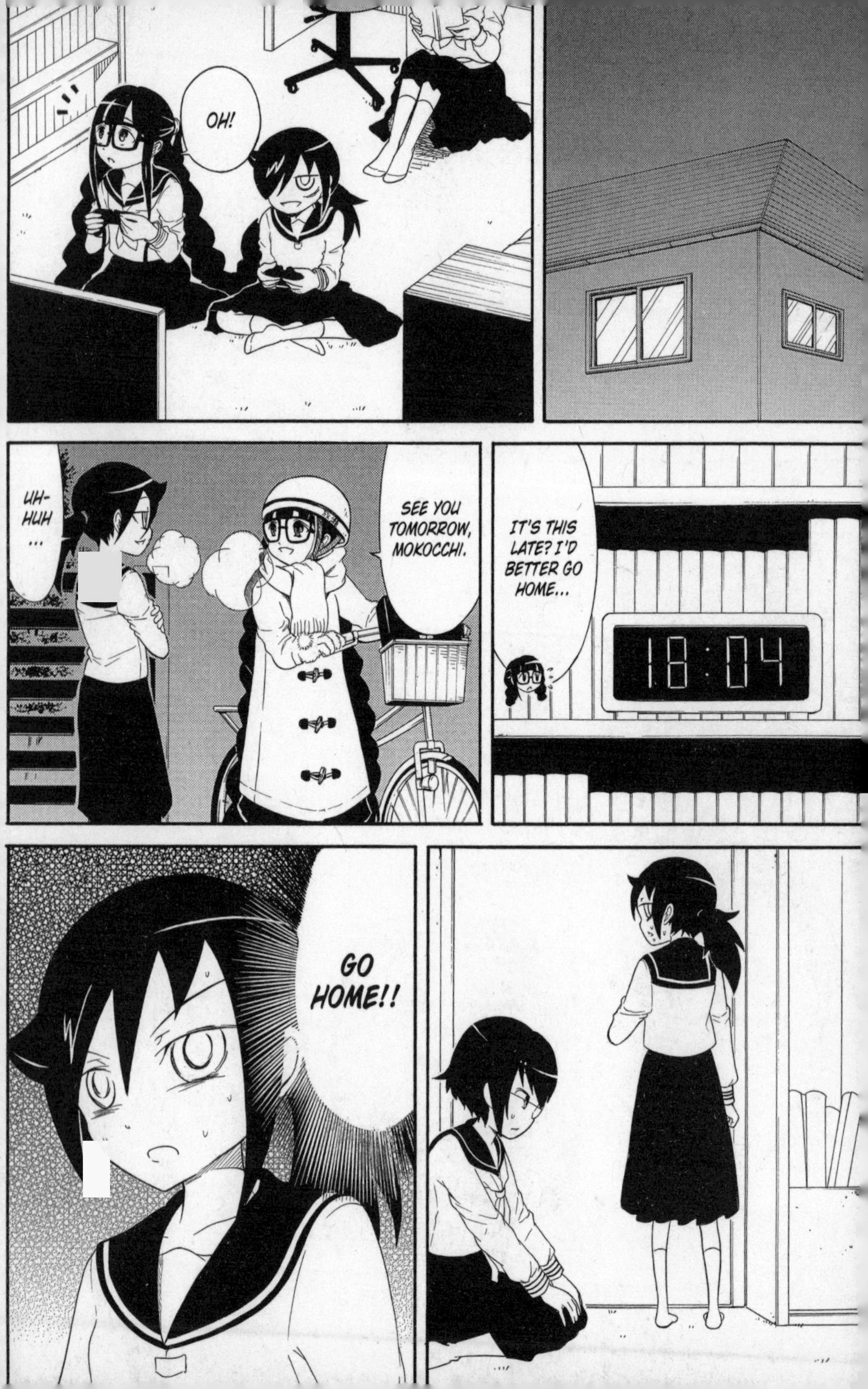
OH!
IT'S THIS LATE? I'D BETTER GO HOME...
18:04
SEE YOU TOMORROW, MOKOCCHI.
UH-HUH...
GO HOME!!

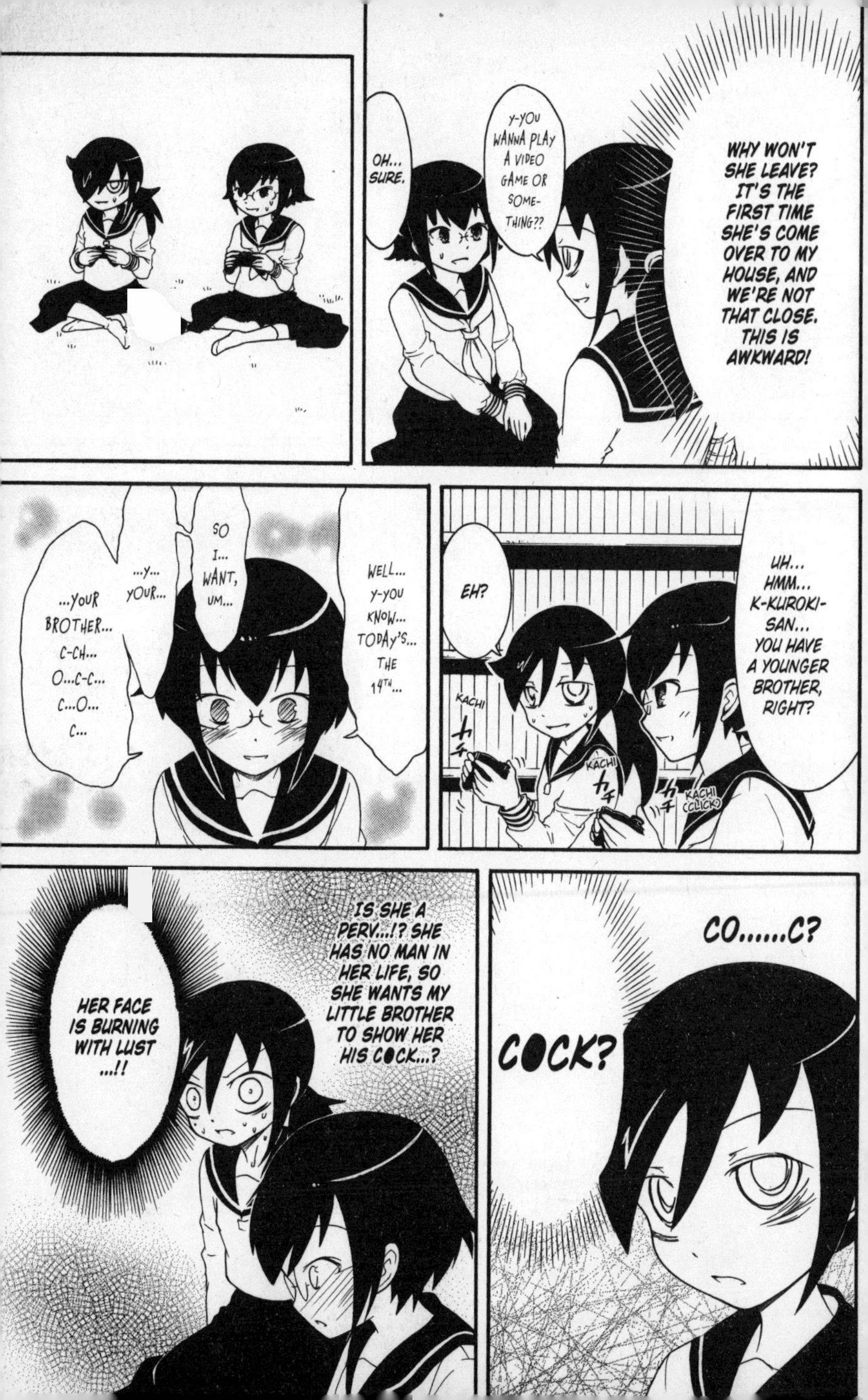
WHY WON'T SHE LEAVE? IT'S THE FIRST TIME SHE'S COME OVER TO MY HOUSE, AND WE'RE NOT THAT CLOSE. THIS IS AWKWARD!
Y-YOU WANNA PLAY A VIDEO GAME OR SOME-THING??
OH... SURE.
UH... HMM... K-KUROKI-SAN... YOU HAVE A YOUNGER BROTHER, RIGHT?
KACHI (CLICK)
KACHI
KACHI
EH?
WELL... Y-YOU KNOW... TODAY'S... THE 14TH...
SO I... WANT, UM...
...Y... YOUR...
...YOUR BROTHER... C-CH... O...C-C... C...O... C...
CO......C?
COCK?
IS SHE A PERV...!? SHE HAS NO MAN IN HER LIFE, SO SHE WANTS MY LITTLE BROTHER TO SHOW HER HIS COCK...?
HER FACE IS BURNING WITH LUST ...!!

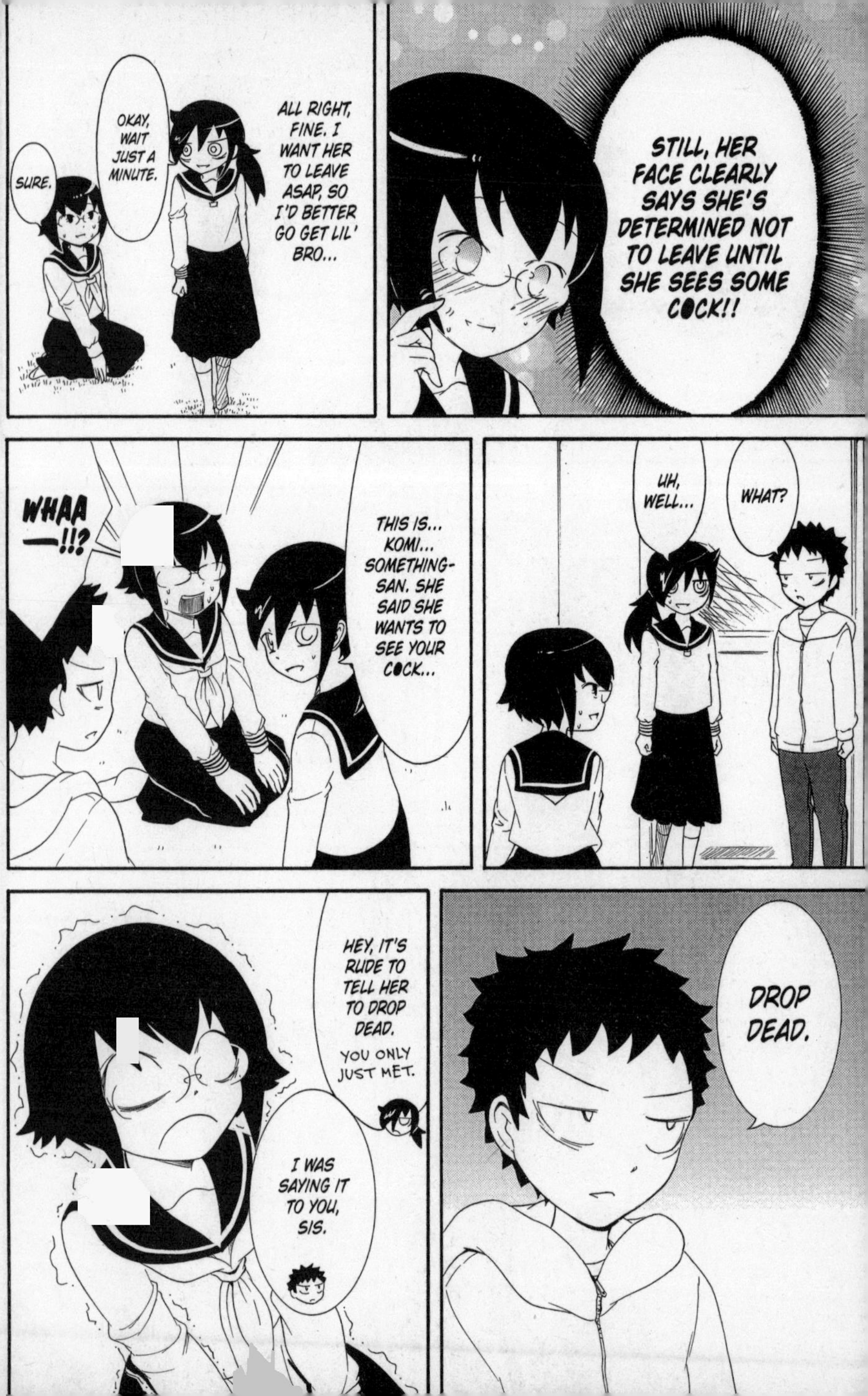
STILL, HER FACE CLEARLY SAYS SHE'S DETERMINED NOT TO LEAVE UNTIL SHE SEES SOME COCK!!
ALL RIGHT, FINE. I WANT HER TO LEAVE ASAP, SO I'D BETTER GO GET LIL' BRO...
OKAY, WAIT JUST A MINUTE.
SURE.
WHAT?
UH, WELL...
THIS IS... KOMI... SOMETHING-SAN. SHE SAID SHE WANTS TO SEE YOUR COCK...
WHAA—!!?
DROP DEAD.
HEY, IT'S RUDE TO TELL HER TO DROP DEAD.
YOU ONLY JUST MET.
I WAS SAYING IT TO YOU, SIS.

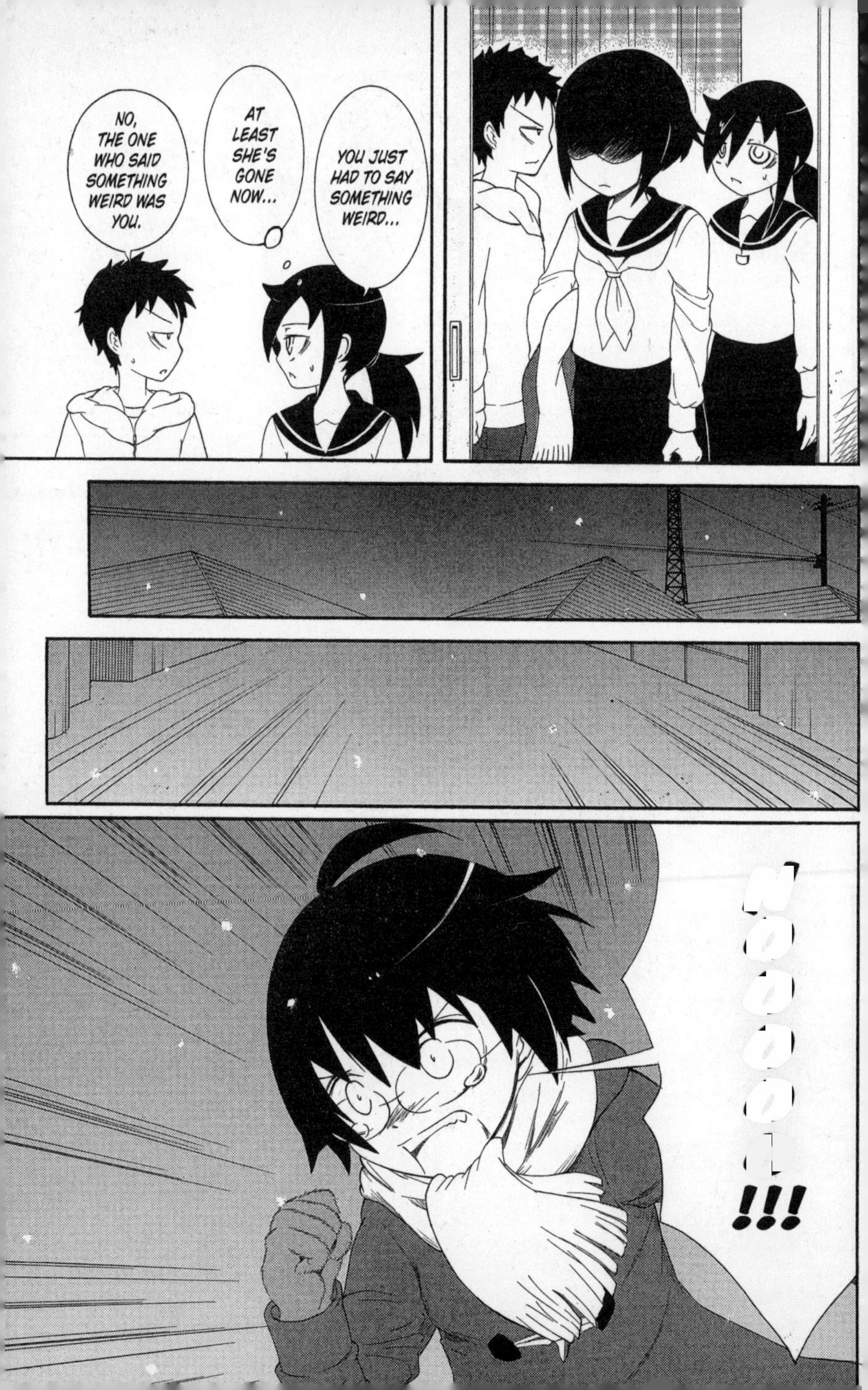
YOU JUST HAD TO SAY SOMETHING WEIRD...
AT LEAST SHE'S GONE NOW...
NO, THE ONE WHO SAID SOMETHING WEIRD WAS YOU.
NOOOOO!!!

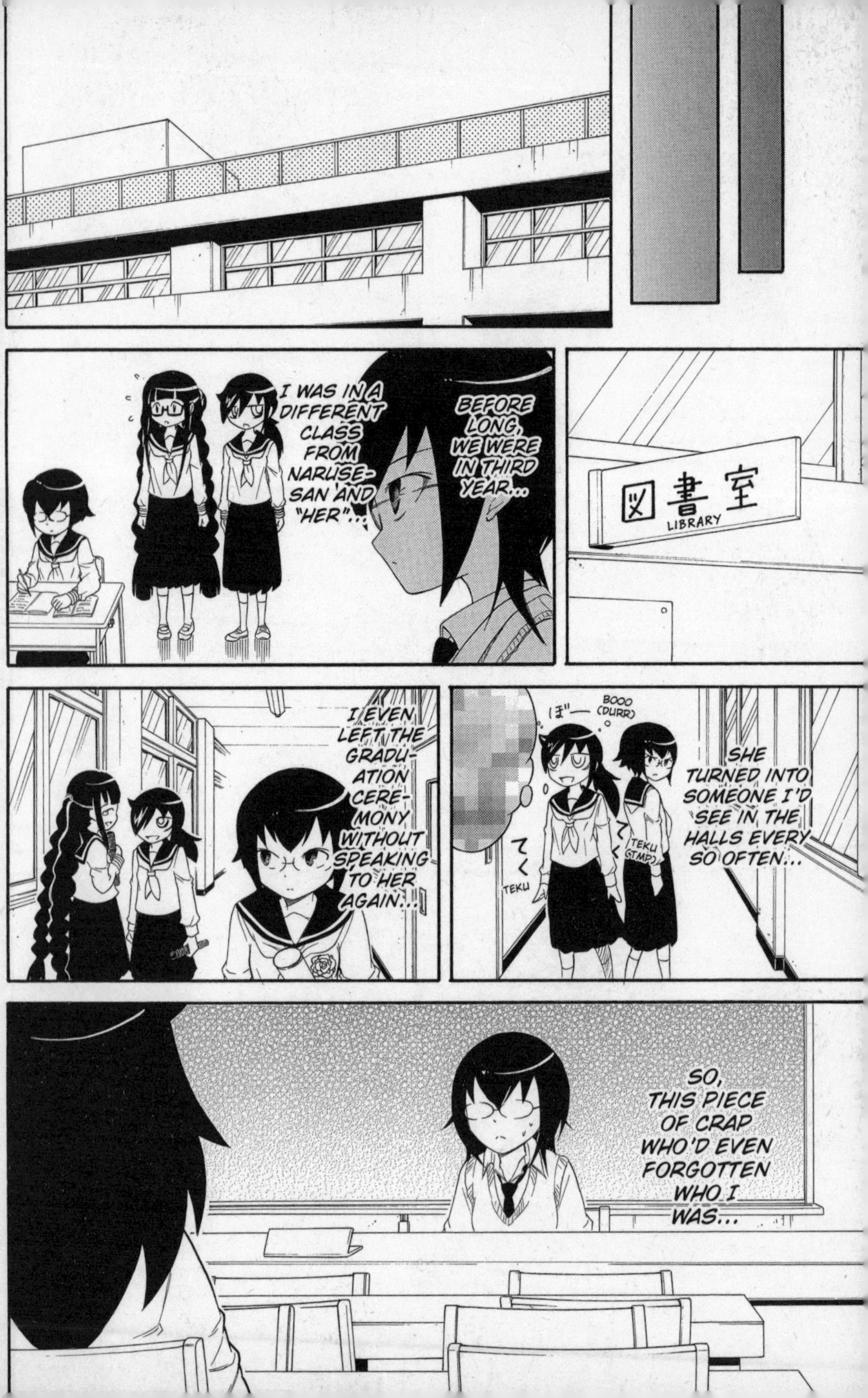
図書室
LIBRARY
BEFORE LONG, WE WERE IN THIRD YEAR...
I WAS IN A DIFFERENT CLASS FROM NARUSE-SAN AND "HER"...
ぼー BOOO (DURR)
SHE TURNED INTO SOMEONE I'D SEE IN THE HALLS EVERY SO OFTEN...
てく TEKU (STMP)
てく TEKU
I EVEN LEFT THE GRADUATION CEREMONY WITHOUT SPEAKING TO HER AGAIN...
SO, THIS PIECE OF CRAP WHO'D EVEN FORGOTTEN WHO I WAS...

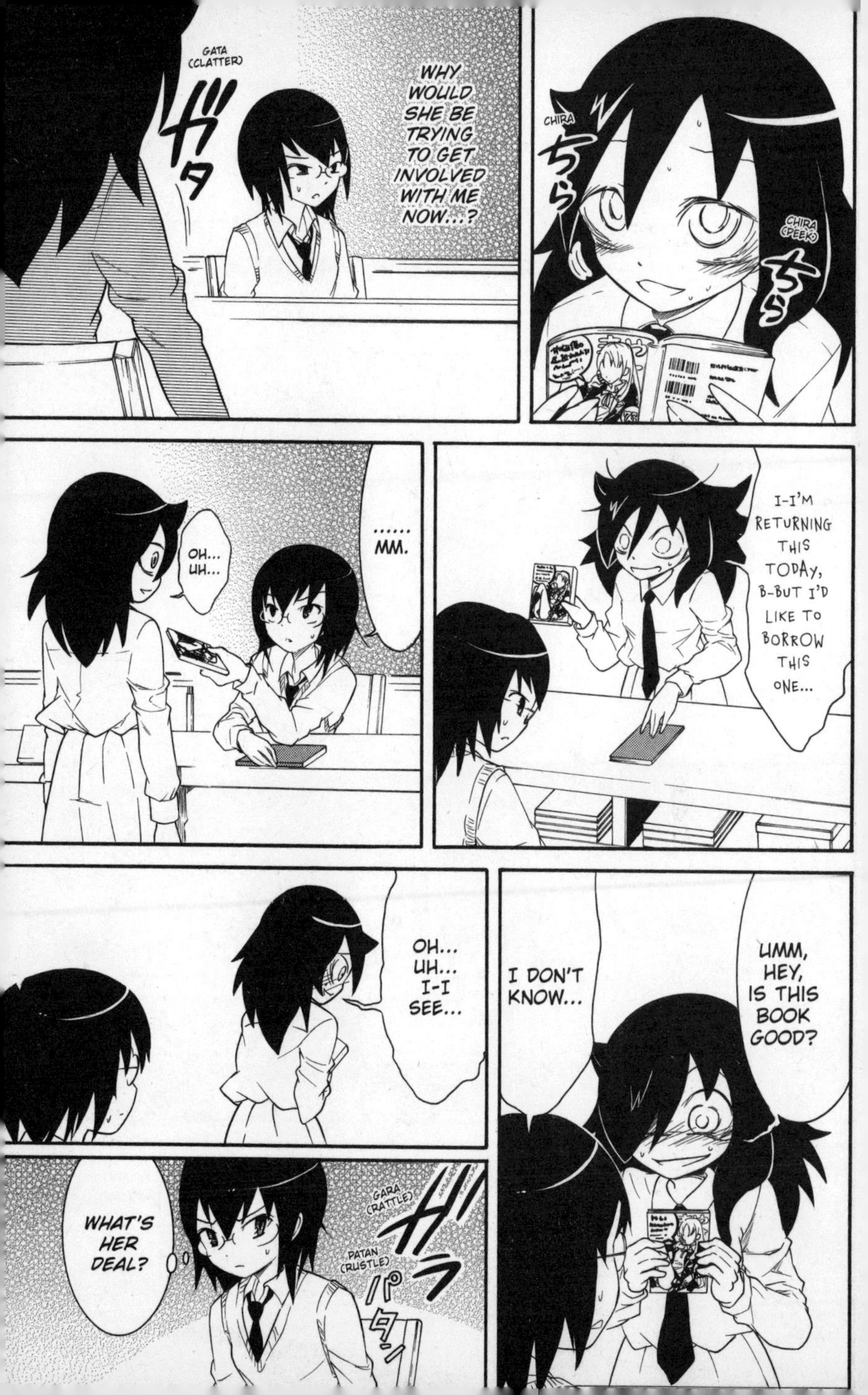

CHIRA
ちら
CHIRA (PEEK)
ちら
WHY WOULD SHE BE TRYING TO GET INVOLVED WITH ME NOW...?
GATA (CLATTER)
ガタ
I-I'M RETURNING THIS TODAY, B-BUT I'D LIKE TO BORROW THIS ONE...
......MM.
OH... UH...
UMM, HEY, IS THIS BOOK GOOD?
I DON'T KNOW...
OH... UH... I-I SEE...
GARA (RATTLE)
ガラ
PATAN (RUSTLE)
パタン
WHAT'S HER DEAL?

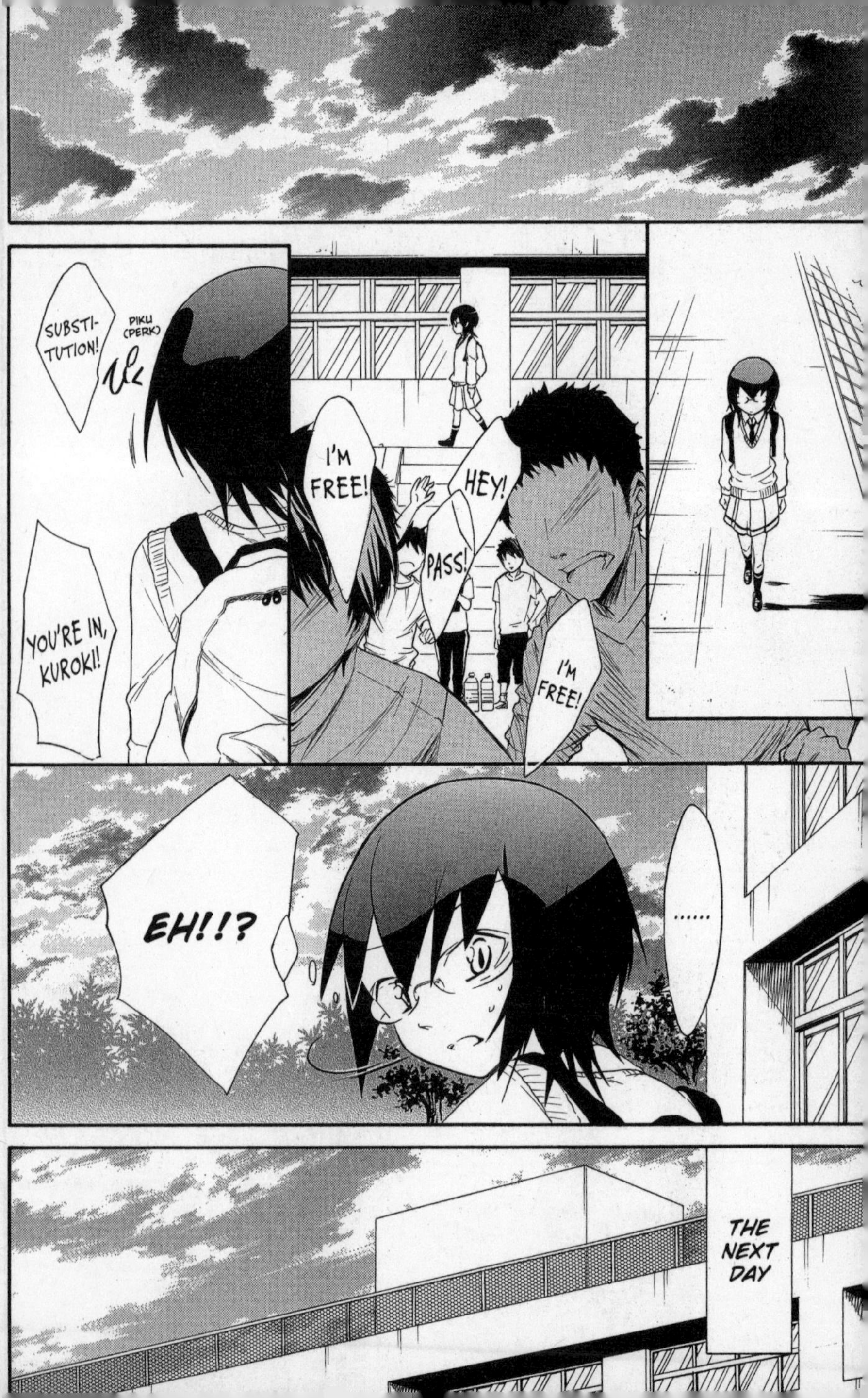
HEY!
I'M FREE!
PASS!
I'M FREE!
SUBSTI-TUTION!
PIKU (PERK)
YOU'RE IN, KUROKI!
......
EH!!?
THE NEXT DAY

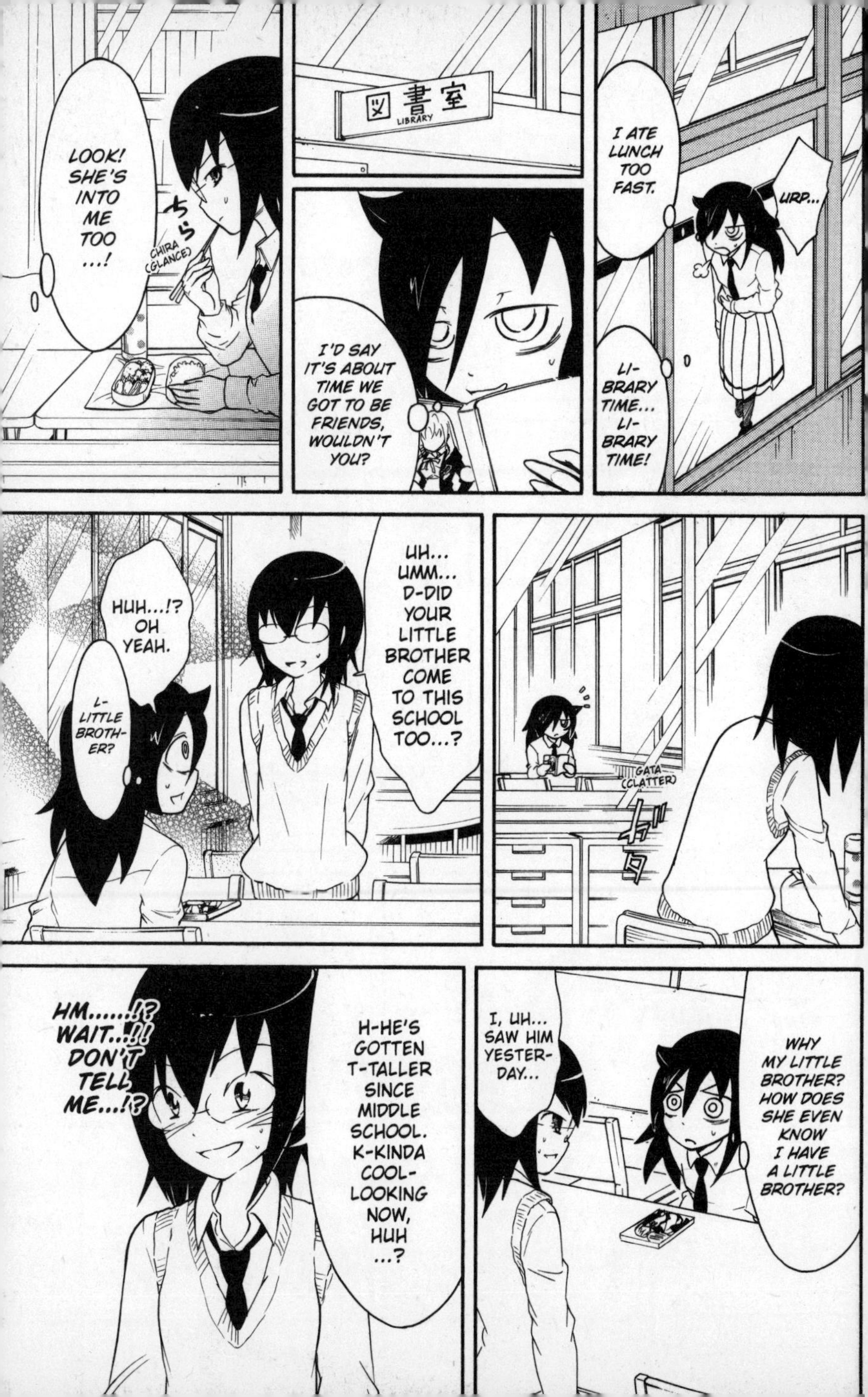

I ATE LUNCH TOO FAST.
URP...
LI-BRARY TIME... LI-BRARY TIME!
図書室
LIBRARY
I'D SAY IT'S ABOUT TIME WE GOT TO BE FRIENDS, WOULDN'T YOU?
ちら
CHIRA (GLANCE)
LOOK! SHE'S INTO ME TOO ...!
GATA (CLATTER)
ガタ
UH... UMM... D-DID YOUR LITTLE BROTHER COME TO THIS SCHOOL TOO...?
HUH...!? OH YEAH.
L-LITTLE BROTHER?
WHY MY LITTLE BROTHER? HOW DOES SHE EVEN KNOW I HAVE A LITTLE BROTHER?
I, UH... SAW HIM YESTERDAY...
H-HE'S GOTTEN T-TALLER SINCE MIDDLE SCHOOL. K-KINDA COOL-LOOKING NOW, HUH ...?
HM......!? WAIT...!! DON'T TELL ME...!?

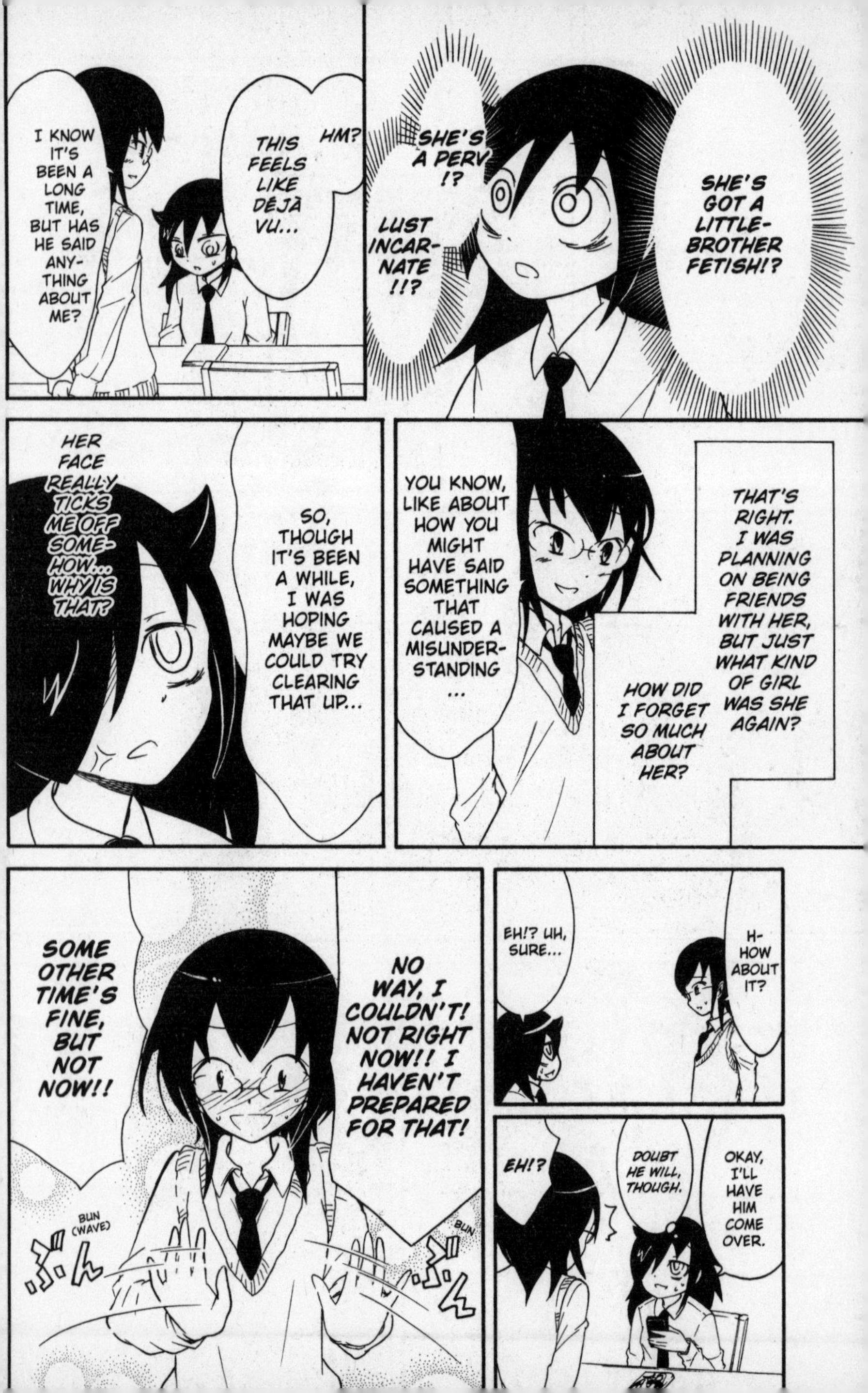
SHE'S GOT A LITTLE-BROTHER FETISH!?
SHE'S A PERV!?
LUST INCARNATE!!?
HM?
THIS FEELS LIKE DÉJÀ VU...
I KNOW IT'S BEEN A LONG TIME, BUT HAS HE SAID ANYTHING ABOUT ME?
THAT'S RIGHT. I WAS PLANNING ON BEING FRIENDS WITH HER, BUT JUST WHAT KIND OF GIRL WAS SHE AGAIN?
HOW DID I FORGET SO MUCH ABOUT HER?
YOU KNOW, LIKE ABOUT HOW YOU MIGHT HAVE SAID SOMETHING THAT CAUSED A MISUNDERSTANDING...
SO, THOUGH IT'S BEEN A WHILE, I WAS HOPING MAYBE WE COULD TRY CLEARING THAT UP...
HER FACE REALLY TICKS ME OFF SOMEHOW... WHY IS THAT?
H-HOW ABOUT IT?
EH!? UH, SURE...
OKAY, I'LL HAVE HIM COME OVER.
DOUBT HE WILL, THOUGH.
EH!?
NO WAY, I COULDN'T! NOT RIGHT NOW!! I HAVEN'T PREPARED FOR THAT!
SOME OTHER TIME'S FINE, BUT NOT NOW!!
BUN
ぶん
BUN (WAVE)
ぶん

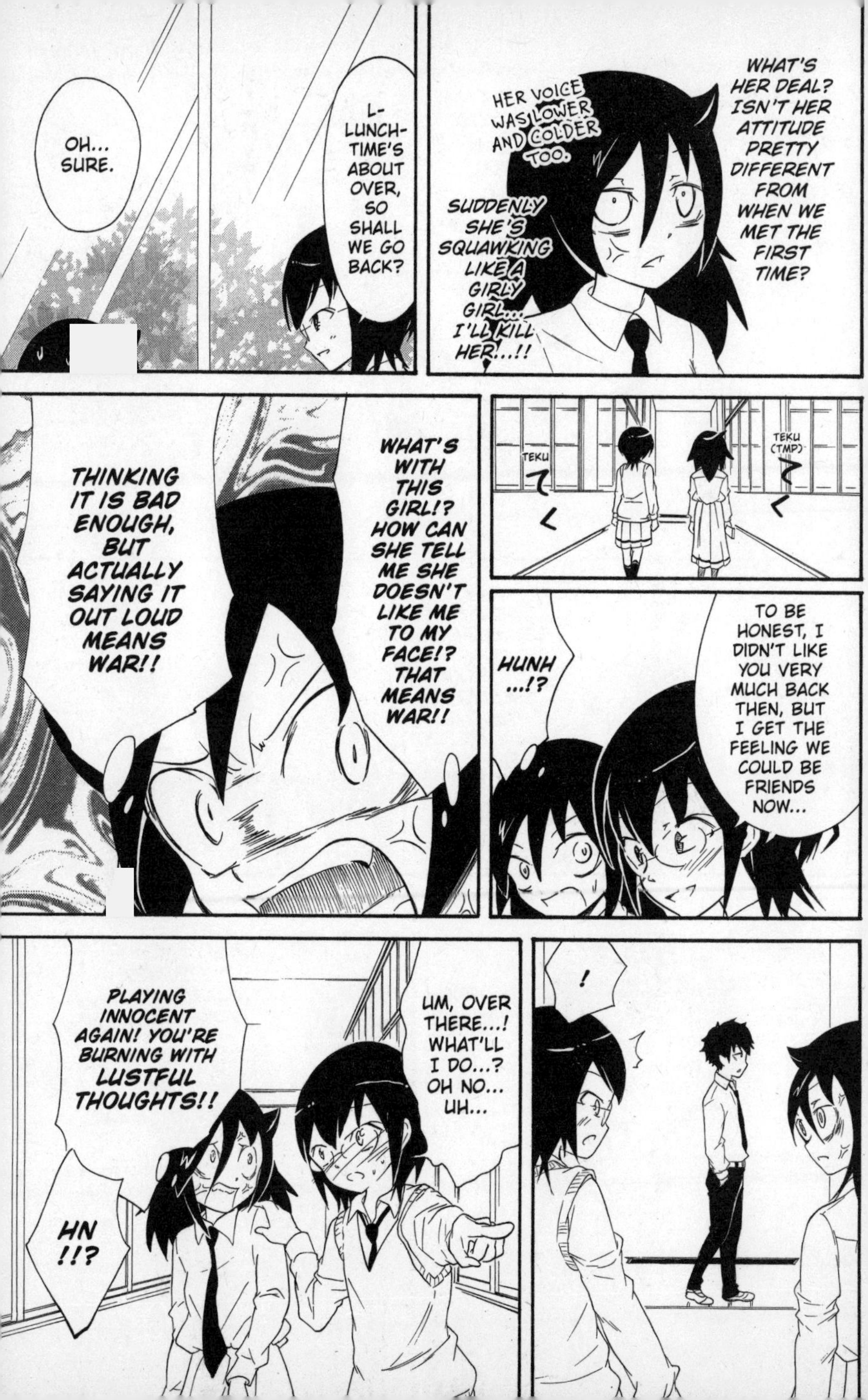
WHAT'S HER DEAL? ISN'T HER ATTITUDE PRETTY DIFFERENT FROM WHEN WE MET THE FIRST TIME?
HER VOICE WAS LOWER AND COLDER TOO.
SUDDENLY SHE'S SQUAWKING LIKE A GIRLY GIRL... I'LL KILL HER...!!
L-LUNCH-TIME'S ABOUT OVER, SO SHALL WE GO BACK?
OH... SURE.
TEKU (TMP)
TEKU
TO BE HONEST, I DIDN'T LIKE YOU VERY MUCH BACK THEN, BUT I GET THE FEELING WE COULD BE FRIENDS NOW...
HUNH ...!?
WHAT'S WITH THIS GIRL!? HOW CAN SHE TELL ME SHE DOESN'T LIKE ME TO MY FACE!? THAT MEANS WAR!!
THINKING IT IS BAD ENOUGH, BUT ACTUALLY SAYING IT OUT LOUD MEANS WAR!!
!
UM, OVER THERE...! WHAT'LL I DO...? OH NO... UH...
PLAYING INNOCENT AGAIN! YOU'RE BURNING WITH LUSTFUL THOUGHTS!!
HN !!?

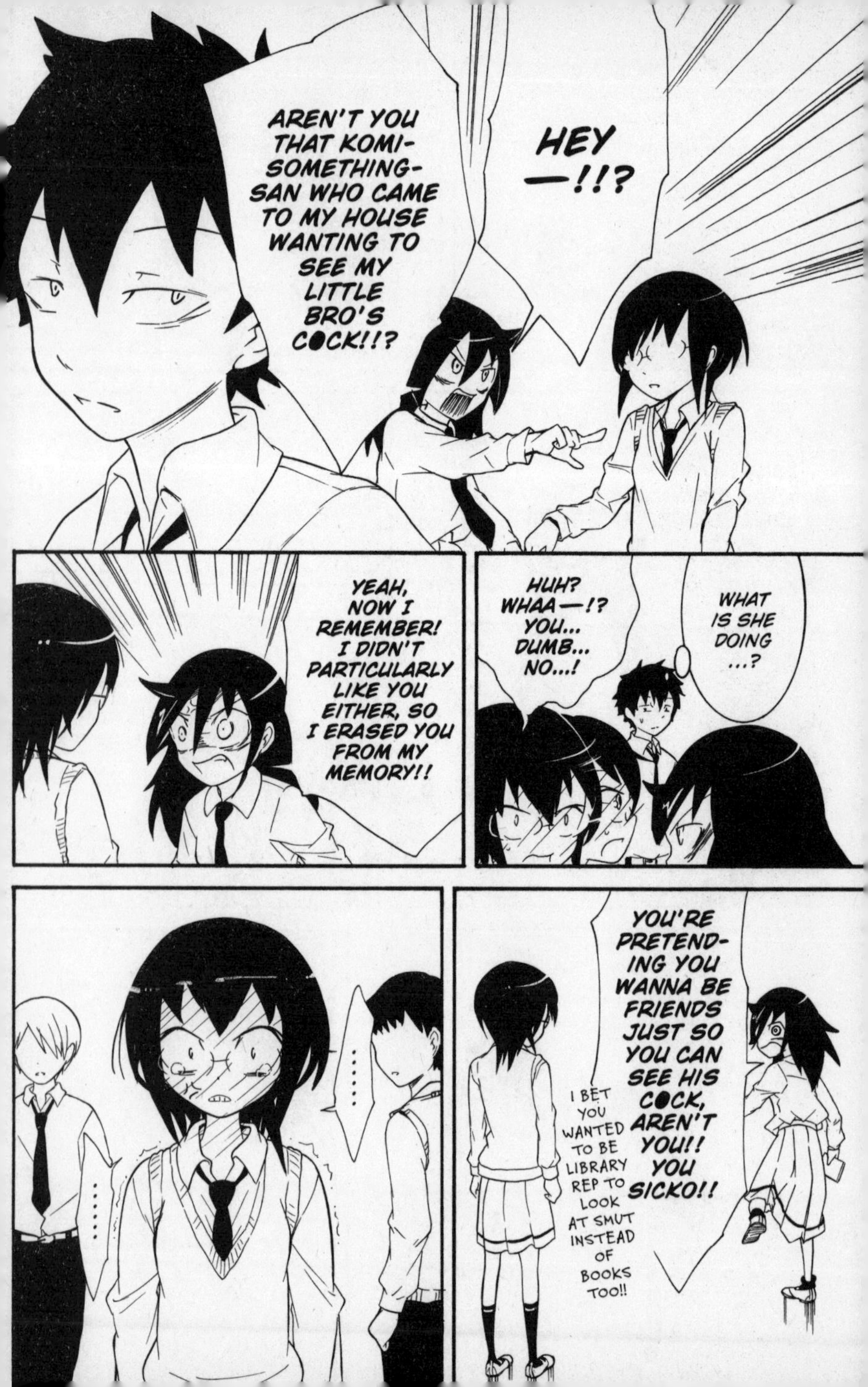
HEY—!!?
AREN'T YOU THAT KOMI-SOMETHING-SAN WHO CAME TO MY HOUSE WANTING TO SEE MY LITTLE BRO'S COCK!!?
WHAT IS SHE DOING ...?
HUH? WHAA—!? YOU... DUMB... NO...!
YEAH, NOW I REMEMBER! I DIDN'T PARTICULARLY LIKE YOU EITHER, SO I ERASED YOU FROM MY MEMORY!!
YOU'RE PRETEND-ING YOU WANNA BE FRIENDS JUST SO YOU CAN SEE HIS COCK, AREN'T YOU!! YOU SICKO!!
I BET YOU WANTED TO BE LIBRARY REP TO LOOK AT SMUT INSTEAD OF BOOKS TOO!!
......
......

No Matter How I Look at It, It's You Guys' Fault I'm Not Popular!

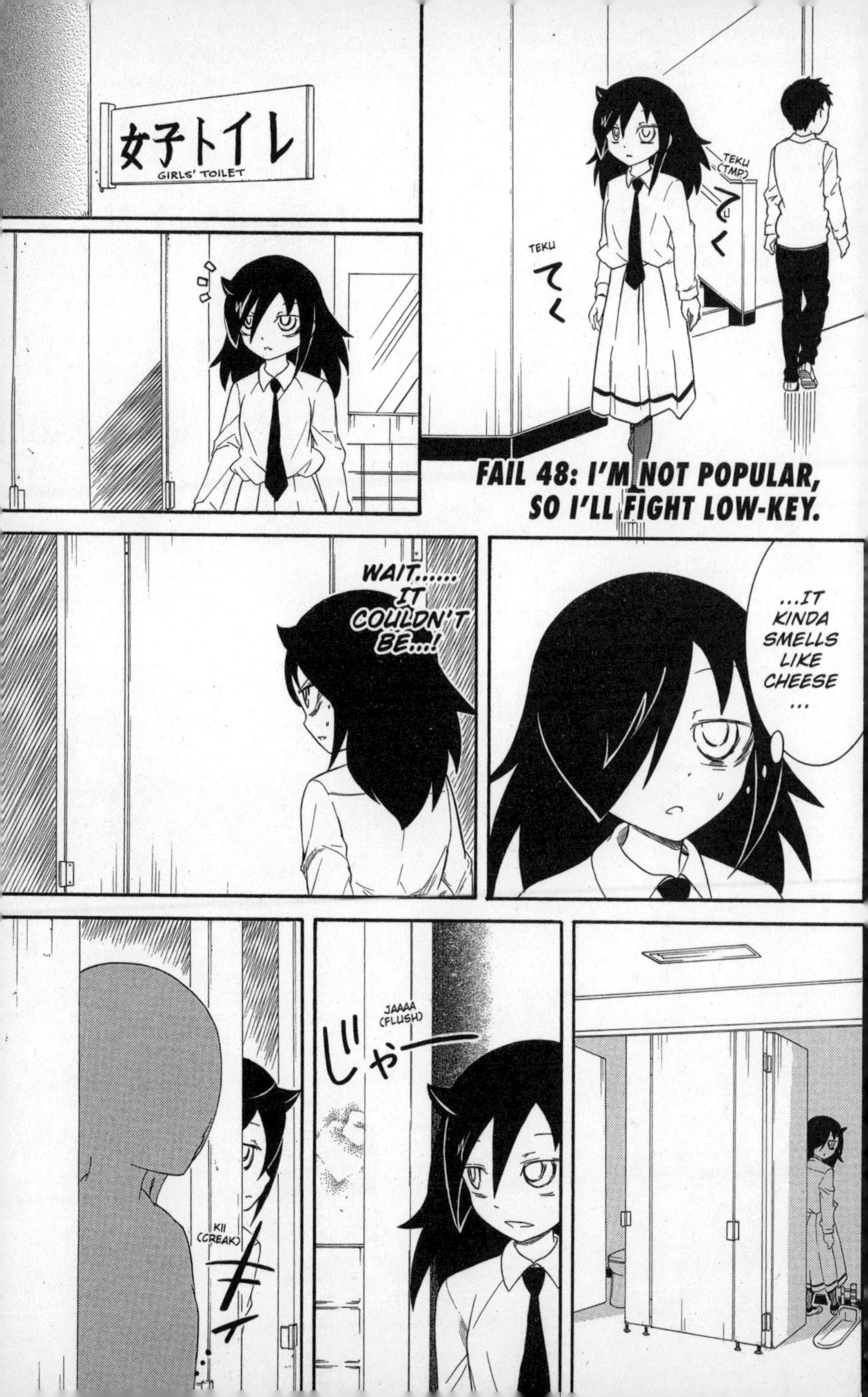
TEKU (TMP)
てく
TEKU
てく
FAIL 48: I'M NOT POPULAR, SO I'LL FIGHT LOW-KEY.
女子トイレ
GIRLS' TOILET
...IT KINDA SMELLS LIKE CHEESE ...
WAIT...... IT COULDN'T BE...!
JAAAA (FLUSH)
じゃー
KII (CREAK)
キィ

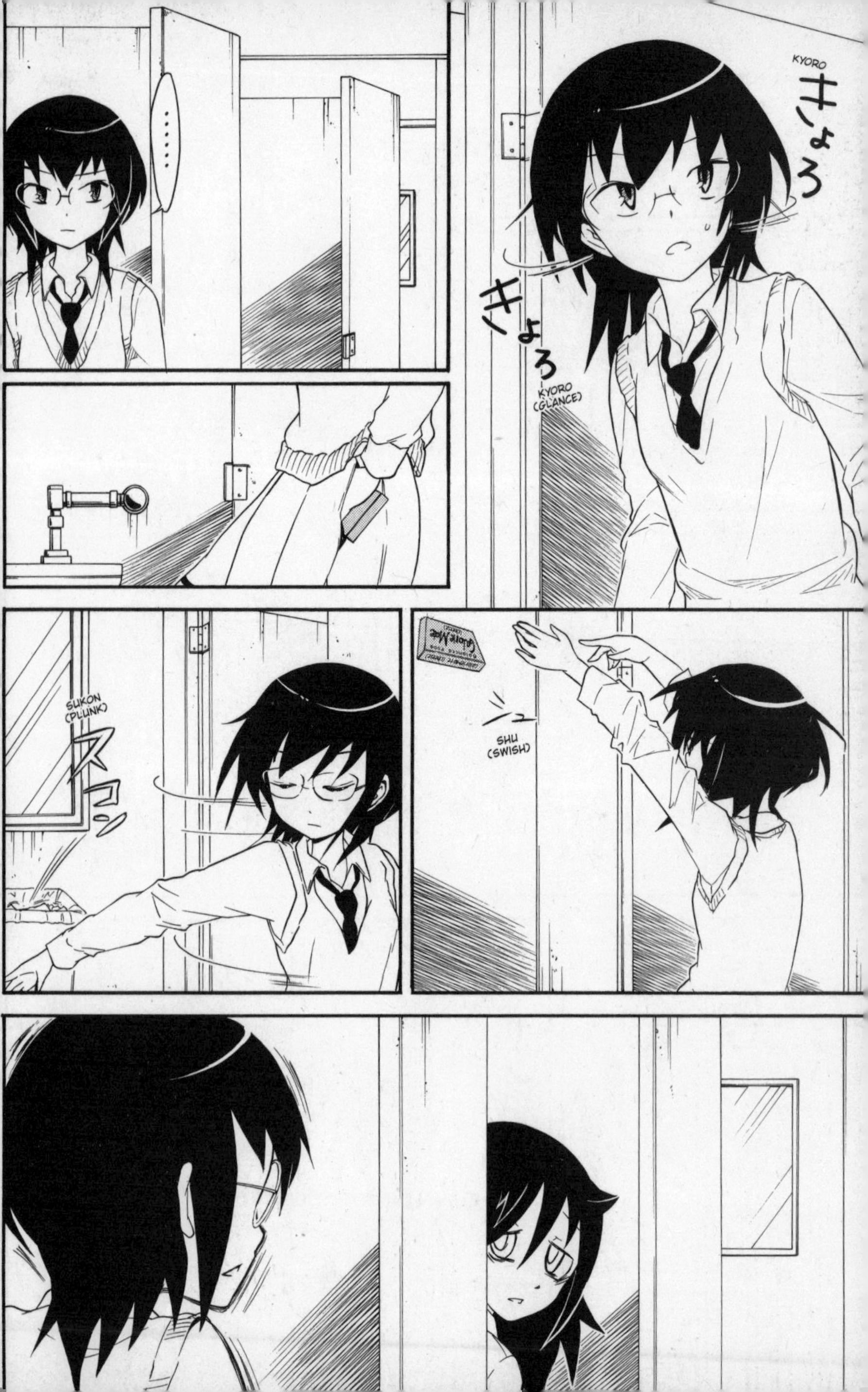
KYORO
きょろ
きょろ
KYORO (GLANCE)
......
SHU (SWISH)
シュ
SUKON (PLUNK)
スコン

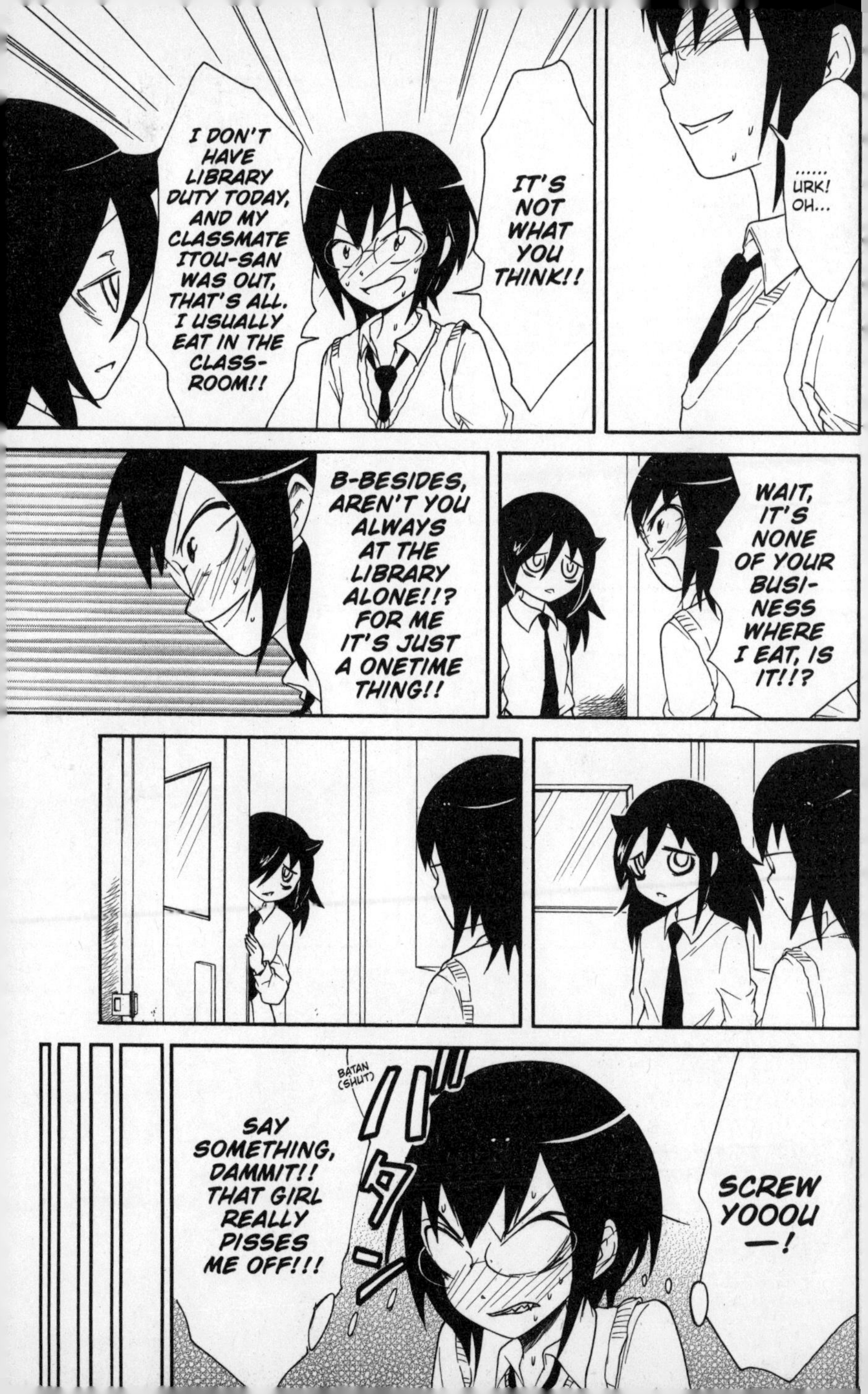
......URK! OH...
IT'S NOT WHAT YOU THINK!!
I DON'T HAVE LIBRARY DUTY TODAY, AND MY CLASSMATE ITOU-SAN WAS OUT, THAT'S ALL. I USUALLY EAT IN THE CLASS-ROOM!!
WAIT, IT'S NONE OF YOUR BUSI-NESS WHERE I EAT, IS IT!!?
B-BESIDES, AREN'T YOU ALWAYS AT THE LIBRARY ALONE!!? FOR ME IT'S JUST A ONETIME THING!!
SCREW YOOOU—!
BATAN (SHUT)
SAY SOMETHING, DAMMIT!! THAT GIRL REALLY PISSES ME OFF!!!

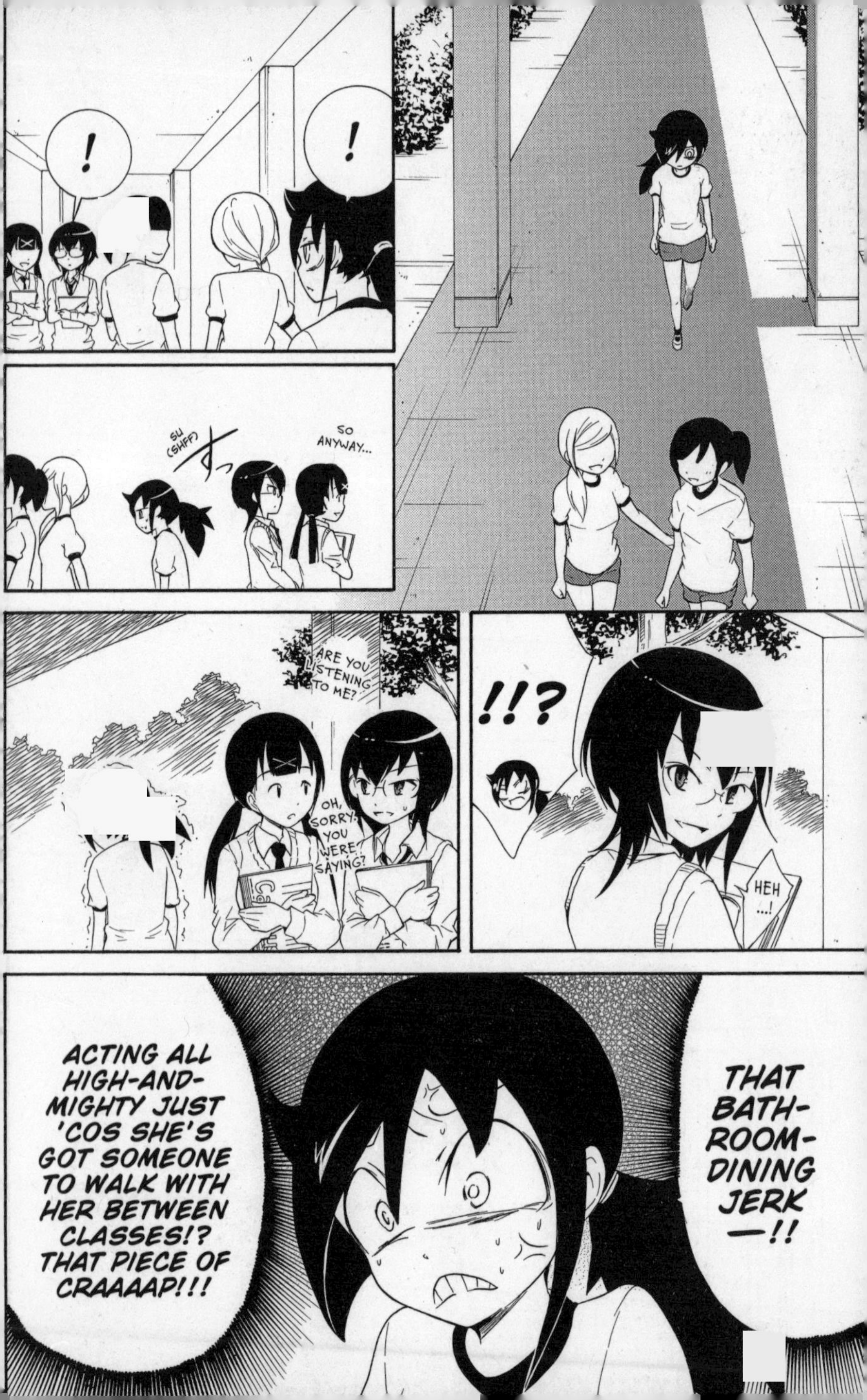
!
!
SO ANYWAY...
SU (SHFF)
すっ
!!?
HEH ...!
ARE YOU LISTENING TO ME?
OH, SORRY. YOU WERE SAYING?
THAT BATH-ROOM-DINING JERK—!!
ACTING ALL HIGH-AND-MIGHTY JUST 'COS SHE'S GOT SOMEONE TO WALK WITH HER BETWEEN CLASSES!? THAT PIECE OF CRAAAAP!!!

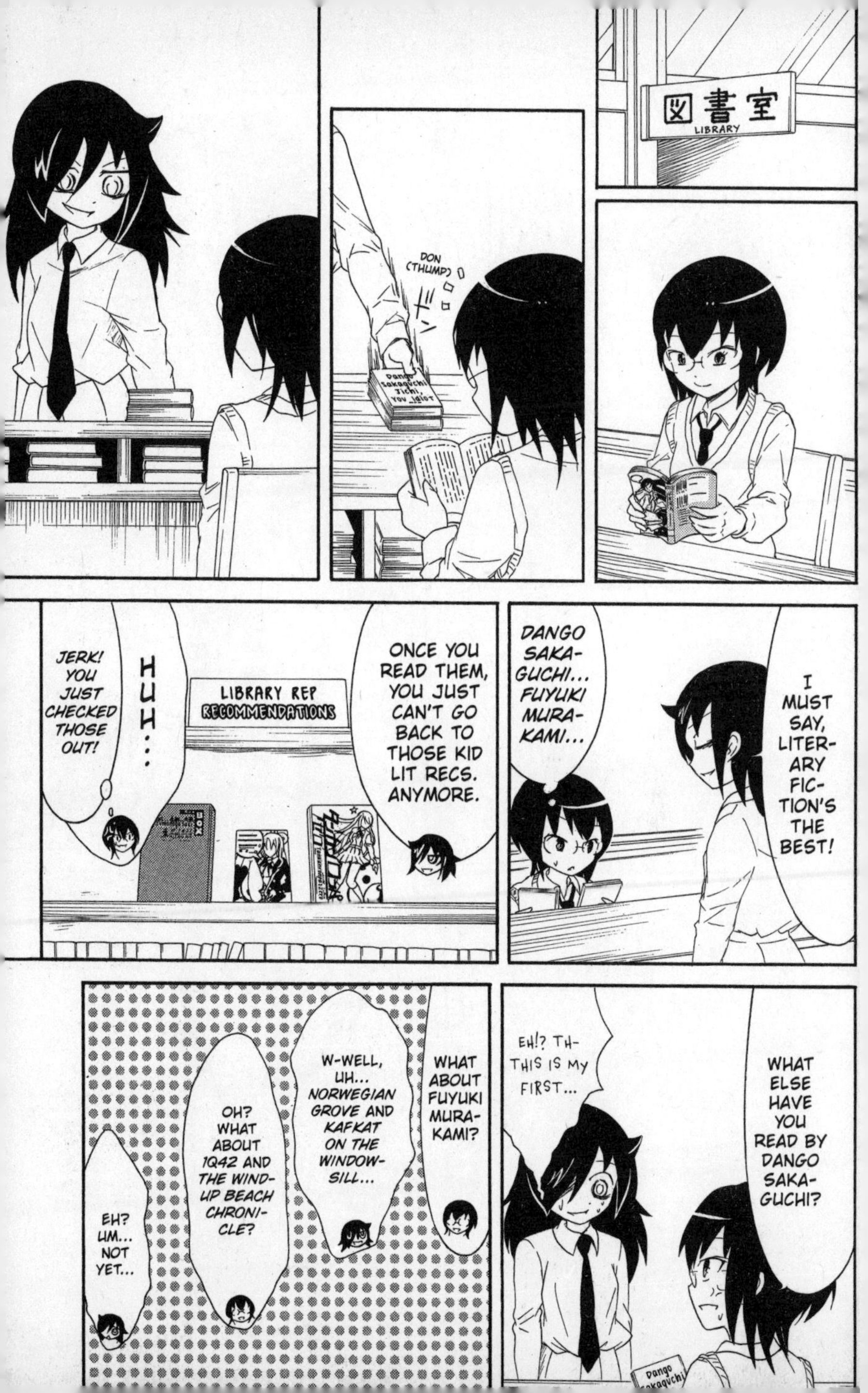
図書室
LIBRARY
DON (THUMP)
I MUST SAY, LITERARY FICTION'S THE BEST!
DANGO SAKAGUCHI... FUYUKI MURAKAMI...
ONCE YOU READ THEM, YOU JUST CAN'T GO BACK TO THOSE KID LIT RECS. ANYMORE.
LIBRARY REP RECOMMENDATIONS
HUH...
JERK! YOU JUST CHECKED THOSE OUT!
WHAT ELSE HAVE YOU READ BY DANGO SAKAGUCHI?
EH!? TH-THIS IS MY FIRST...
Dango Sakaguchi
WHAT ABOUT FUYUKI MURAKAMI?
W-WELL, UH... NORWEGIAN GROVE AND KAFKAT ON THE WINDOWSILL...
OH? WHAT ABOUT 1Q42 AND THE WIND-UP BEACH CHRONICLE?
EH? UM... NOT YET...

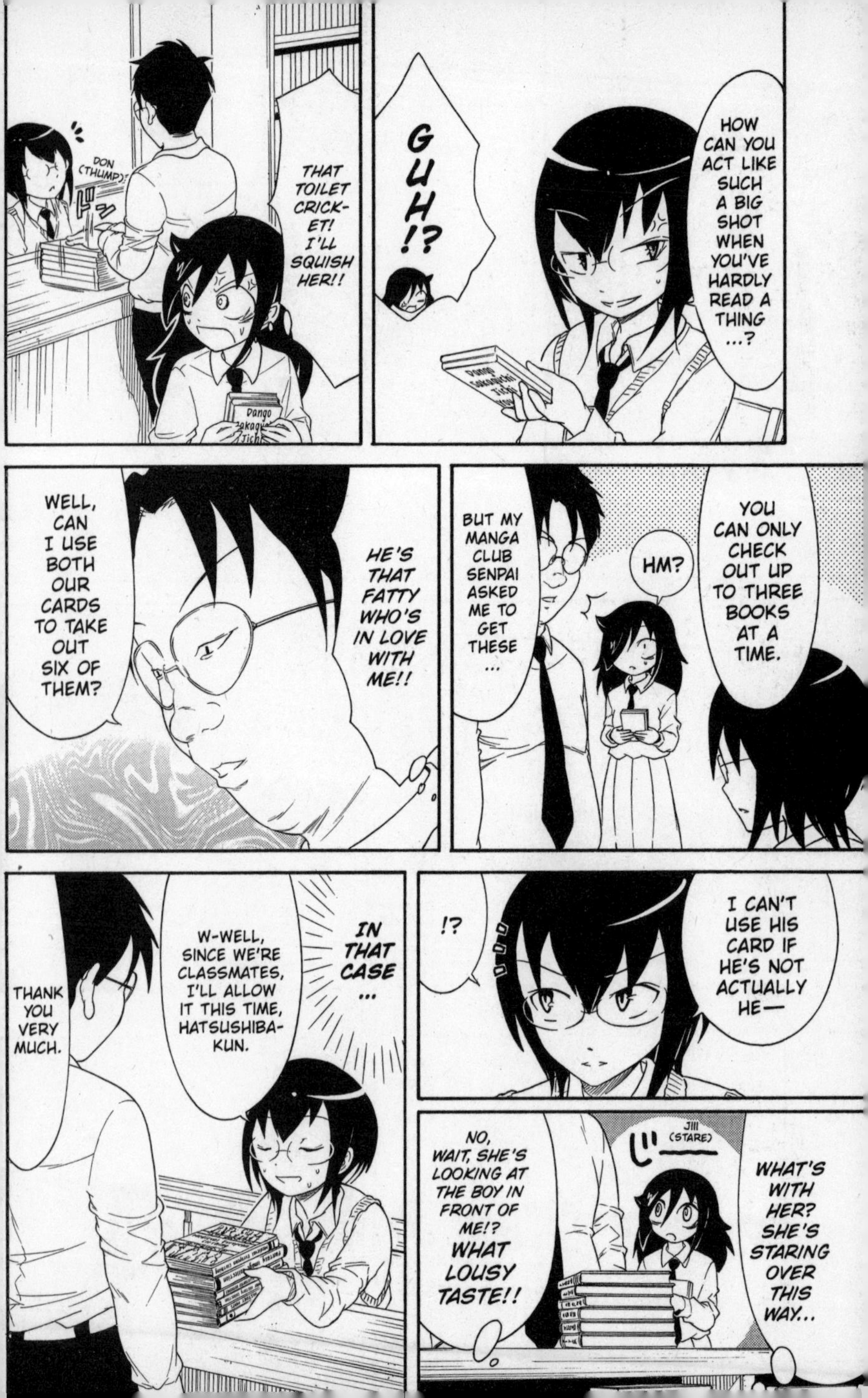
HOW CAN YOU ACT LIKE SUCH A BIG SHOT WHEN YOU'VE HARDLY READ A THING...?
GUH!?
THAT TOILET CRICKET! I'LL SQUISH HER!!
DON (THUMP)!?
YOU CAN ONLY CHECK OUT UP TO THREE BOOKS AT A TIME.
HM?
BUT MY MANGA CLUB SENPAI ASKED ME TO GET THESE...
HE'S THAT FATTY WHO'S IN LOVE WITH ME!!
WELL, CAN I USE BOTH OUR CARDS TO TAKE OUT SIX OF THEM?
I CAN'T USE HIS CARD IF HE'S NOT ACTUALLY HE—
!?
WHAT'S WITH HER? SHE'S STARING OVER THIS WAY...
JIII (STARE)
NO, WAIT, SHE'S LOOKING AT THE BOY IN FRONT OF ME!? WHAT LOUSY TASTE!!
IN THAT CASE...
W-WELL, SINCE WE'RE CLASSMATES, I'LL ALLOW IT THIS TIME, HATSUSHIBA-KUN.
THANK YOU VERY MUCH.

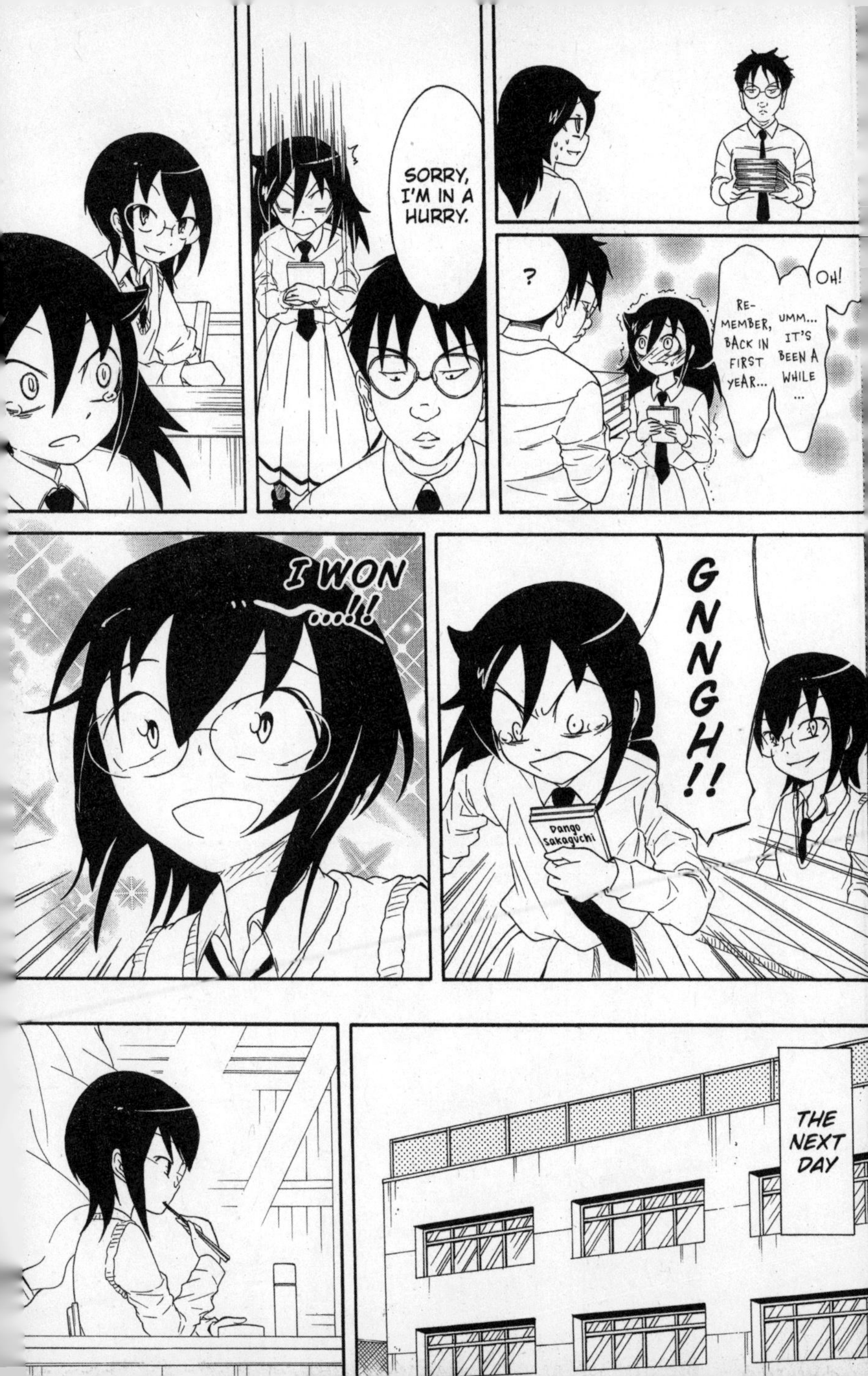
?
OH!
UMM... IT'S BEEN A WHILE ...
RE-MEMBER, BACK IN FIRST YEAR...
SORRY, I'M IN A HURRY.
GNNGH!!
Dango Sakaguchi
I WON ...!!
THE NEXT DAY

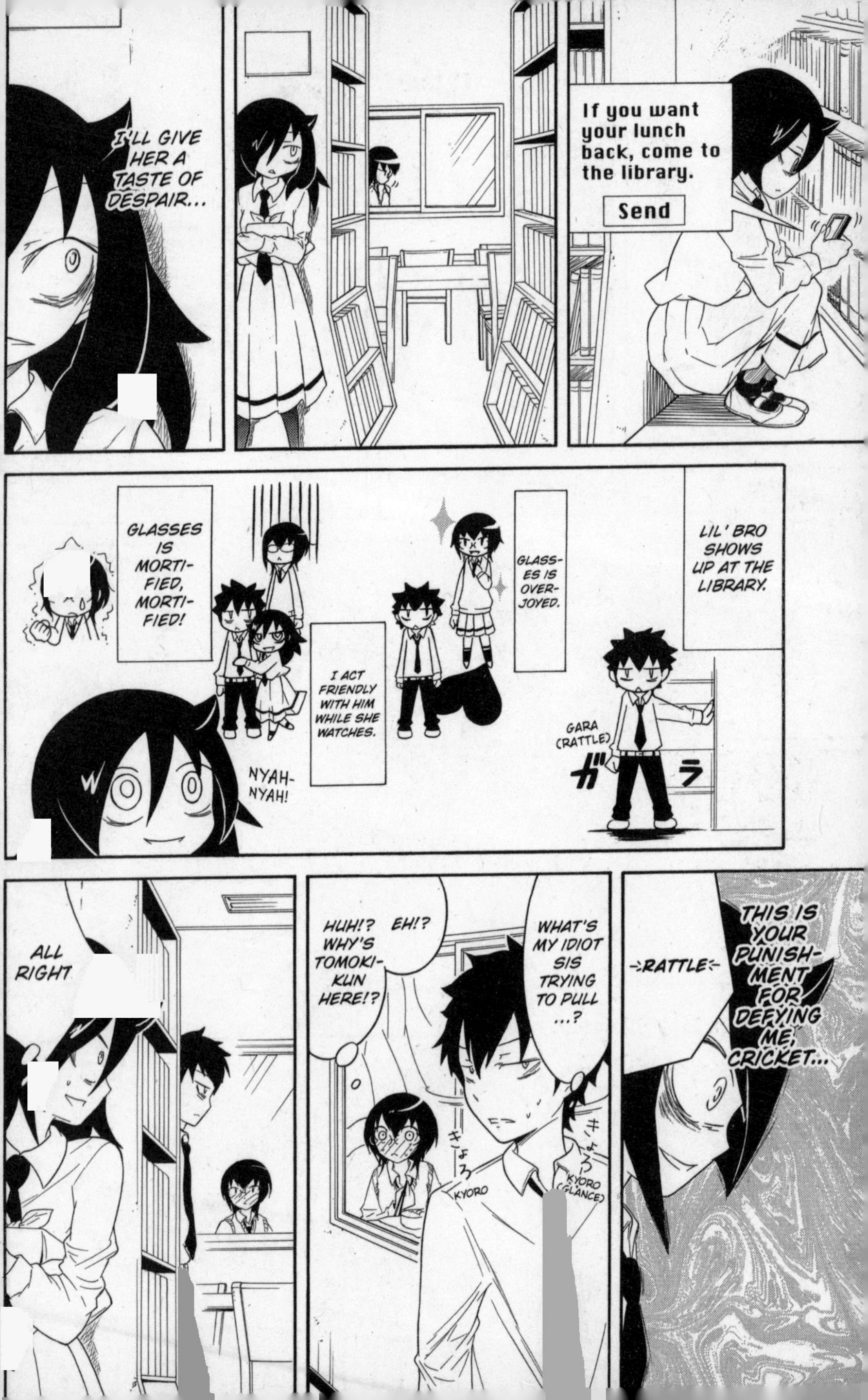
If you want your lunch back, come to the library.
Send
I'LL GIVE HER A TASTE OF DESPAIR...
LIL' BRO SHOWS UP AT THE LIBRARY.
GARA (RATTLE)
ガラ
GLASS-ES IS OVER-JOYED.
I ACT FRIENDLY WITH HIM WHILE SHE WATCHES.
NYAH-NYAH!
GLASSES IS MORTI-FIED, MORTI-FIED!
THIS IS YOUR PUNISH-MENT FOR DEFYING ME, CRICKET...
-RATTLE-
WHAT'S MY IDIOT SIS TRYING TO PULL ...?
きょろ!
KYORO (GLANCE)
EH!?
HUH!? WHY'S TOMOKI-KUN HERE!?
きょろ
KYORO
ALL RIGHT

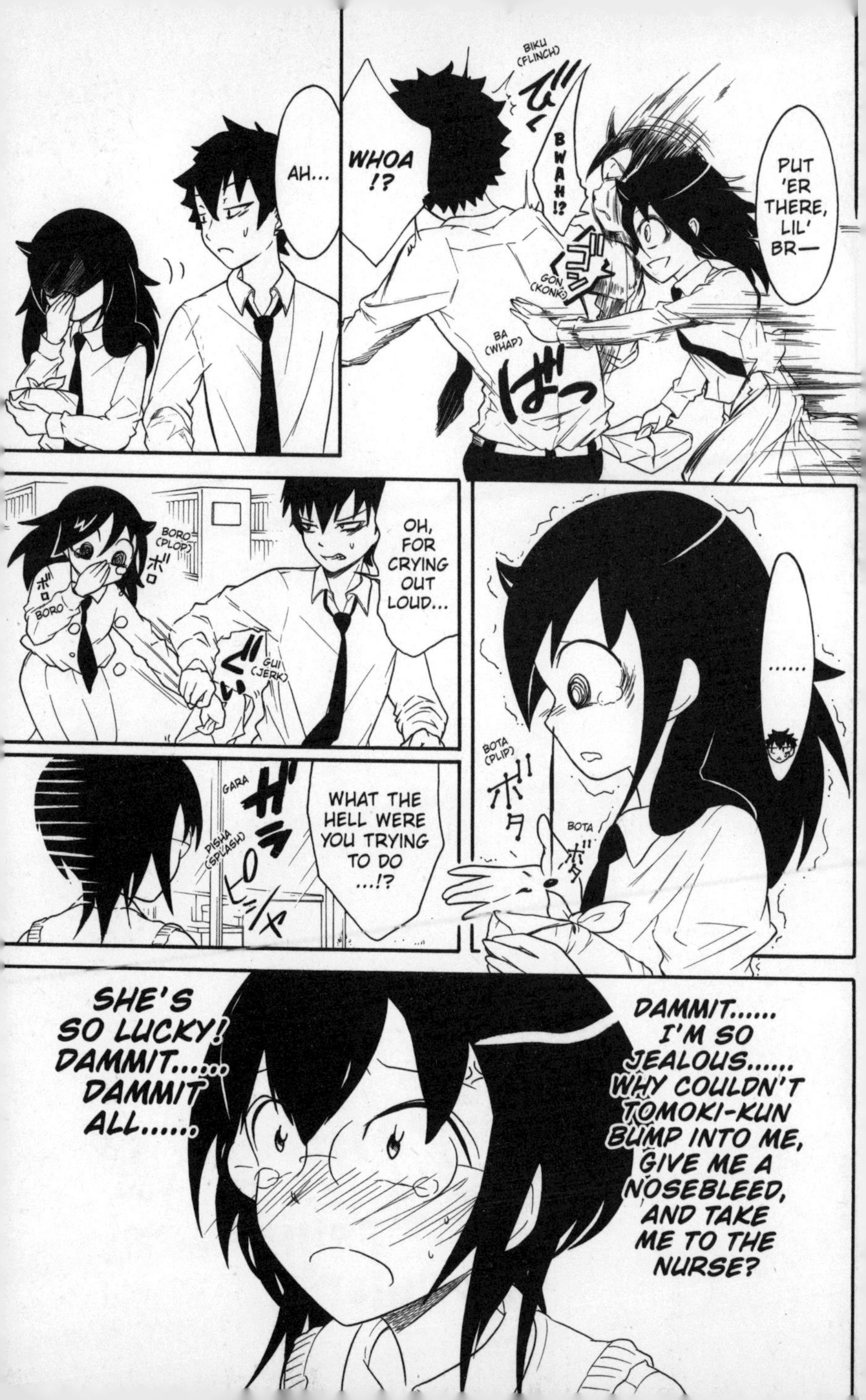
PUT 'ER THERE, LIL' BR—
BIKU (FLINCH)
びく
BWAH!?
GON (KONK)
ゴン
WHOA !?
BA (WHAP)
ばっ
AH...
......
BOTA (PLIP)
ボタ
BOTA
ボタ
OH, FOR CRYING OUT LOUD...
BORO (PLOP)
ボロ
BORO
ボロ
GUI (JERK)
ぐい
WHAT THE HELL WERE YOU TRYING TO DO ...!?
GARA
ガラ
PISHA (SPLASH)
ピシャ
DAMMIT...... I'M SO JEALOUS...... WHY COULDN'T TOMOKI-KUN BUMP INTO ME, GIVE ME A NOSEBLEED, AND TAKE ME TO THE NURSE?
SHE'S SO LUCKY! DAMMIT...... DAMMIT ALL......

No Matter How I Look at It, It's You Guys' Fault I'm Not Popular!

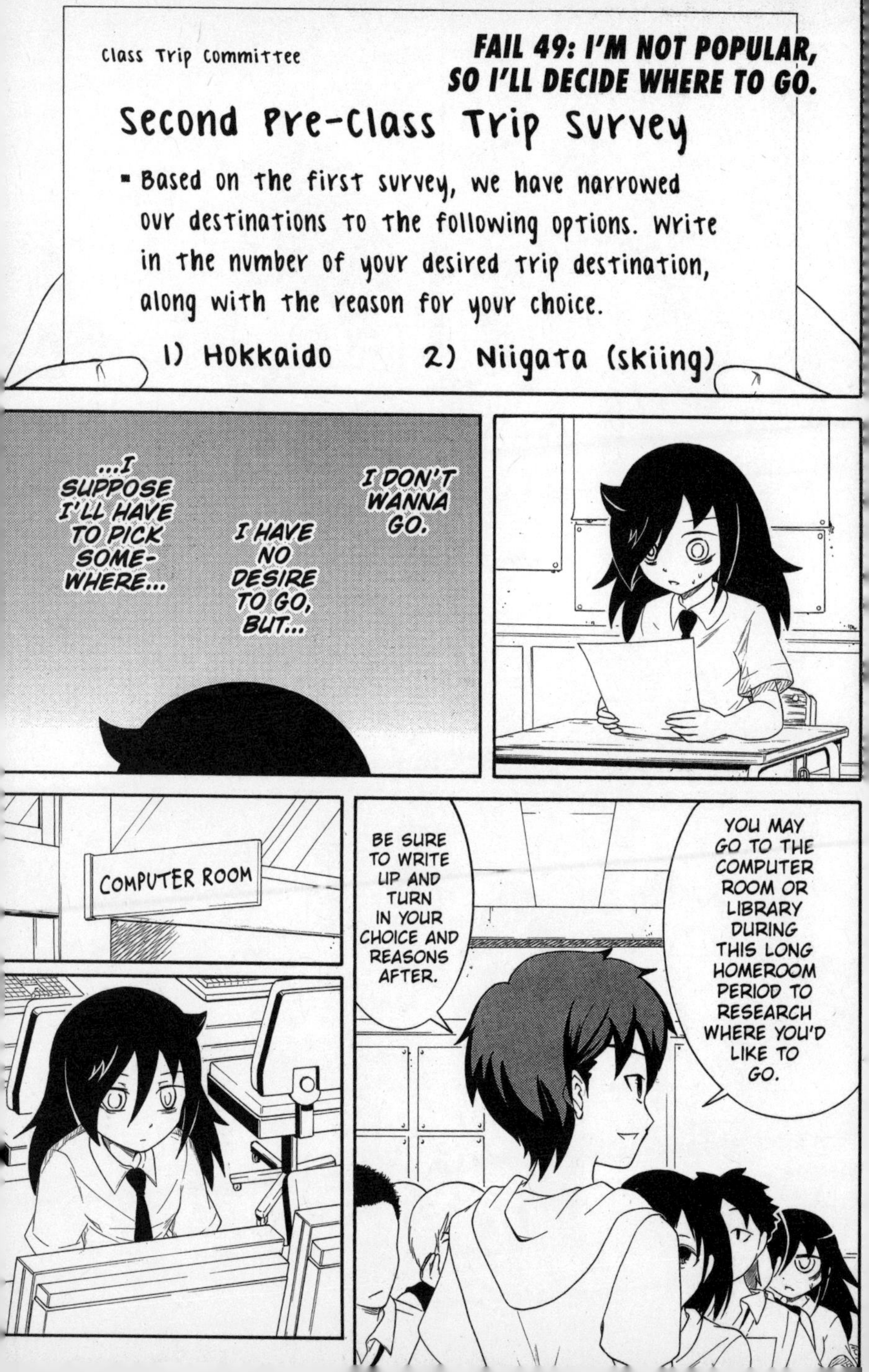
FAIL 49: I'M NOT POPULAR, SO I'LL DECIDE WHERE TO GO.
Class Trip Committee
Second Pre-Class Trip Survey
- Based on the first survey, we have narrowed our destinations to the following options. Write in the number of your desired trip destination, along with the reason for your choice.
1) Hokkaido
2) Niigata (skiing)
I DON'T WANNA GO.
I HAVE NO DESIRE TO GO, BUT...
...I SUPPOSE I'LL HAVE TO PICK SOME-WHERE...
YOU MAY GO TO THE COMPUTER ROOM OR LIBRARY DURING THIS LONG HOMEROOM PERIOD TO RESEARCH WHERE YOU'D LIKE TO GO.
BE SURE TO WRITE UP AND TURN IN YOUR CHOICE AND REASONS AFTER.
COMPUTER ROOM

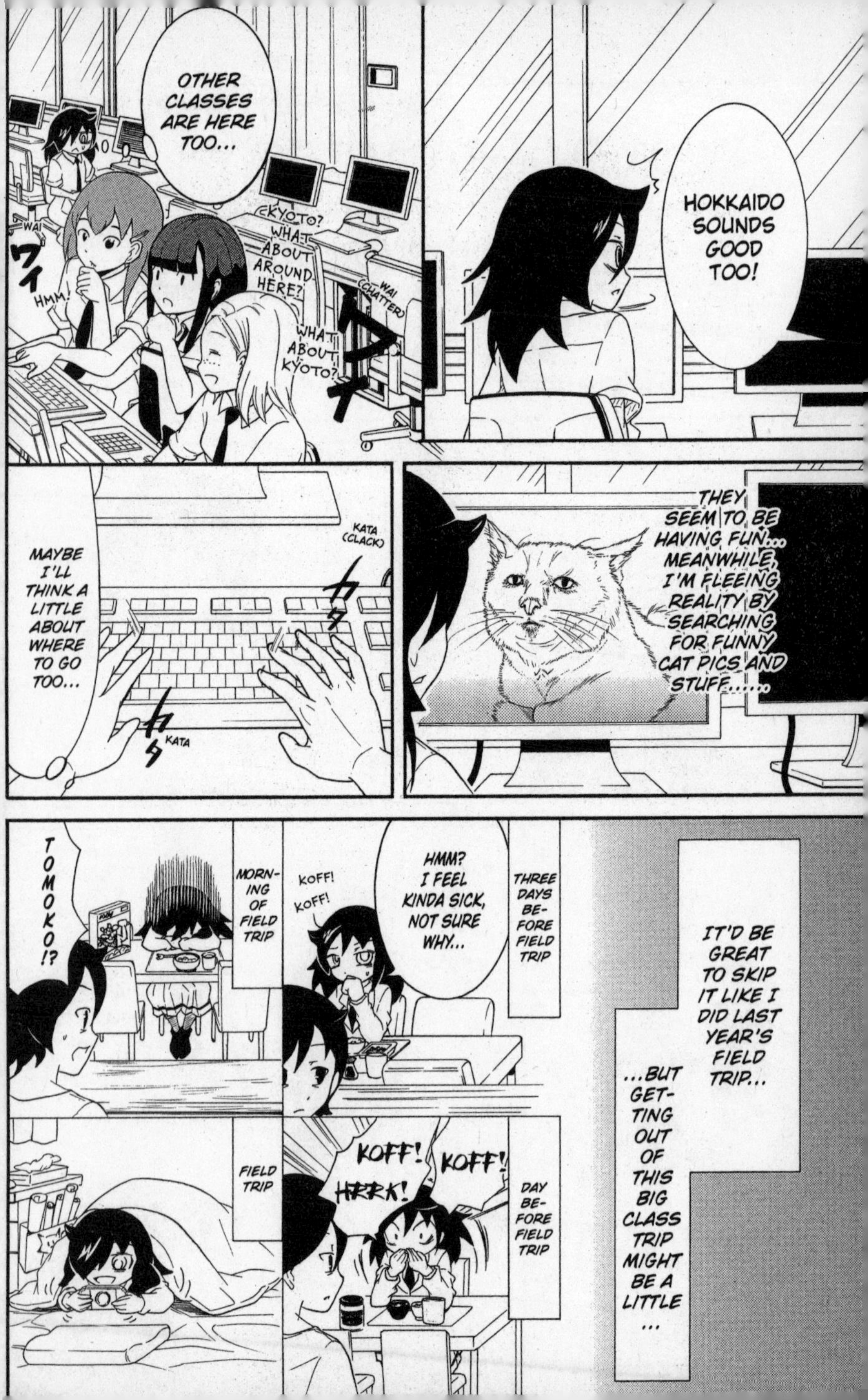
HOKKAIDO SOUNDS GOOD TOO!
OTHER CLASSES ARE HERE TOO...
KYOTO? WHAT ABOUT AROUND HERE?
WAI (CHATTER)
WHAT ABOUT KYOTO?
WAI
HMM!
THEY SEEM TO BE HAVING FUN... MEANWHILE, I'M FLEEING REALITY BY SEARCHING FOR FUNNY CAT PICS AND STUFF......
KATA (CLACK)
MAYBE I'LL THINK A LITTLE ABOUT WHERE TO GO TOO...
KATA
IT'D BE GREAT TO SKIP IT LIKE I DID LAST YEAR'S FIELD TRIP...
...BUT GETTING OUT OF THIS BIG CLASS TRIP MIGHT BE A LITTLE ...
THREE DAYS BEFORE FIELD TRIP
HMM? I FEEL KINDA SICK, NOT SURE WHY...
KOFF! KOFF!
DAY BEFORE FIELD TRIP
KOFF! KOFF!
HRRK!
MORNING OF FIELD TRIP
TOMOKO!?
FIELD TRIP

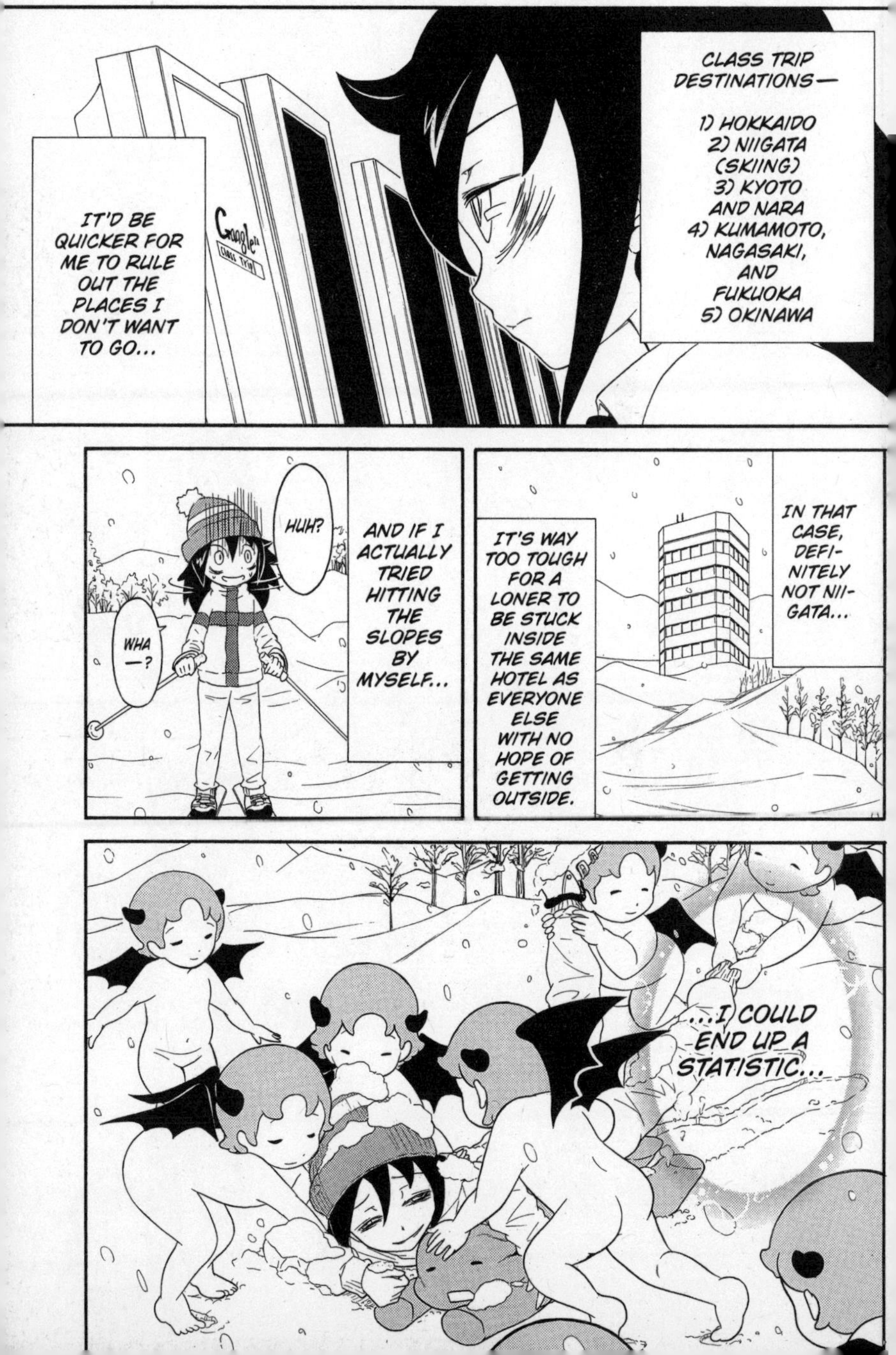
CLASS TRIP DESTINATIONS—
1) HOKKAIDO
2) NIIGATA (SKIING)
3) KYOTO AND NARA
4) KUMAMOTO, NAGASAKI, AND FUKUOKA
5) OKINAWA
IT'D BE QUICKER FOR ME TO RULE OUT THE PLACES I DON'T WANT TO GO...
IN THAT CASE, DEFINITELY NOT NIIGATA...
IT'S WAY TOO TOUGH FOR A LONER TO BE STUCK INSIDE THE SAME HOTEL AS EVERYONE ELSE WITH NO HOPE OF GETTING OUTSIDE.
AND IF I ACTUALLY TRIED HITTING THE SLOPES BY MYSELF...
HUH?
WHA—?
...I COULD END UP A STATISTIC...

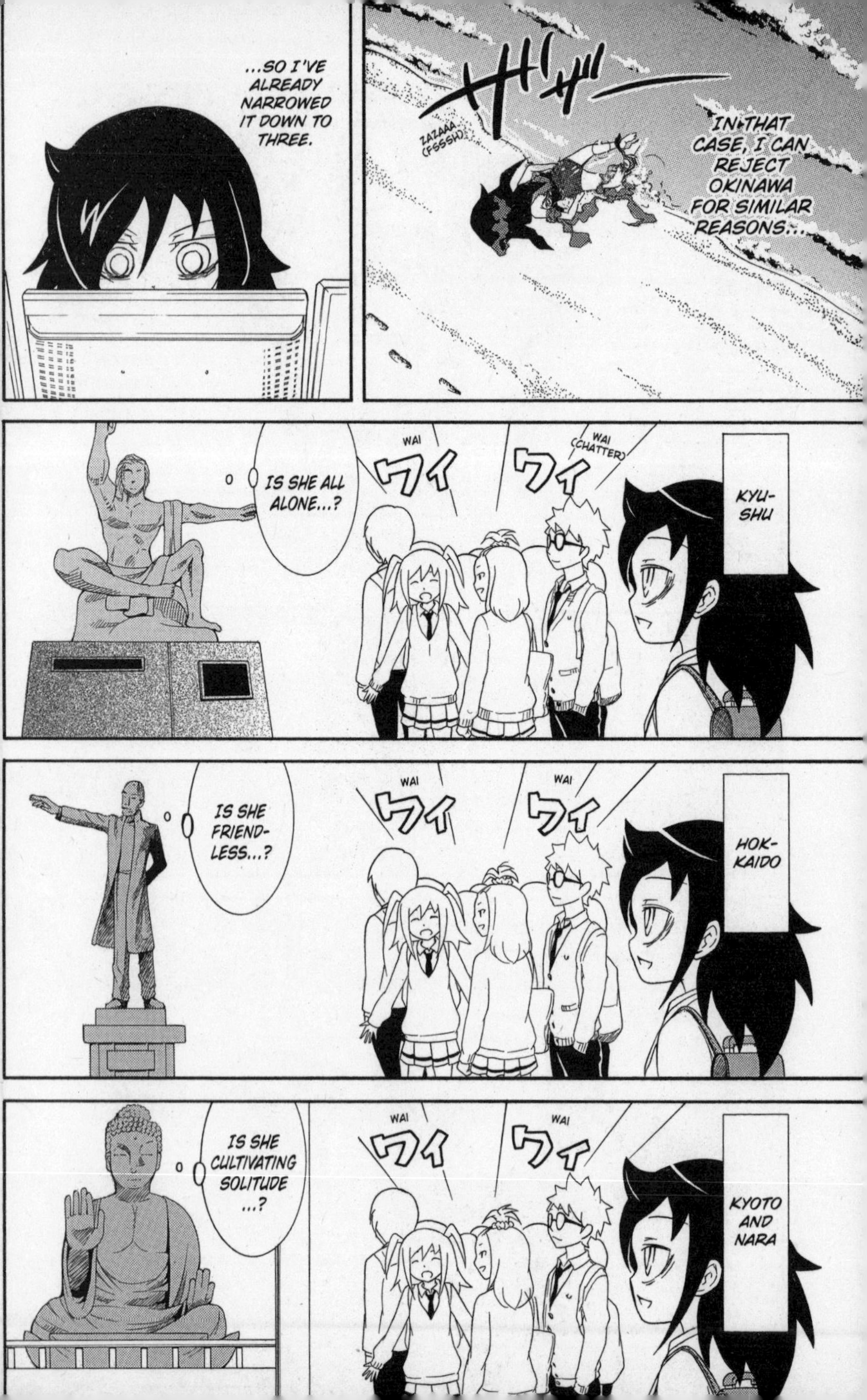
IN THAT CASE, I CAN REJECT OKINAWA FOR SIMILAR REASONS...
ZAZAAA (FSSSH)
...SO I'VE ALREADY NARROWED IT DOWN TO THREE.
KYU-SHU
WAI (CHATTER)
ワイ
WAI
ワイ
IS SHE ALL ALONE...?
HOK-KAIDO
WAI
ワイ
WAI
ワイ
IS SHE FRIEND-LESS...?
KYOTO AND NARA
WAI
ワイ
WAI
ワイ
IS SHE CULTIVATING SOLITUDE ...?

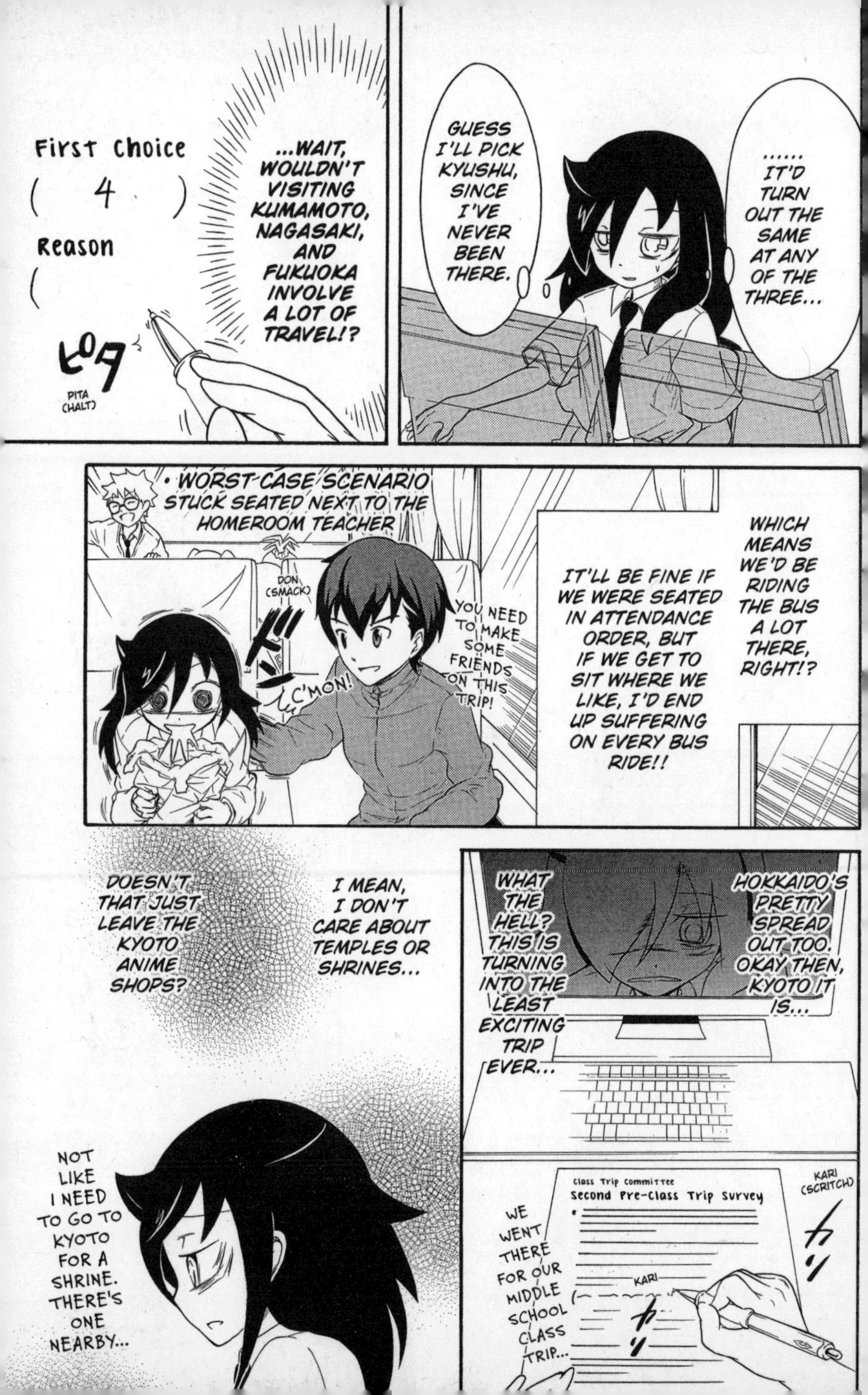
......IT'D TURN OUT THE SAME AT ANY OF THE THREE...
GUESS I'LL PICK KYUSHU, SINCE I'VE NEVER BEEN THERE.
...WAIT, WOULDN'T VISITING KUMAMOTO, NAGASAKI, AND FUKUOKA INVOLVE A LOT OF TRAVEL!?
First Choice
(4)
Reason
(
PITA (HALT)
WHICH MEANS WE'D BE RIDING THE BUS A LOT THERE, RIGHT!?
IT'LL BE FINE IF WE WERE SEATED IN ATTENDANCE ORDER, BUT IF WE GET TO SIT WHERE WE LIKE, I'D END UP SUFFERING ON EVERY BUS RIDE!!
YOU NEED TO MAKE SOME FRIENDS ON THIS TRIP!
C'MON!
DON (SMACK)
• WORST CASE SCENARIO STUCK SEATED NEXT TO THE HOMEROOM TEACHER
HOKKAIDO'S PRETTY SPREAD OUT TOO. OKAY THEN, KYOTO IT IS...
WHAT THE HELL? THIS IS TURNING INTO THE LEAST EXCITING TRIP EVER...
KARI (SCRITCH)
Class Trip Committee
Second Pre-Class Trip Survey
WE WENT THERE FOR OUR MIDDLE SCHOOL CLASS TRIP...
KARI
I MEAN, I DON'T CARE ABOUT TEMPLES OR SHRINES...
DOESN'T THAT JUST LEAVE THE KYOTO ANIME SHOPS?
NOT LIKE I NEED TO GO TO KYOTO FOR A SHRINE. THERE'S ONE NEARBY...

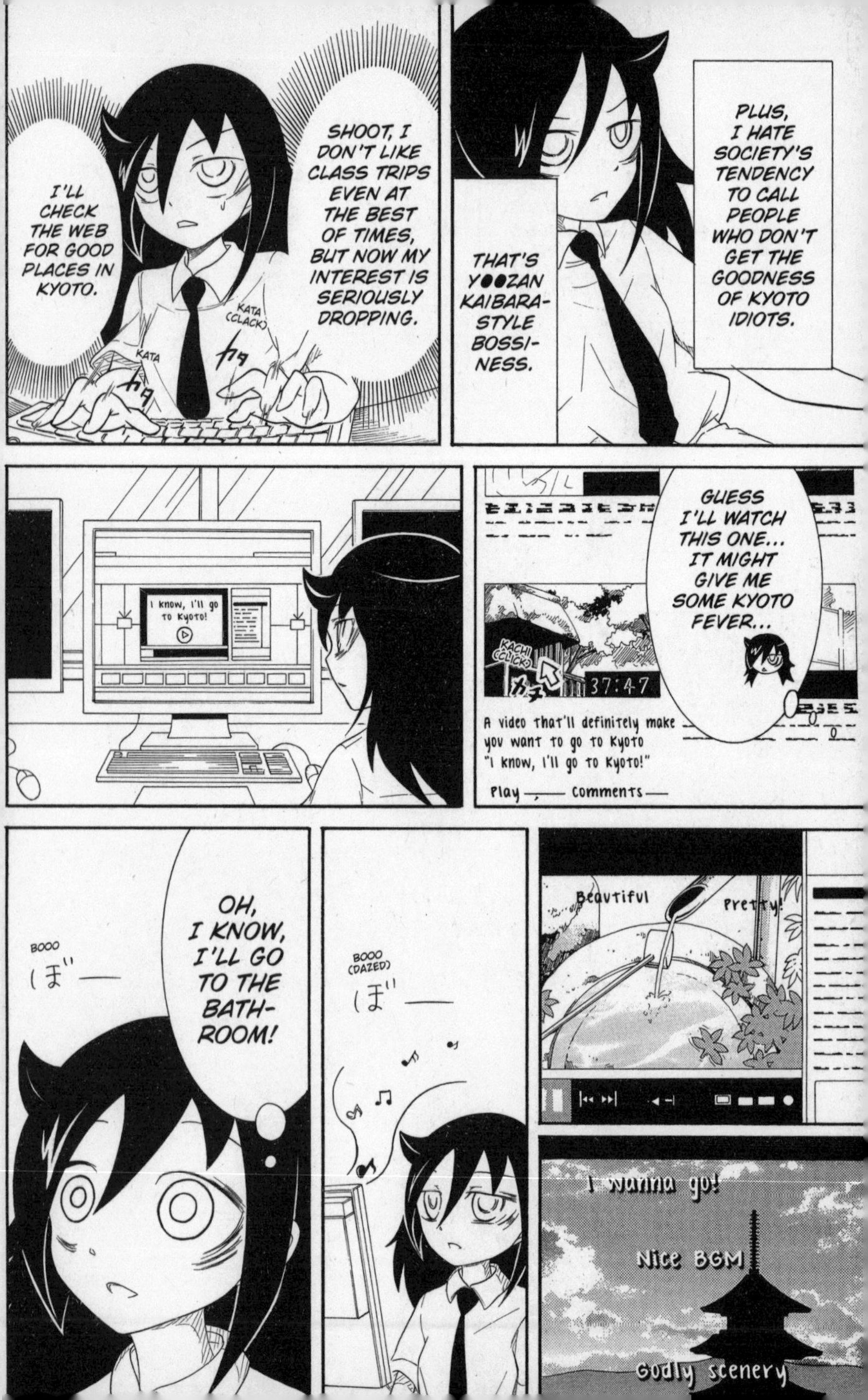
PLUS, I HATE SOCIETY'S TENDENCY TO CALL PEOPLE WHO DON'T GET THE GOODNESS OF KYOTO IDIOTS.
THAT'S Y●●ZAN KAIBARA-STYLE BOSSINESS.
SHOOT, I DON'T LIKE CLASS TRIPS EVEN AT THE BEST OF TIMES, BUT NOW MY INTEREST IS SERIOUSLY DROPPING.
KATA (CLACK)
カタ
I'LL CHECK THE WEB FOR GOOD PLACES IN KYOTO.
KATA
カタ
GUESS I'LL WATCH THIS ONE... IT MIGHT GIVE ME SOME KYOTO FEVER...
KACHI (CLICK)
カチ
37:47
A video that'll definitely make you want to go to Kyoto
"I know, I'll go to Kyoto!"
Play — Comments —
I know, I'll go to Kyoto!
Pretty!
Beautiful
I wanna go!
Nice BGM
Godly scenery
BOOO (DAZED)
ぼー
OH, I KNOW, I'LL GO TO THE BATHROOM!
BOOO
ぼー

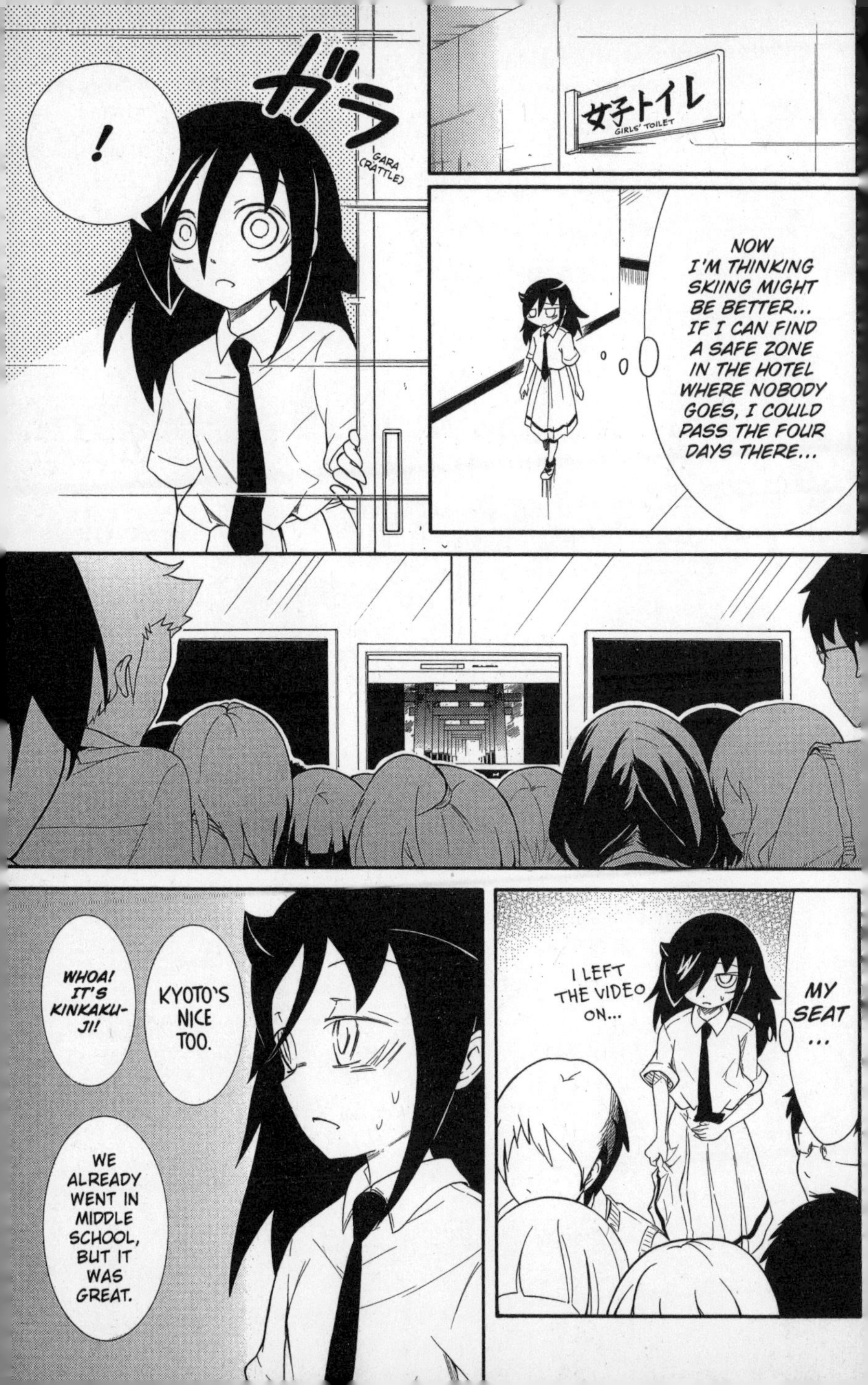
女子トイレ
GIRLS' TOILET
NOW I'M THINKING SKIING MIGHT BE BETTER... IF I CAN FIND A SAFE ZONE IN THE HOTEL WHERE NOBODY GOES, I COULD PASS THE FOUR DAYS THERE...
ガラ
GARA (RATTLE)
!
MY SEAT ...
I LEFT THE VIDEO ON...
KYOTO'S NICE TOO.
WHOA! IT'S KINKAKU-JI!
WE ALREADY WENT IN MIDDLE SCHOOL, BUT IT WAS GREAT.

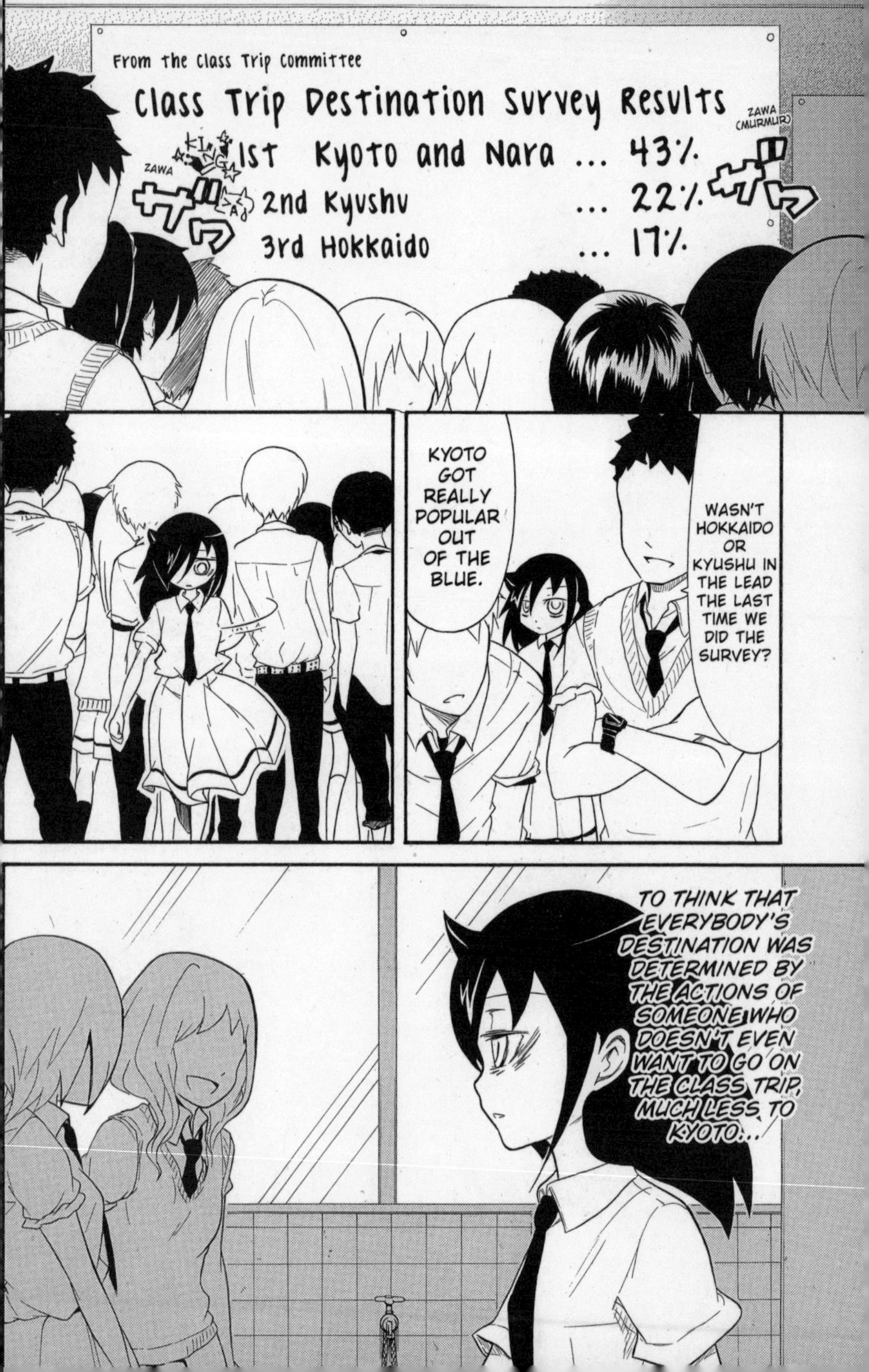
From the Class Trip Committee
Class Trip Destination Survey Results
1st Kyoto and Nara ... 43%
2nd Kyushu ... 22%
3rd Hokkaido ... 17%
ZAWA (MURMUR)
ZAWA
WASN'T HOKKAIDO OR KYUSHU IN THE LEAD THE LAST TIME WE DID THE SURVEY?
KYOTO GOT REALLY POPULAR OUT OF THE BLUE.
TO THINK THAT EVERYBODY'S DESTINATION WAS DETERMINED BY THE ACTIONS OF SOMEONE WHO DOESN'T EVEN WANT TO GO ON THE CLASS TRIP, MUCH LESS TO KYOTO...

No Matter How I
Look at It, It's You
Guys' Fault I'm Not
Popular!

FAIL 50: I'M NOT POPULAR, SO I'LL HANG OUT BY MYSELF IN A TWILIT CLASSROOM.

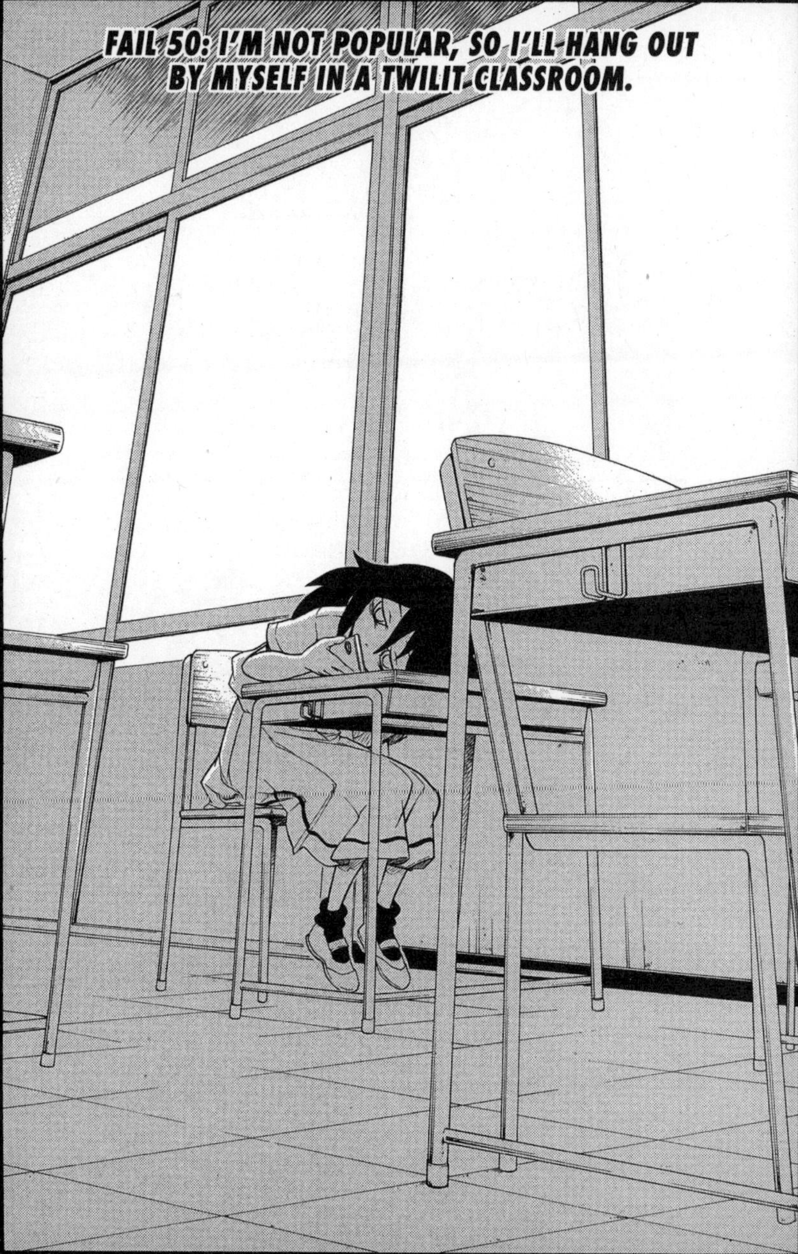

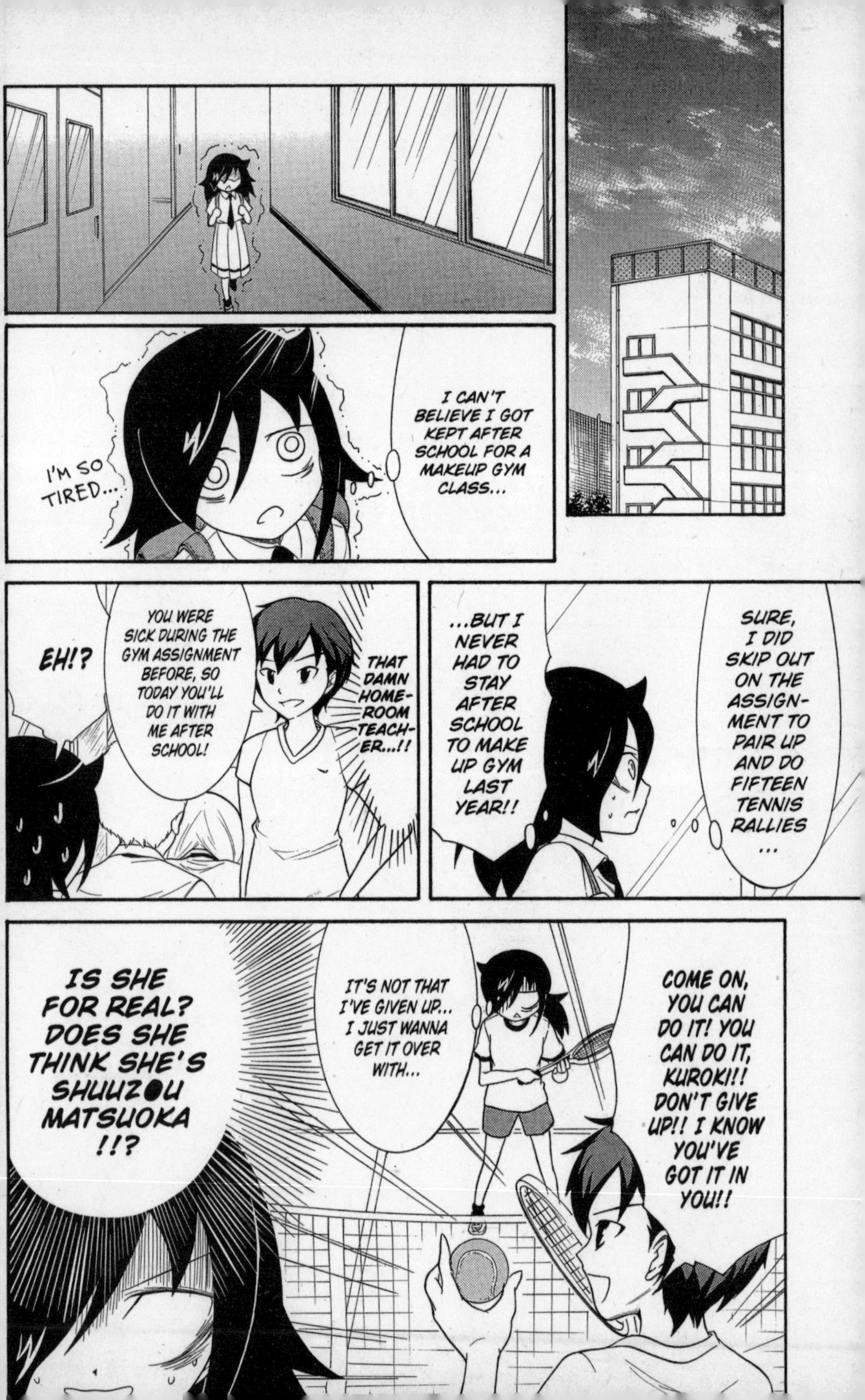
I CAN'T BELIEVE I GOT KEPT AFTER SCHOOL FOR A MAKEUP GYM CLASS...
I'M SO TIRED...
SURE, I DID SKIP OUT ON THE ASSIGN-MENT TO PAIR UP AND DO FIFTEEN TENNIS RALLIES...
...BUT I NEVER HAD TO STAY AFTER SCHOOL TO MAKE UP GYM LAST YEAR!!
YOU WERE SICK DURING THE GYM ASSIGNMENT BEFORE, SO TODAY YOU'LL DO IT WITH ME AFTER SCHOOL!
EH!?
THAT DAMN HOME-ROOM TEACH-ER...!!
COME ON, YOU CAN DO IT! YOU CAN DO IT, KUROKI!! DON'T GIVE UP!! I KNOW YOU'VE GOT IT IN YOU!!
IT'S NOT THAT I'VE GIVEN UP... I JUST WANNA GET IT OVER WITH...
IS SHE FOR REAL? DOES SHE THINK SHE'S SHUUZOU MATSUOKA!!?

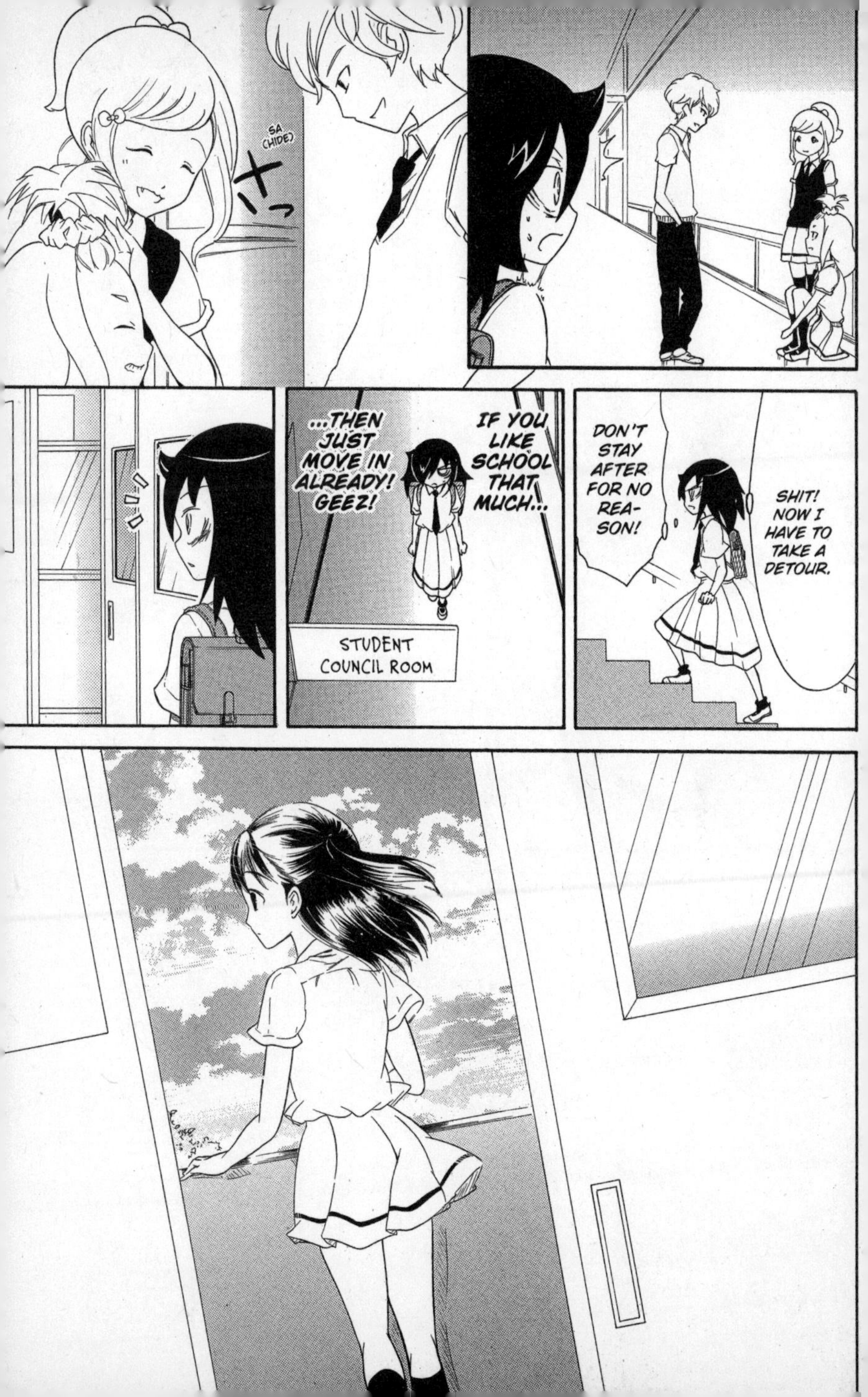
SA (HIDE)
さっ
SHIT! NOW I HAVE TO TAKE A DETOUR.
DON'T STAY AFTER FOR NO REA-SON!
IF YOU LIKE SCHOOL THAT MUCH...
...THEN JUST MOVE IN ALREADY! GEEZ!
STUDENT COUNCIL ROOM

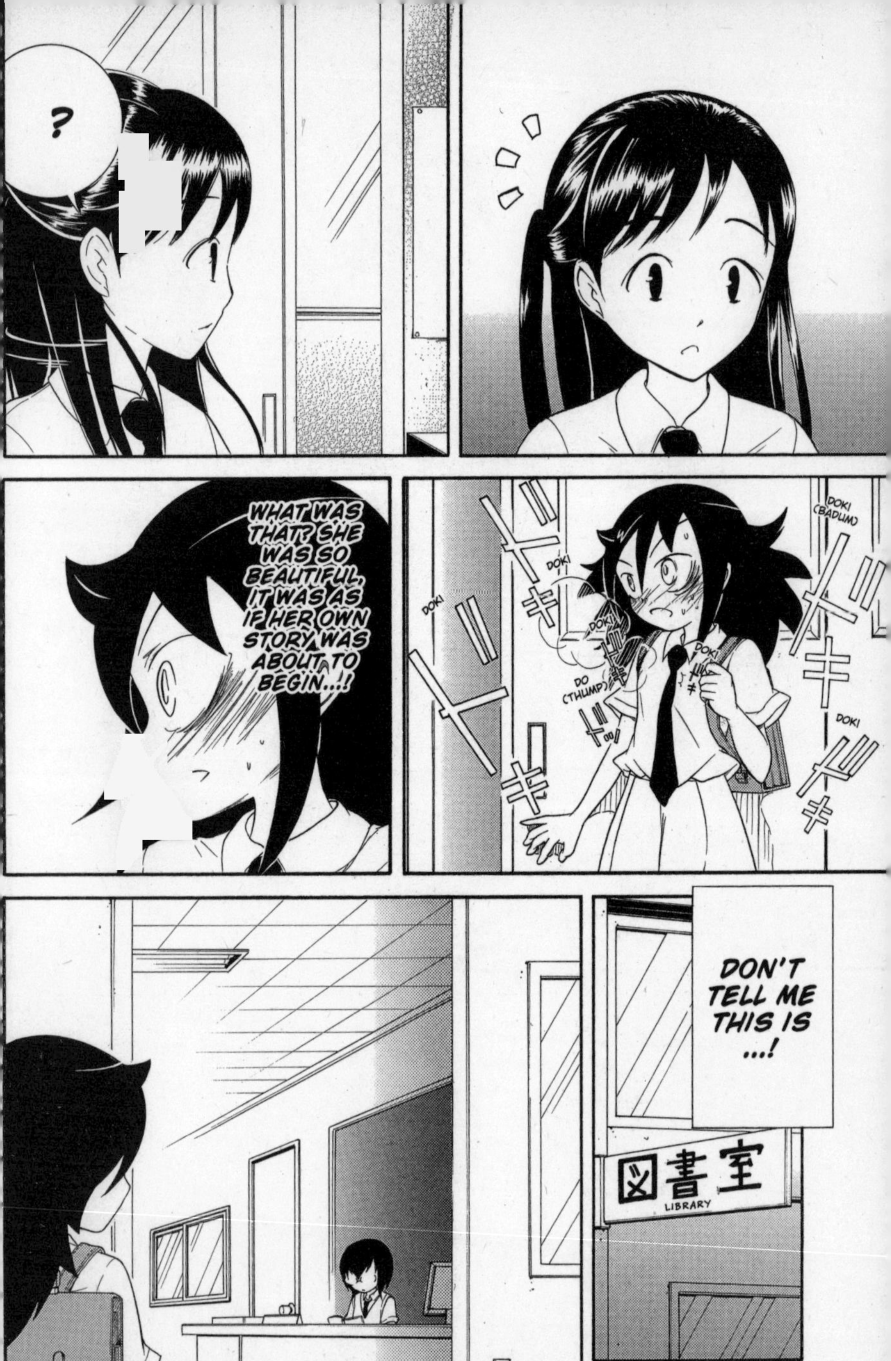
?
DOKI (BADUM)
DOKI
DOKI
DOKI
DOKI
DO (THUMP)
DOKI
WHAT WAS THAT? SHE WAS SO BEAUTIFUL, IT WAS AS IF HER OWN STORY WAS ABOUT TO BEGIN...!
DON'T TELL ME THIS IS ...!
図書室
LIBRARY

BOOK: KII'S JOURNEY

THAT'S IT!! WHEN ALONE IN A TWILIT CLASSROOM ENVIRONMENT, A PRETTY GIRL GETS EVEN PRETTIER! SO BY THAT MATH, EVEN AN AVERAGE GIRL LOOKS GOOD!

HUNH!?

......

!?

KASHA (SNAP)

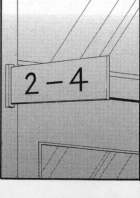

2 - 4

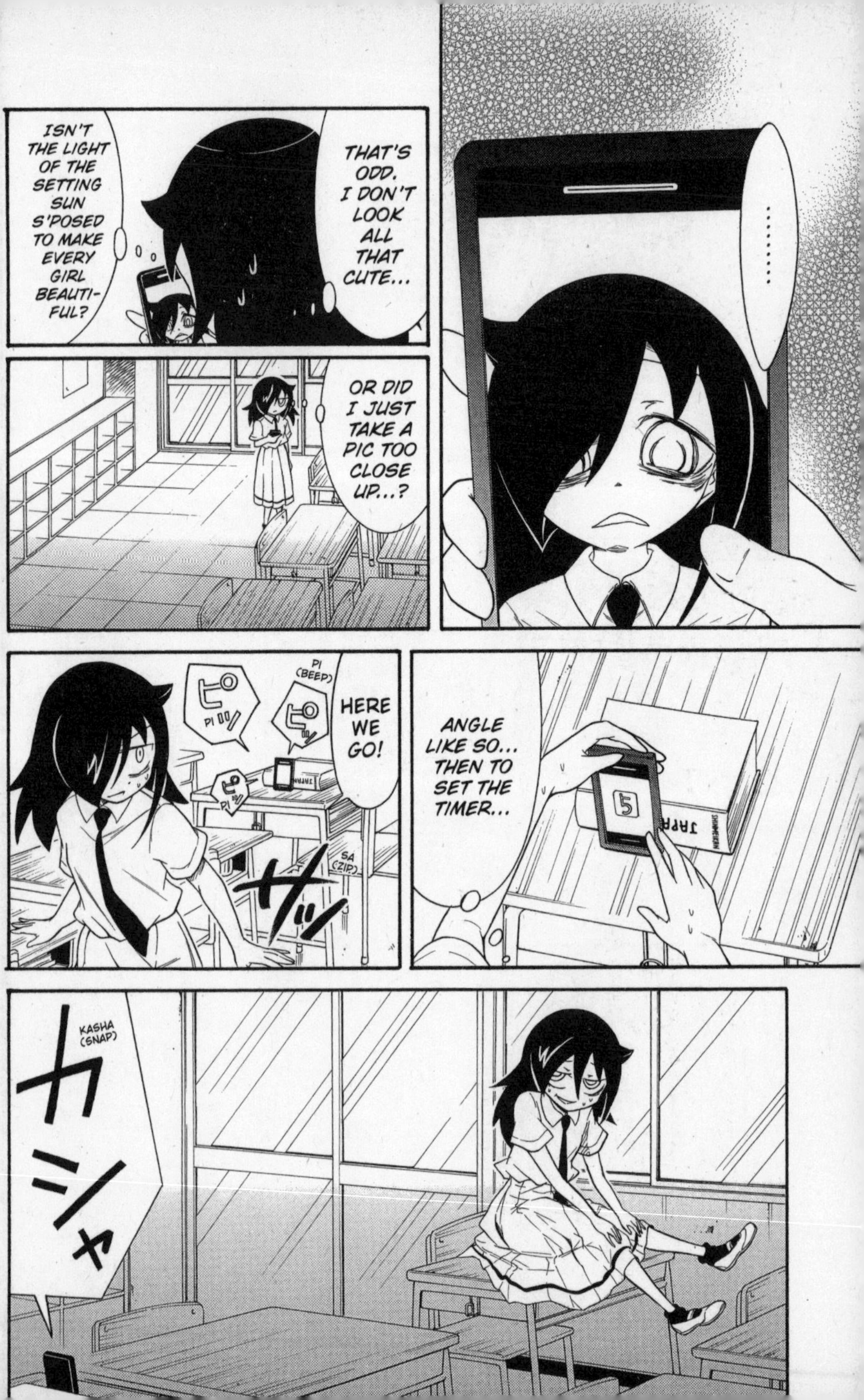
……
THAT'S ODD. I DON'T LOOK ALL THAT CUTE...
ISN'T THE LIGHT OF THE SETTING SUN S'POSED TO MAKE EVERY GIRL BEAUTI-FUL?
OR DID I JUST TAKE A PIC TOO CLOSE UP...?
ANGLE LIKE SO... THEN TO SET THE TIMER...
HERE WE GO!
PI (BEEP)
PI
PI
SA (ZIP)
KASHA (SNAP)

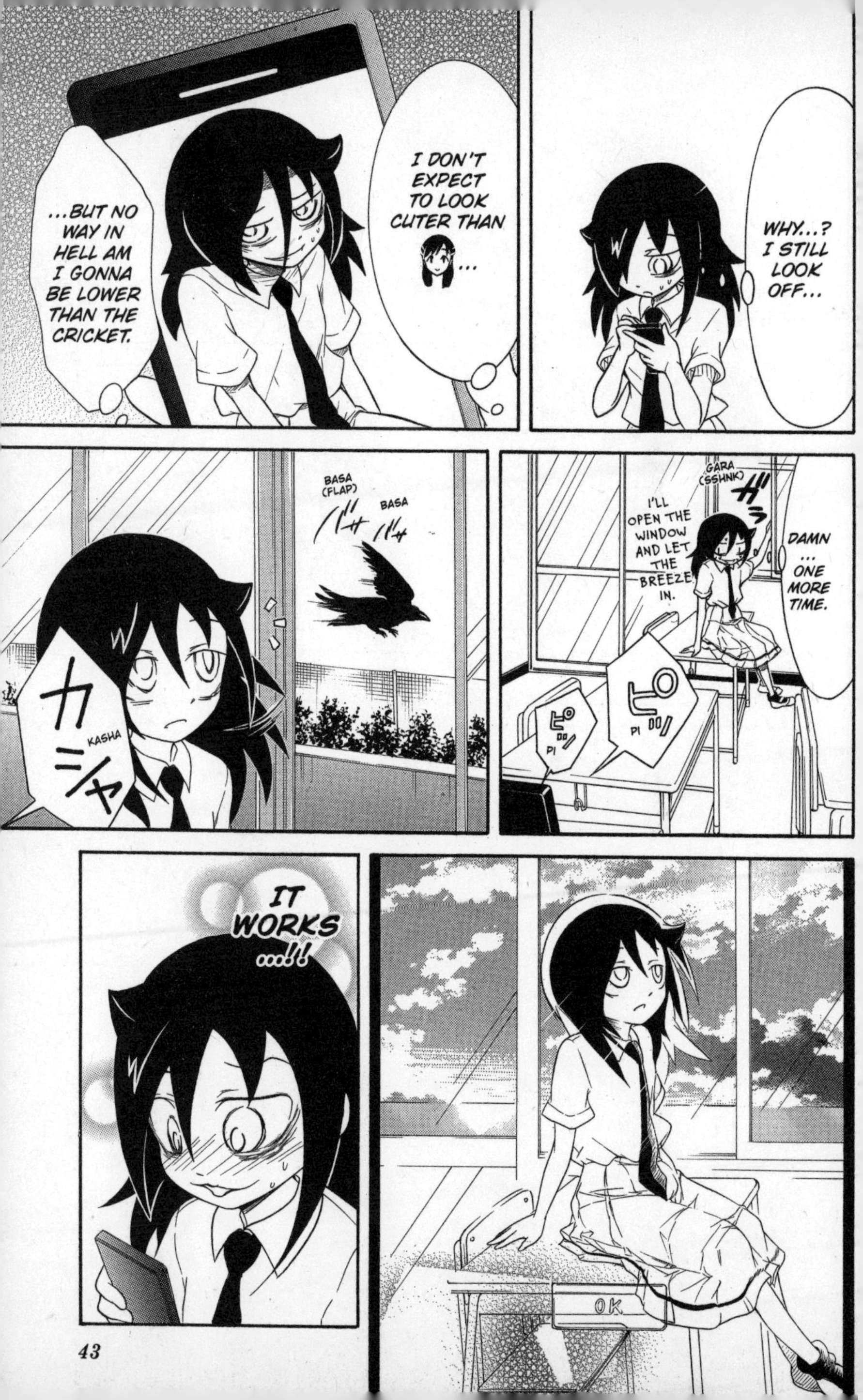
WHY...? I STILL LOOK OFF...
I DON'T EXPECT TO LOOK CUTER THAN ...
...BUT NO WAY IN HELL AM I GONNA BE LOWER THAN THE CRICKET.
DAMN... ONE MORE TIME.
I'LL OPEN THE WINDOW AND LET THE BREEZE IN.
GARA (SSHNK)
PI
PI
BASA (FLAP)
BASA
KASHA
OK
IT WORKS...!!

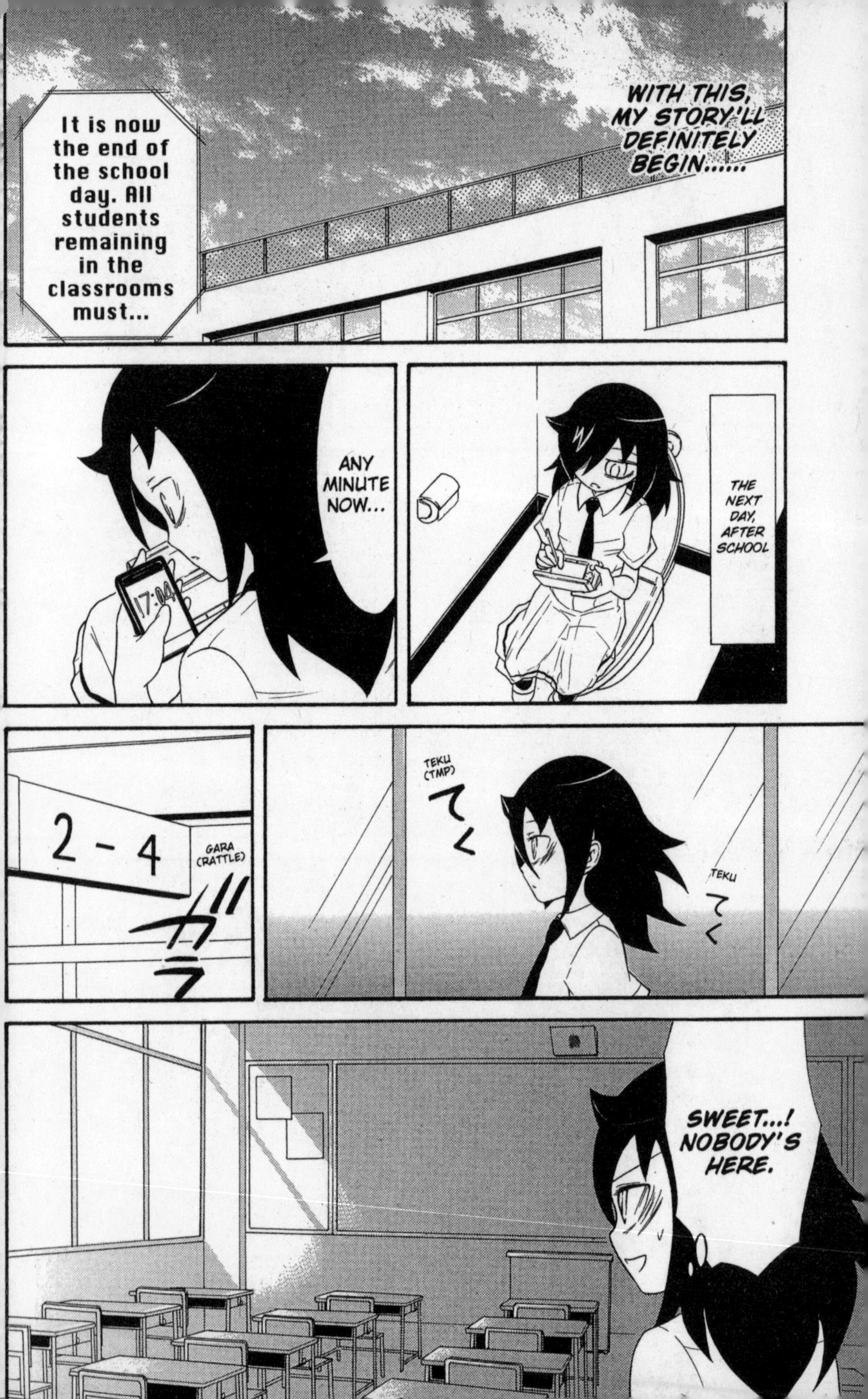
WITH THIS, MY STORY'LL DEFINITELY BEGIN......
It is now the end of the school day. All students remaining in the classrooms must...
THE NEXT DAY, AFTER SCHOOL
ANY MINUTE NOW...
17:04
TEKU (TMP)
てく
TEKU
てく
2 - 4
GARA (RATTLE)
ガラ
SWEET...! NOBODY'S HERE.

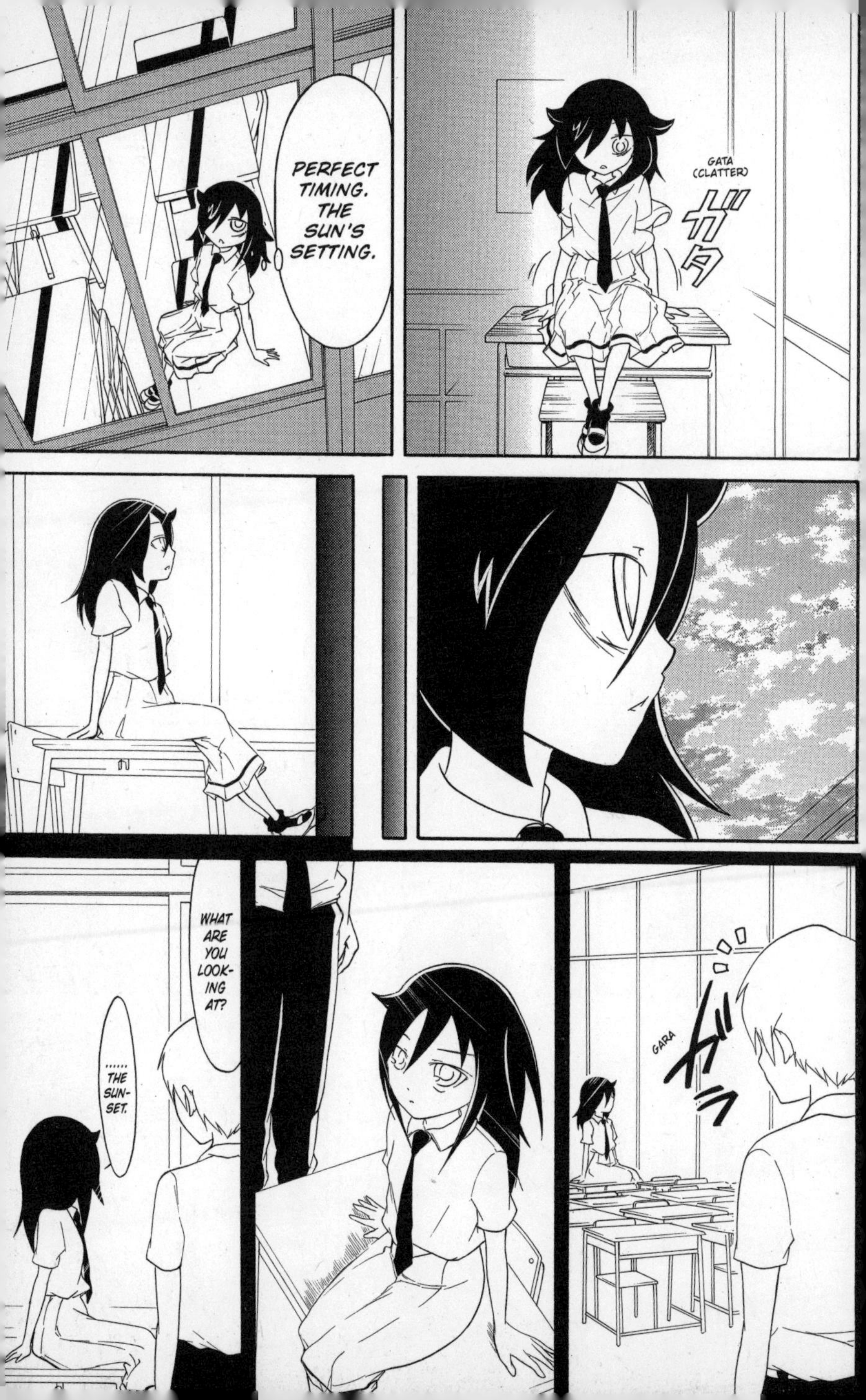
GATA (CLATTER)
ガタ
PERFECT TIMING. THE SUN'S SETTING.
GARA
ガラ
WHAT ARE YOU LOOKING AT?
......THE SUN-SET.

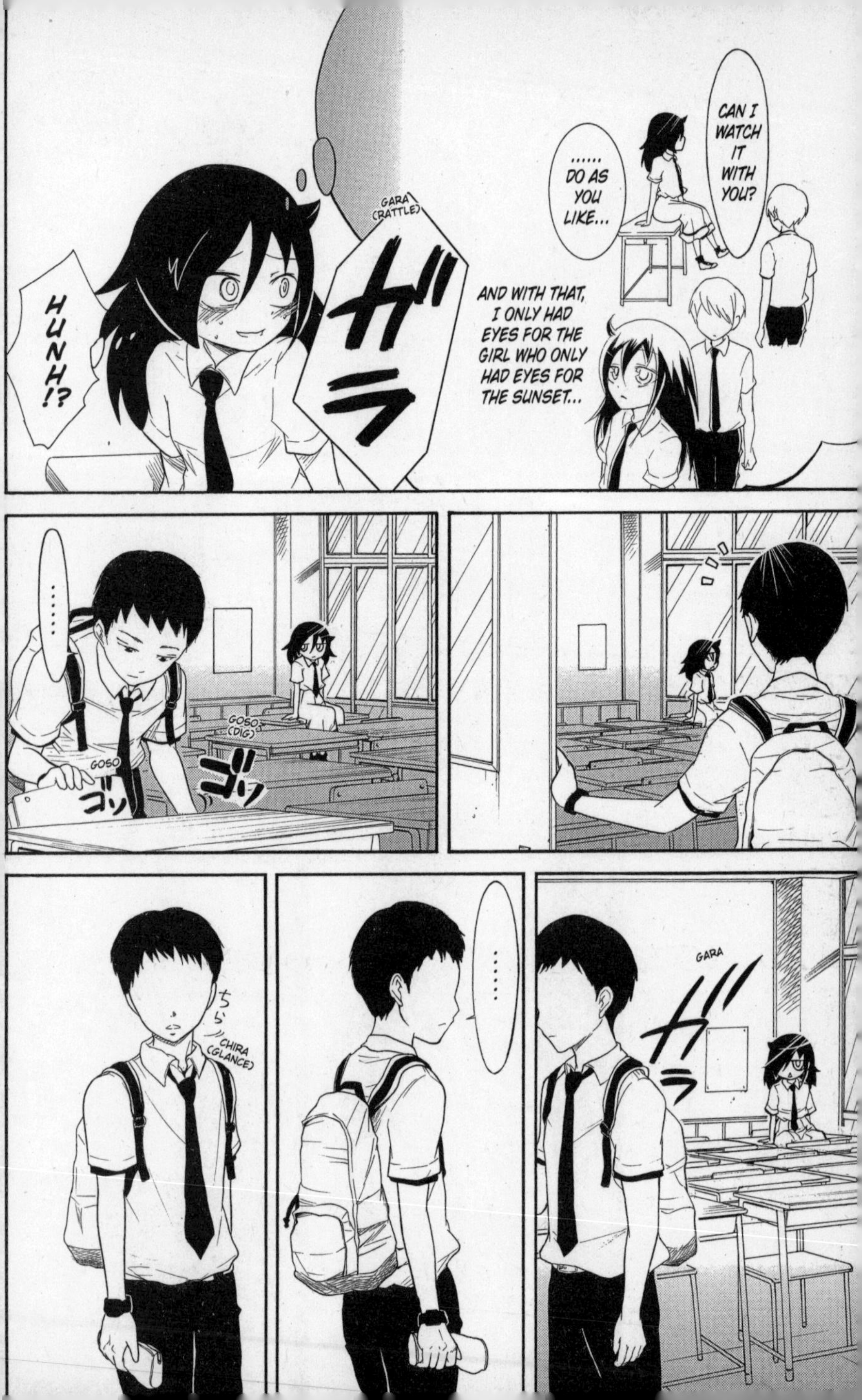
CAN I WATCH IT WITH YOU?
...... DO AS YOU LIKE...
AND WITH THAT, I ONLY HAD EYES FOR THE GIRL WHO ONLY HAD EYES FOR THE SUNSET...
GARA (RATTLE)
ガラ
HUNH!?
......
GOSO (DIG)
ゴソ
GOSO
ゴソ
GARA
ガラ
......
ちら
CHIRA (GLANCE)

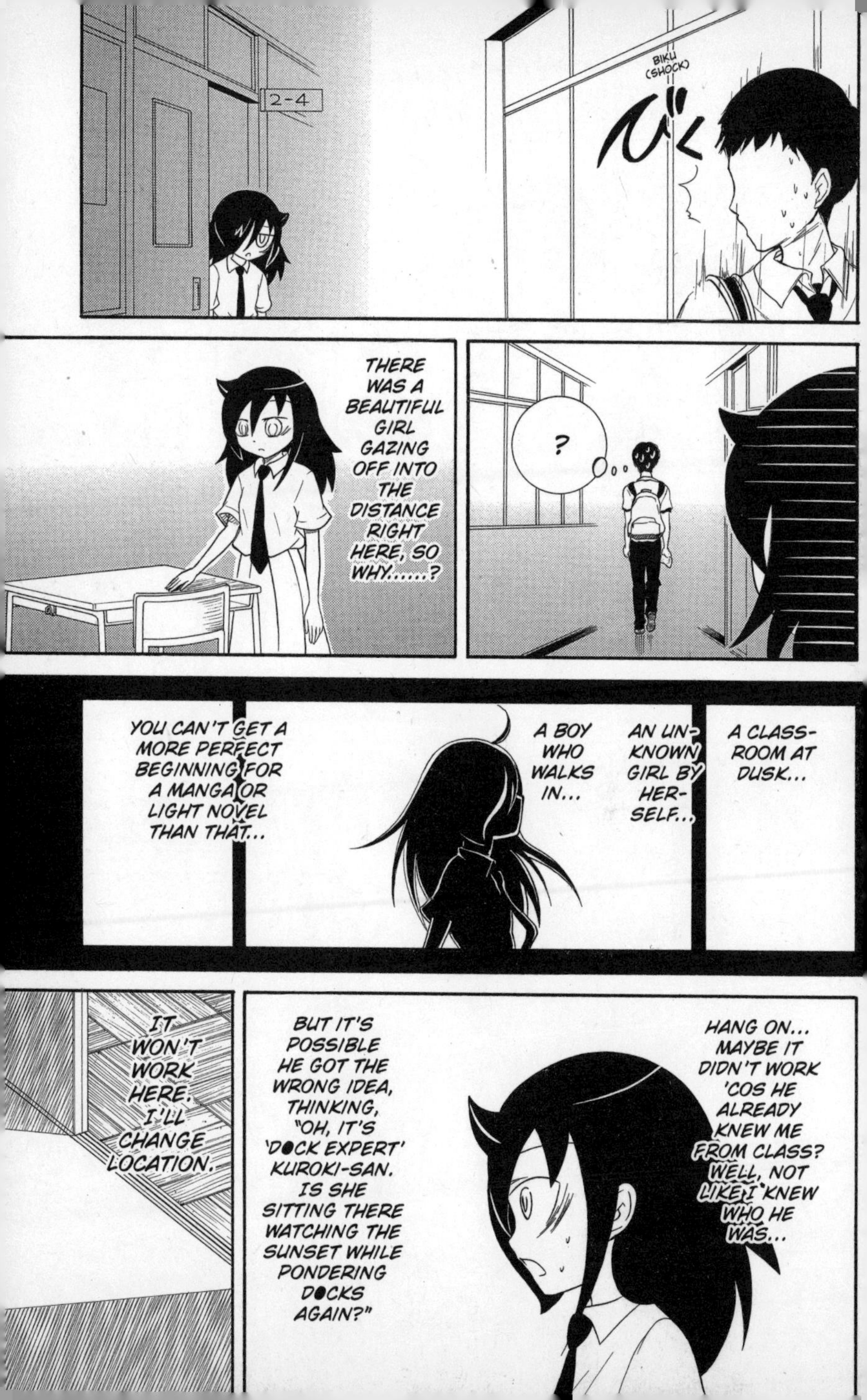
BIKU (SHOCK)
びく
?
THERE WAS A BEAUTIFUL GIRL GAZING OFF INTO THE DISTANCE RIGHT HERE, SO WHY......?
A CLASS-ROOM AT DUSK...
AN UN-KNOWN GIRL BY HER-SELF...
A BOY WHO WALKS IN...
YOU CAN'T GET A MORE PERFECT BEGINNING FOR A MANGA OR LIGHT NOVEL THAN THAT...
HANG ON... MAYBE IT DIDN'T WORK 'COS HE ALREADY KNEW ME FROM CLASS? WELL, NOT LIKE I KNEW WHO HE WAS...
BUT IT'S POSSIBLE HE GOT THE WRONG IDEA, THINKING, "OH, IT'S 'DOCK EXPERT' KUROKI-SAN. IS SHE SITTING THERE WATCHING THE SUNSET WHILE PONDERING DOCKS AGAIN?"
IT WON'T WORK HERE. I'LL CHANGE LOCATION.

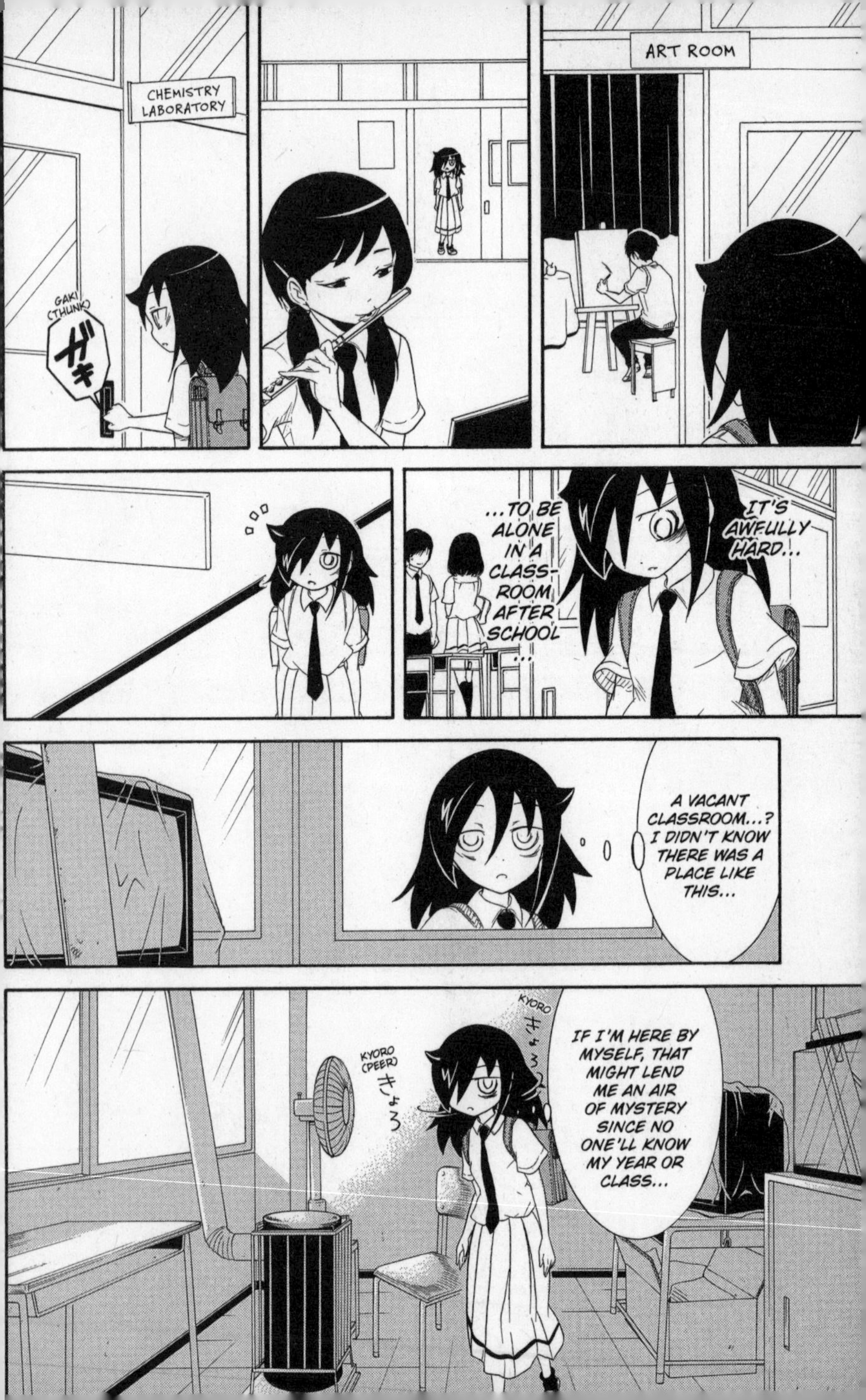
ART ROOM
CHEMISTRY LABORATORY
GAKI (THUNK)
ガキ
IT'S AWFULLY HARD...
...TO BE ALONE IN A CLASSROOM AFTER SCHOOL...
A VACANT CLASSROOM...? I DIDN'T KNOW THERE WAS A PLACE LIKE THIS...
KYORO
きょろ
IF I'M HERE BY MYSELF, THAT MIGHT LEND ME AN AIR OF MYSTERY SINCE NO ONE'LL KNOW MY YEAR OR CLASS...
KYORO (PEER)
きょろ

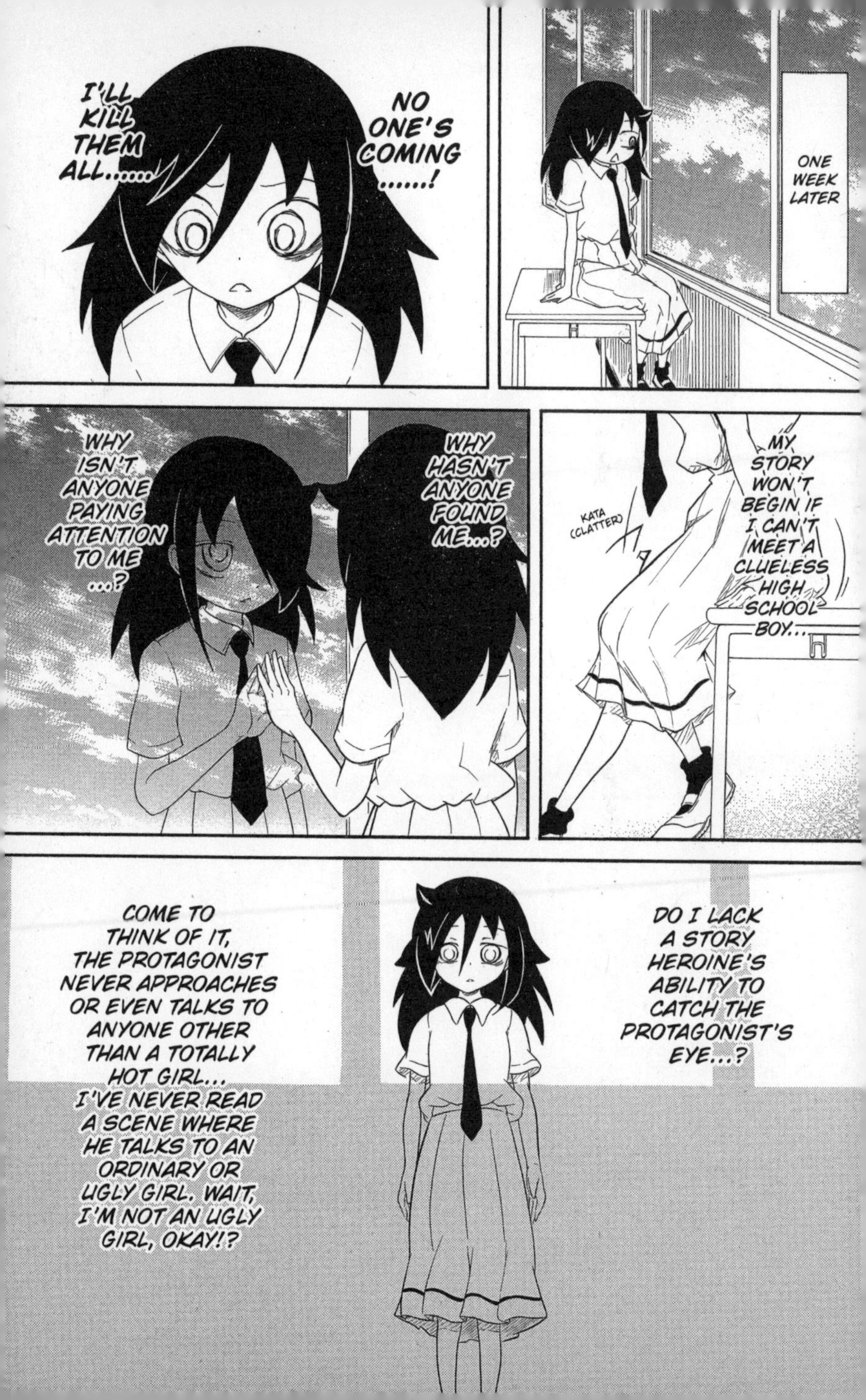
ONE WEEK LATER
NO ONE'S COMING......!
I'LL KILL THEM ALL......
MY STORY WON'T BEGIN IF I CAN'T MEET A CLUELESS HIGH SCHOOL BOY...
KATA (CLATTER)
WHY HASN'T ANYONE FOUND ME...?
WHY ISN'T ANYONE PAYING ATTENTION TO ME...?
DO I LACK A STORY HEROINE'S ABILITY TO CATCH THE PROTAGONIST'S EYE...?
COME TO THINK OF IT, THE PROTAGONIST NEVER APPROACHES OR EVEN TALKS TO ANYONE OTHER THAN A TOTALLY HOT GIRL... I'VE NEVER READ A SCENE WHERE HE TALKS TO AN ORDINARY OR UGLY GIRL. WAIT, I'M NOT AN UGLY GIRL, OKAY!?

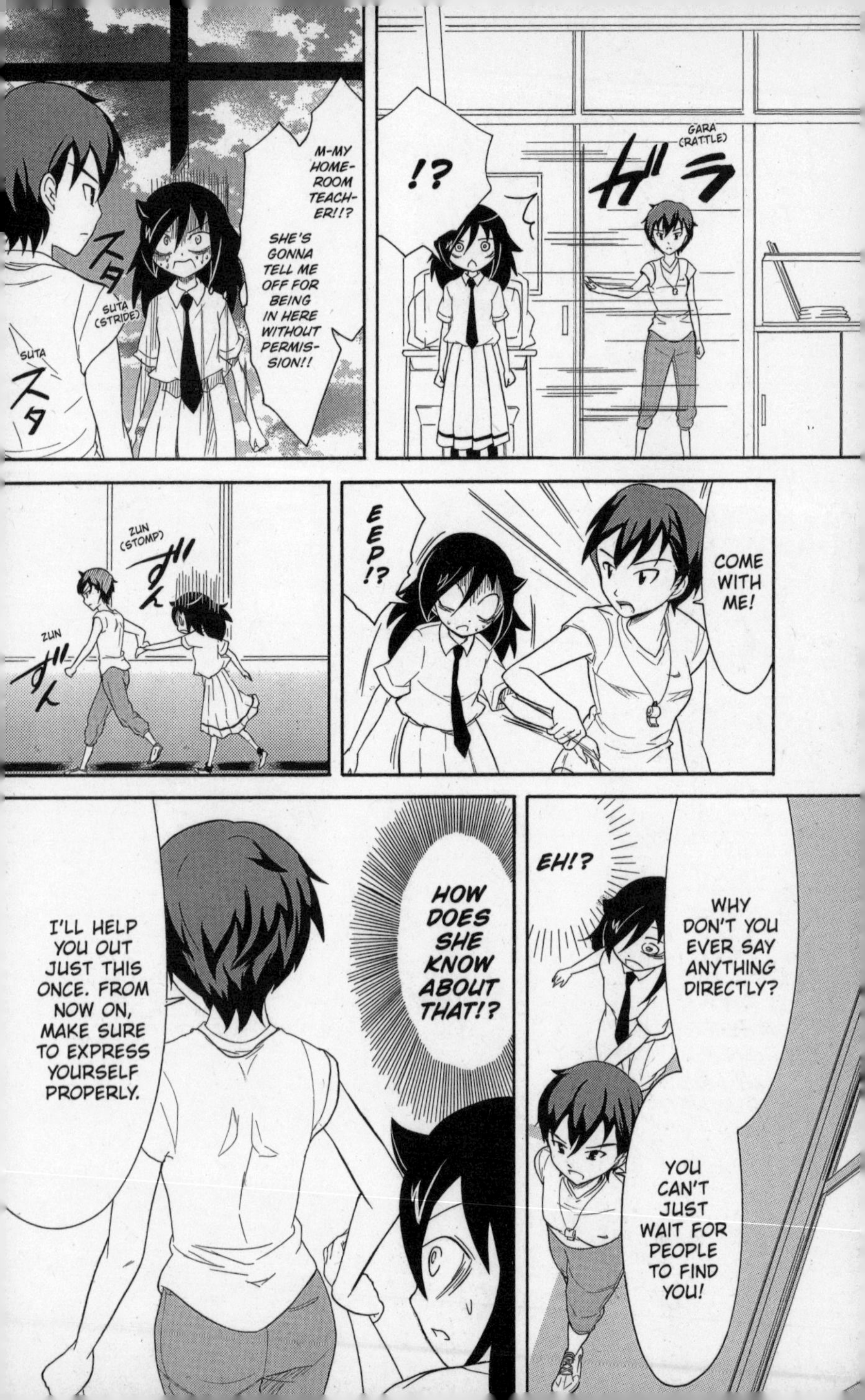
GARA (RATTLE)
ガラ
!?
M-MY HOMEROOM TEACHER!!?
SHE'S GONNA TELL ME OFF FOR BEING IN HERE WITHOUT PERMISSION!!
SUTA (STRIDE)
スタ
SUTA
スタ
COME WITH ME!
EEP!?
ZUN (STOMP)
ずん
ZUN
ずん
WHY DON'T YOU EVER SAY ANYTHING DIRECTLY?
EH!?
YOU CAN'T JUST WAIT FOR PEOPLE TO FIND YOU!
HOW DOES SHE KNOW ABOUT THAT!?
I'LL HELP YOU OUT JUST THIS ONCE. FROM NOW ON, MAKE SURE TO EXPRESS YOURSELF PROPERLY.

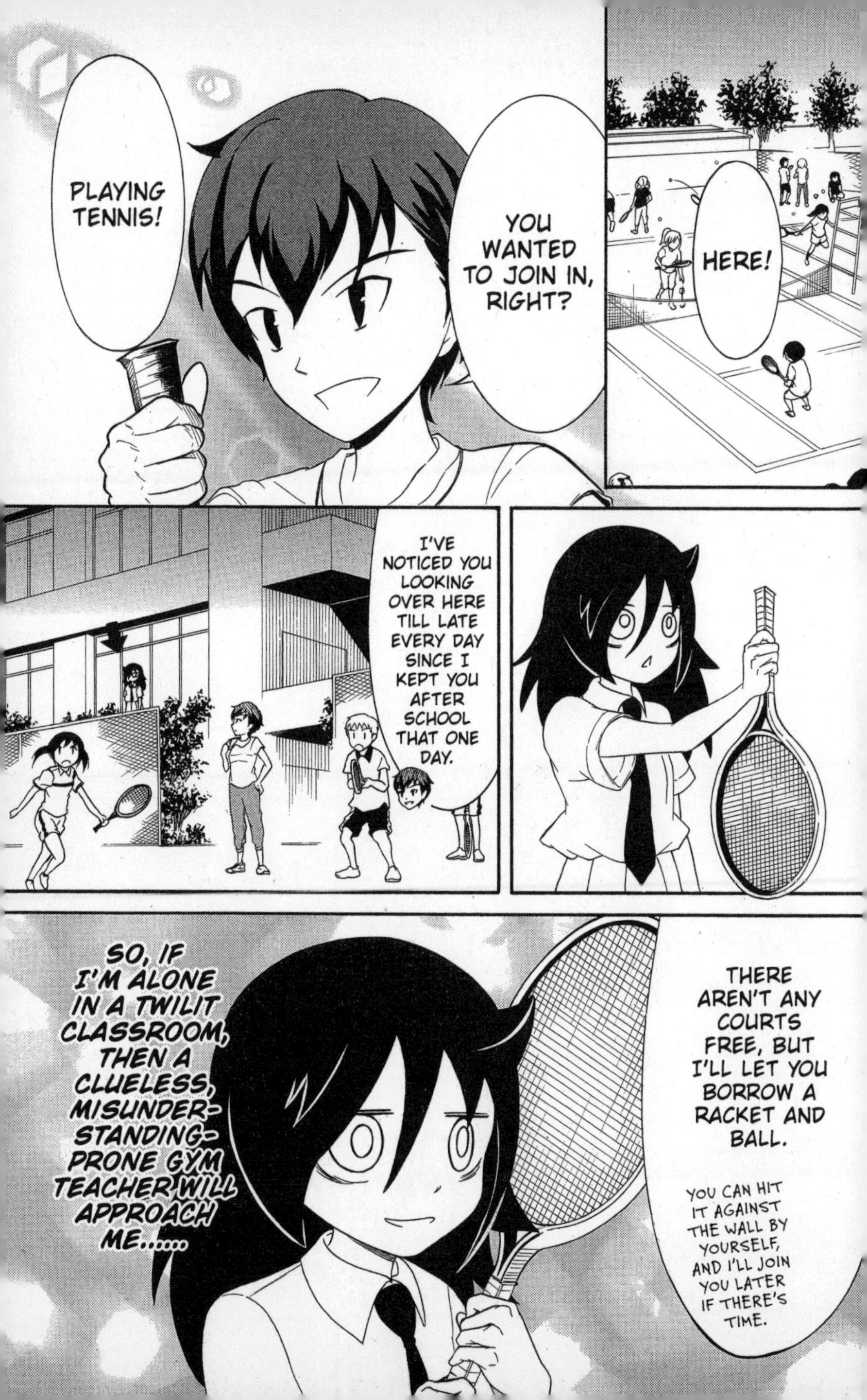

HERE!
YOU WANTED TO JOIN IN, RIGHT?
PLAYING TENNIS!
I'VE NOTICED YOU LOOKING OVER HERE TILL LATE EVERY DAY SINCE I KEPT YOU AFTER SCHOOL THAT ONE DAY.
THERE AREN'T ANY COURTS FREE, BUT I'LL LET YOU BORROW A RACKET AND BALL.
YOU CAN HIT IT AGAINST THE WALL BY YOURSELF, AND I'LL JOIN YOU LATER IF THERE'S TIME.
SO, IF I'M ALONE IN A TWILIT CLASSROOM, THEN A CLUELESS, MISUNDERSTANDING-PRONE GYM TEACHER WILL APPROACH ME......

No Matter How I Look at It, It's You Guys' Fault I'm Not Popular!

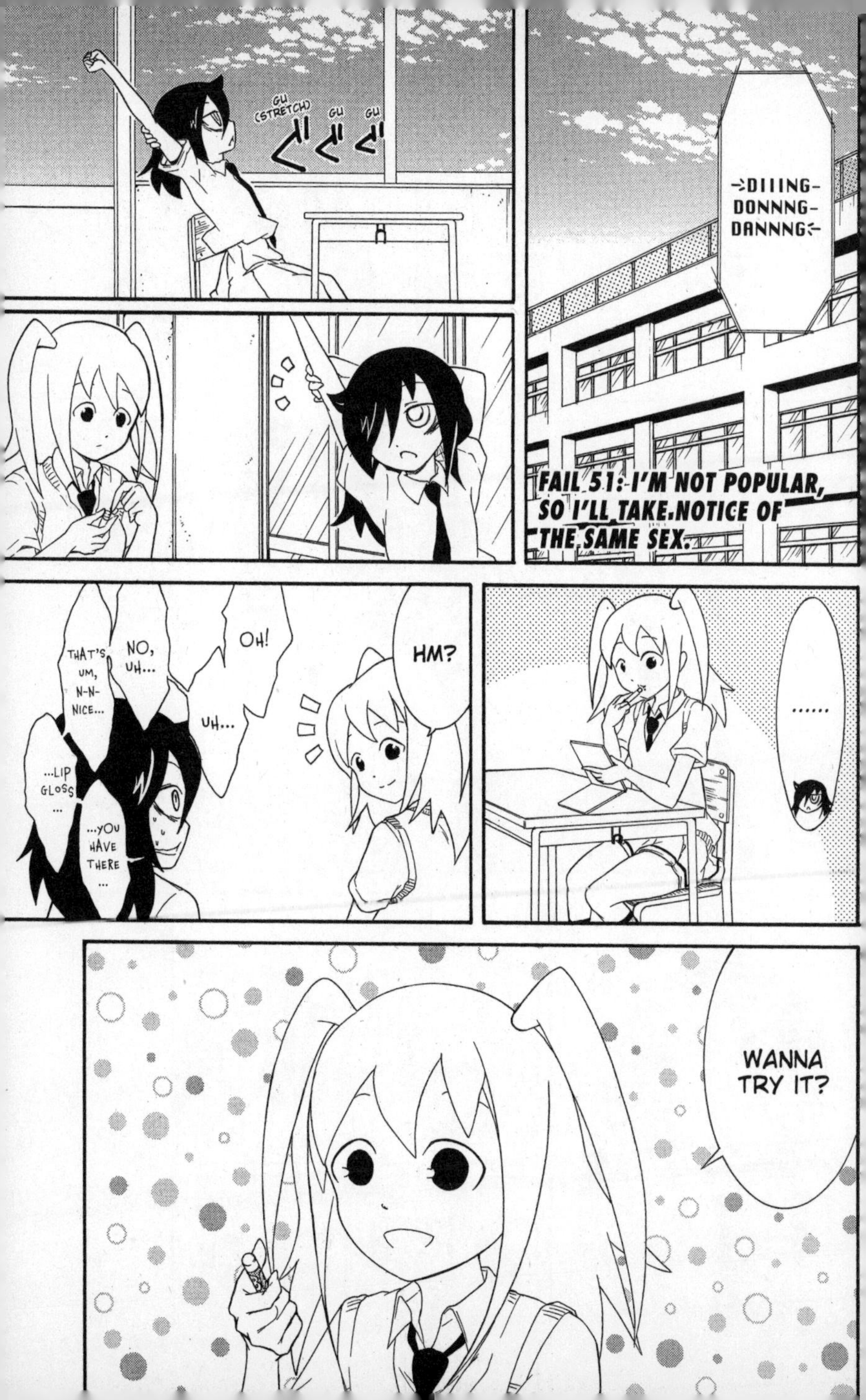

-DIIING-DONNNG-DANNNG-
FAIL 51: I'M NOT POPULAR, SO I'LL TAKE NOTICE OF THE SAME SEX.
GU (STRETCH) GU GU
......
HM?
OH!
UH...
NO, UH...
THAT'S UM, N-N-NICE...
...LIP GLOSS...
...YOU HAVE THERE...
WANNA TRY IT?

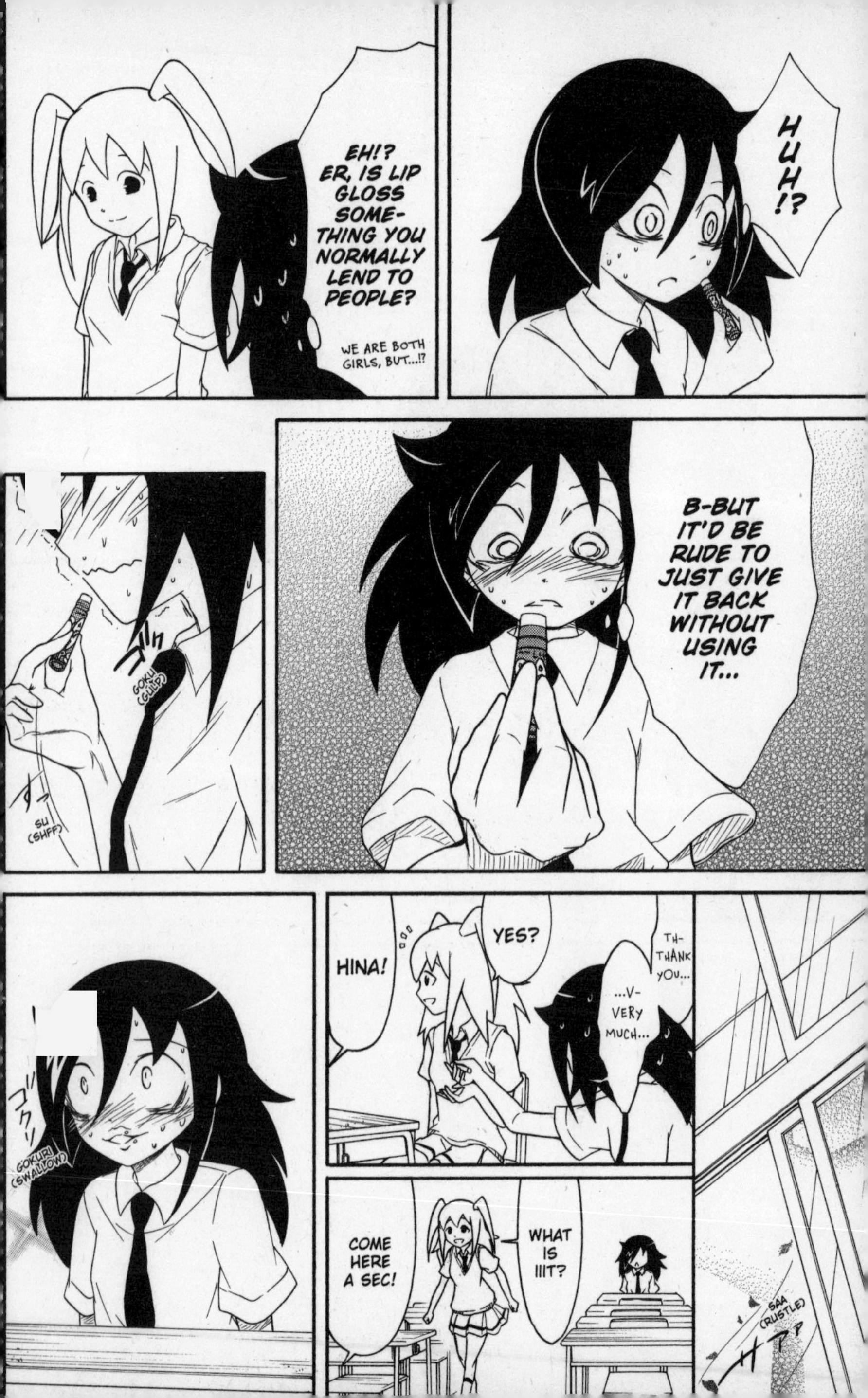
HUH!?
EH!? ER, IS LIP GLOSS SOME-THING YOU NORMALLY LEND TO PEOPLE?
WE ARE BOTH GIRLS, BUT...!?
B-BUT IT'D BE RUDE TO JUST GIVE IT BACK WITHOUT USING IT...
GOKU (GULP)
SU (SHFF)
SAA (RUSTLE)
TH-THANK YOU...
...V-VERY MUCH...
YES?
HINA!
WHAT IS IIIT?
COME HERE A SEC!
GOKURI (SWALLOW)

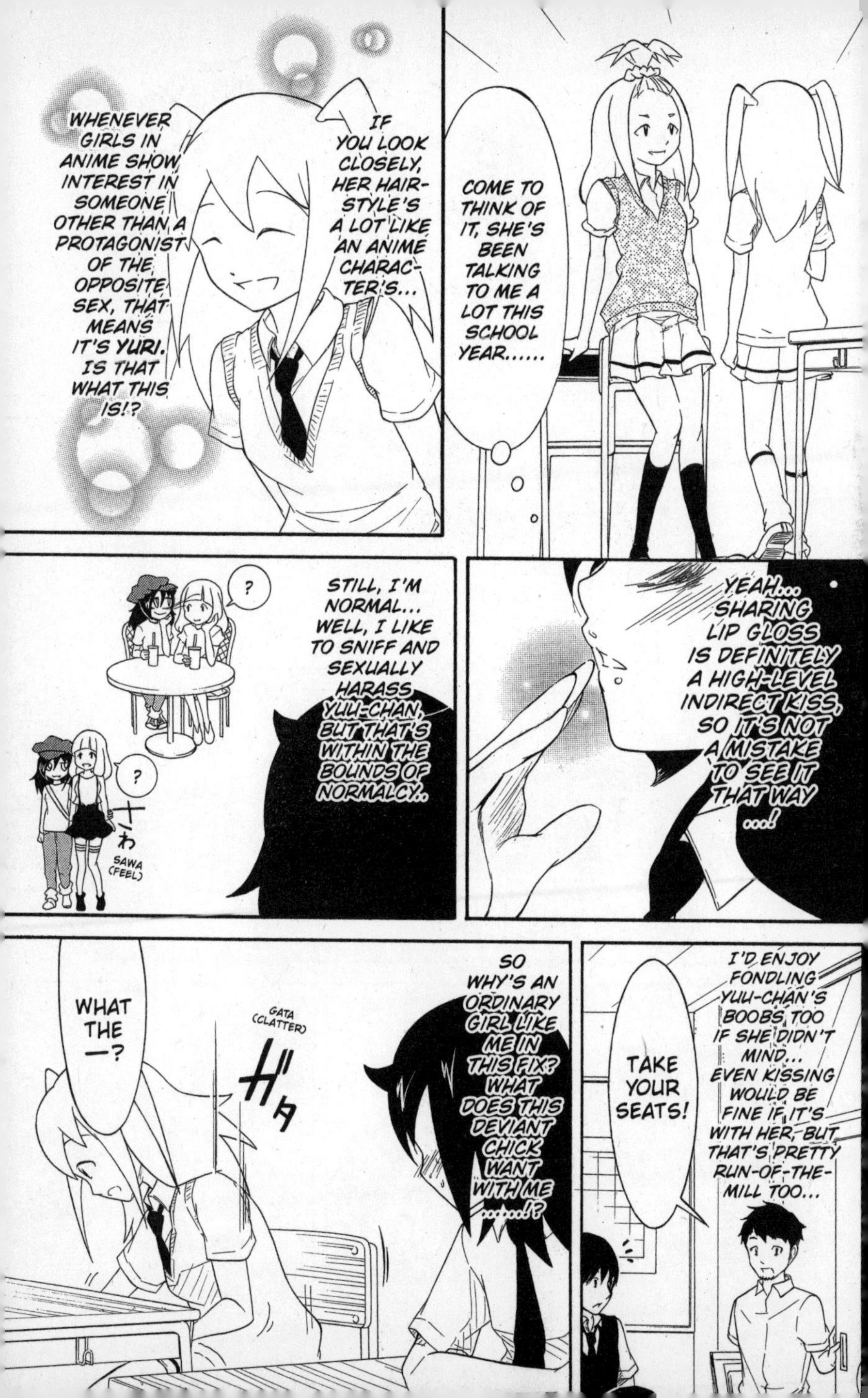
COME TO THINK OF IT, SHE'S BEEN TALKING TO ME A LOT THIS SCHOOL YEAR......
IF YOU LOOK CLOSELY, HER HAIR-STYLE'S A LOT LIKE AN ANIME CHARAC-TER'S...
WHENEVER GIRLS IN ANIME SHOW INTEREST IN SOMEONE OTHER THAN A PROTAGONIST OF THE OPPOSITE SEX, THAT MEANS IT'S YURI. IS THAT WHAT THIS IS!?
YEAH... SHARING LIP GLOSS IS DEFINITELY A HIGH-LEVEL INDIRECT KISS, SO IT'S NOT A MISTAKE TO SEE IT THAT WAY...!
STILL, I'M NORMAL... WELL, I LIKE TO SNIFF AND SEXUALLY HARASS YUU-CHAN, BUT THAT'S WITHIN THE BOUNDS OF NORMALCY..
?
?
さわ
SAWA (FEEL)
I'D ENJOY FONDLING YUU-CHAN'S BOOBS TOO IF SHE DIDN'T MIND... EVEN KISSING WOULD BE FINE IF IT'S WITH HER, BUT THAT'S PRETTY RUN-OF-THE-MILL TOO...
TAKE YOUR SEATS!
SO WHY'S AN ORDINARY GIRL LIKE ME IN THIS FIX? WHAT DOES THIS DEVIANT CHICK WANT WITH ME......!?
ガタ
GATA (CLATTER)
WHAT THE—?

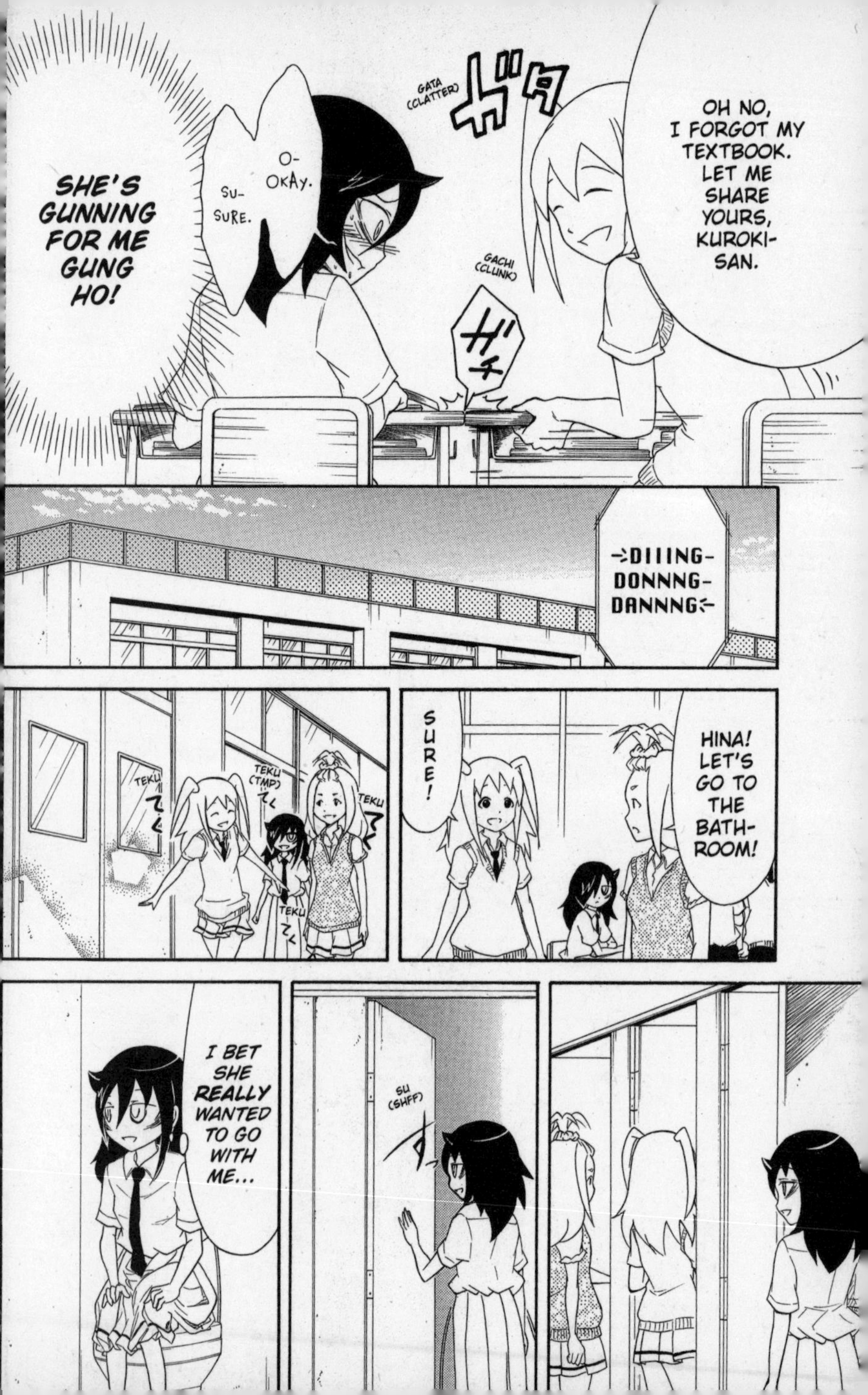
OH NO, I FORGOT MY TEXTBOOK. LET ME SHARE YOURS, KUROKI-SAN.
GATA (CLATTER)
O- OKAY.
SU- SURE.
GACHI (CLUNK)
SHE'S GUNNING FOR ME GUNG HO!
-DIIING-DONNNG-DANNNG-
HINA! LET'S GO TO THE BATH-ROOM!
SURE!
TEKU
TEKU (TMP)
TEKU
TEKU
SU (SHFF)
I BET SHE REALLY WANTED TO GO WITH ME...

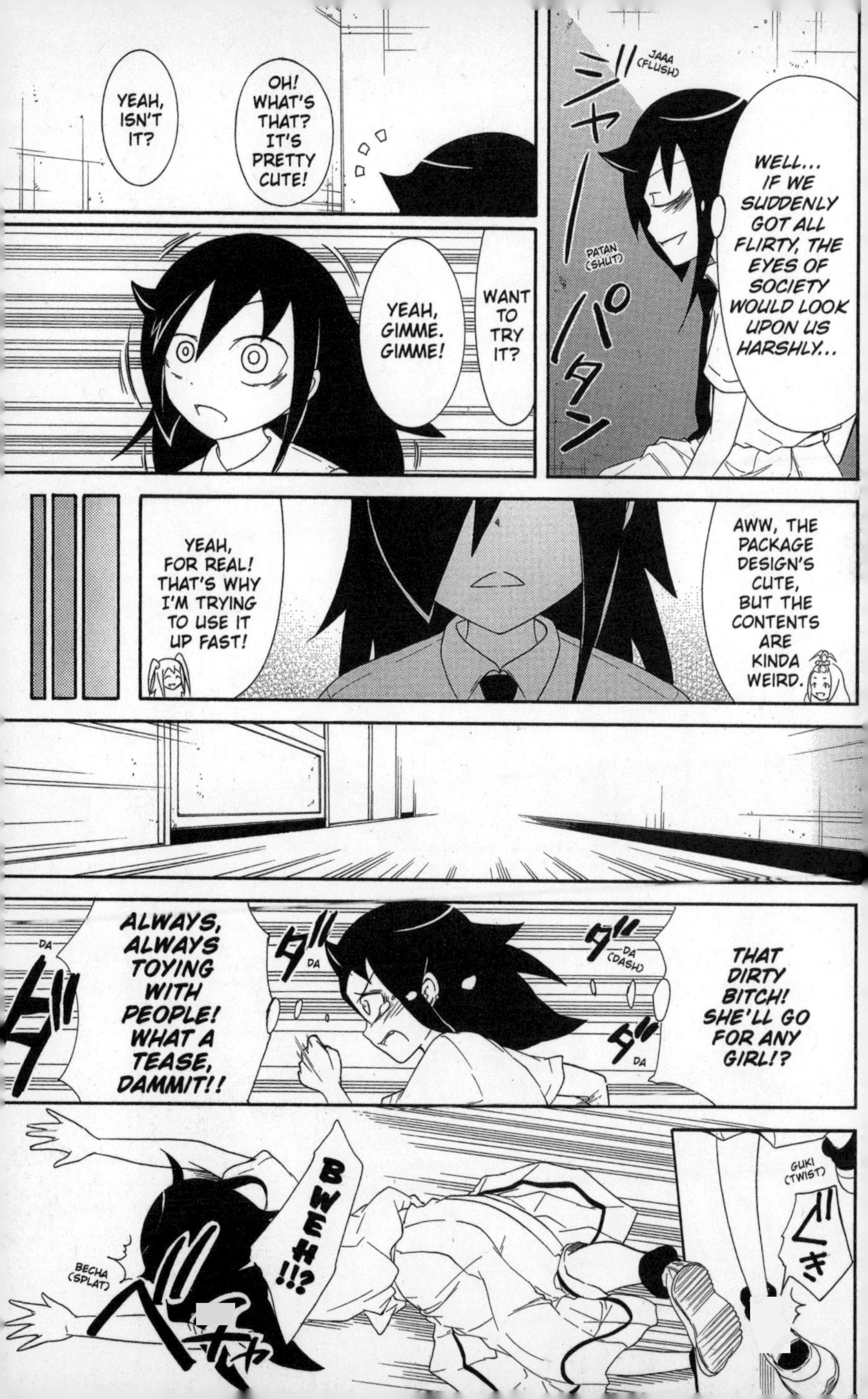

JAAA (FLUSH)
ジャー
WELL... IF WE SUDDENLY GOT ALL FLIRTY, THE EYES OF SOCIETY WOULD LOOK UPON US HARSHLY...
PATAN (SHUT)
パタン
OH! WHAT'S THAT? IT'S PRETTY CUTE!
YEAH, ISN'T IT?
WANT TO TRY IT?
YEAH, GIMME. GIMME!
AWW, THE PACKAGE DESIGN'S CUTE, BUT THE CONTENTS ARE KINDA WEIRD.
YEAH, FOR REAL! THAT'S WHY I'M TRYING TO USE IT UP FAST!
THAT DIRTY BITCH! SHE'LL GO FOR ANY GIRL!?
DA (DASH)
DA
DA
ALWAYS, ALWAYS TOYING WITH PEOPLE! WHAT A TEASE, DAMMIT!!
DA
GUKI (TWIST)
BWEH!!?
BECHA (SPLAT)

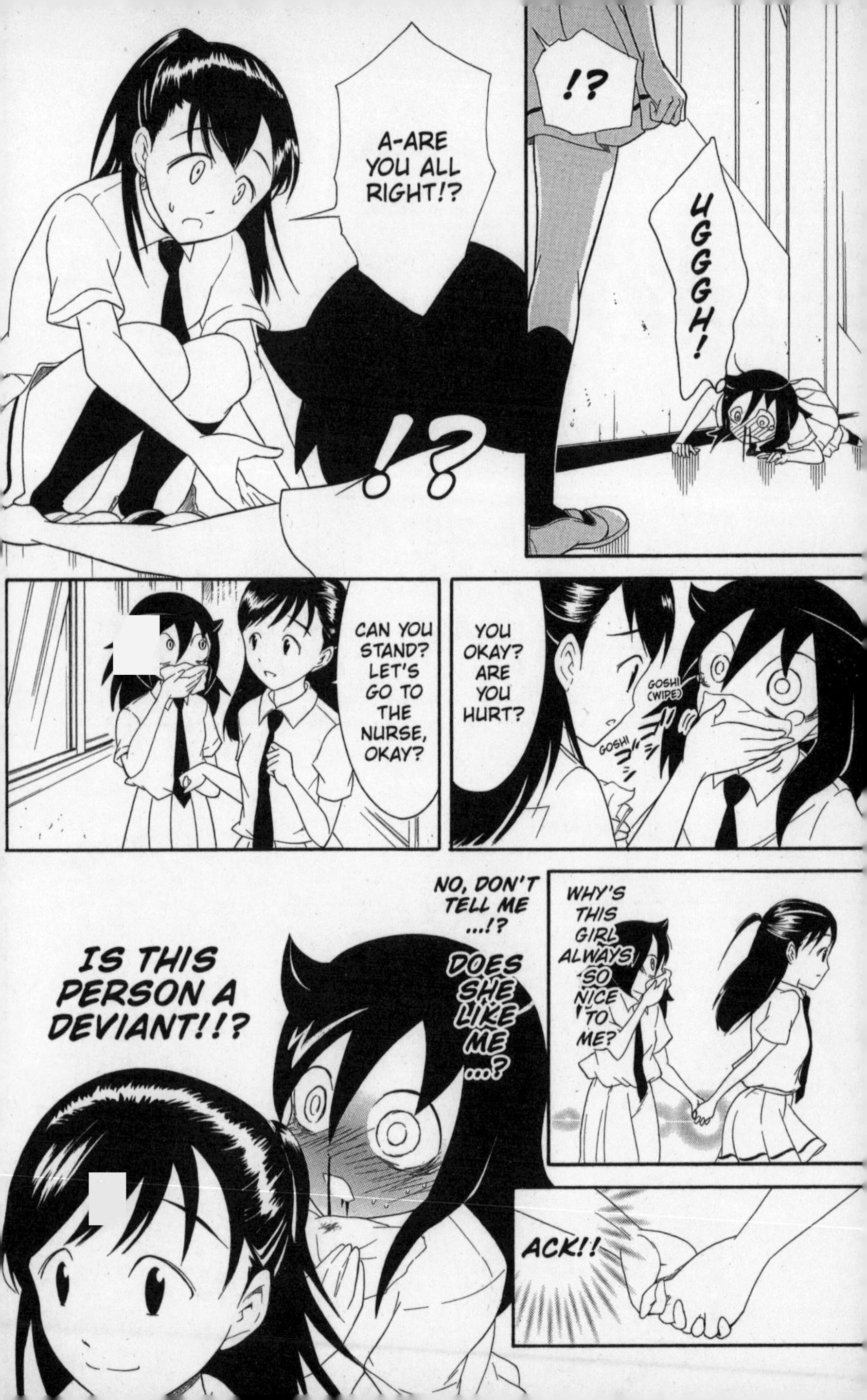
!?
UGGGH!
A-ARE YOU ALL RIGHT!?
!?
YOU OKAY? ARE YOU HURT?
GOSHI (WIPE)
GOSHI
CAN YOU STAND? LET'S GO TO THE NURSE, OKAY?
WHY'S THIS GIRL ALWAYS SO NICE TO ME?
ACK!!
NO, DON'T TELL ME ...!?
DOES SHE LIKE ME ...?
IS THIS PERSON A DEVIANT!!?

No Matter How I Look at It, It's You Guys' Fault I'm Not Popular!

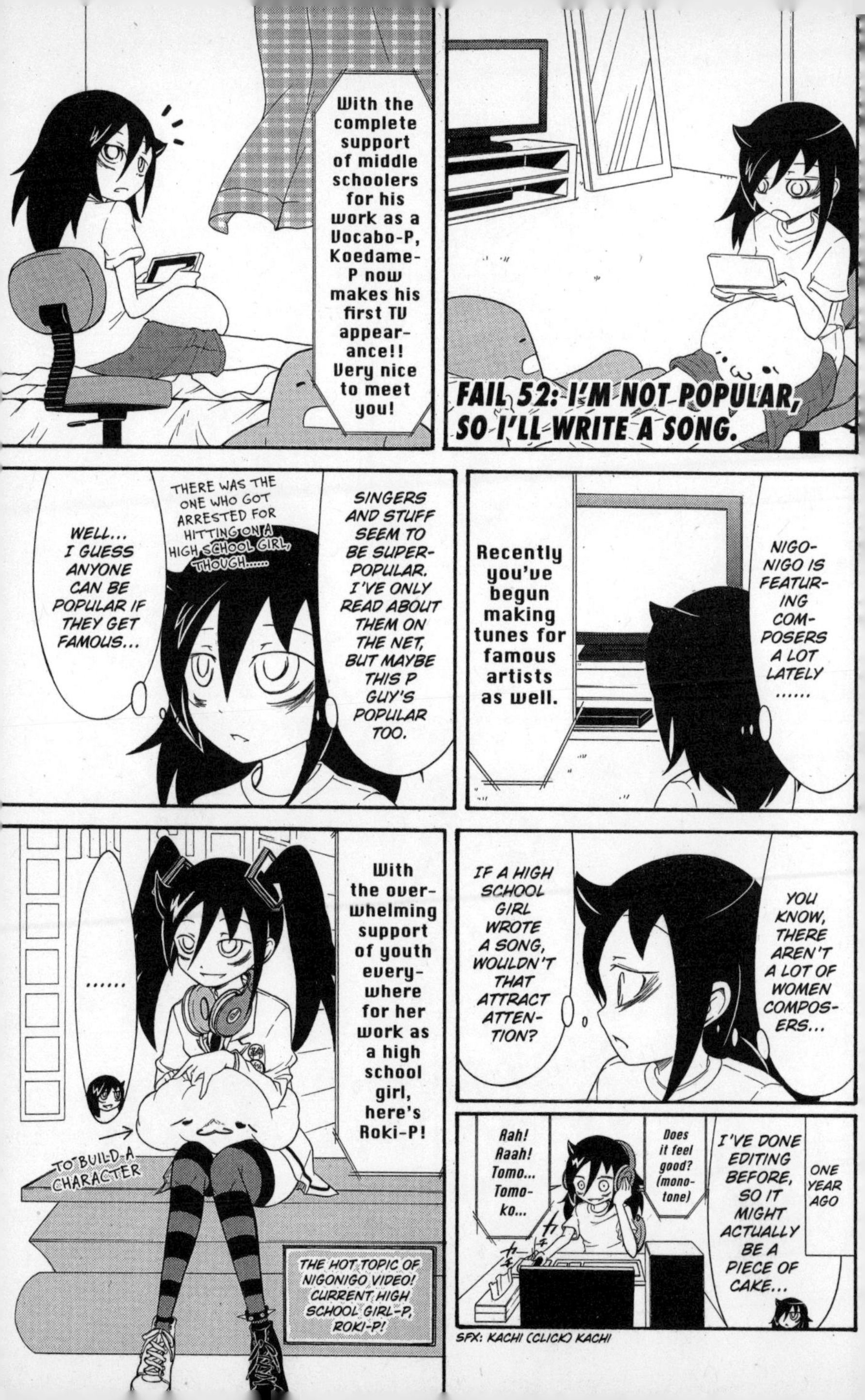
FAIL 52: I'M NOT POPULAR, SO I'LL WRITE A SONG.
With the complete support of middle schoolers for his work as a Vocabo-P, Koedame-P now makes his first TV appearance!! Very nice to meet you!
NIGO-NIGO IS FEATURING COMPOSERS A LOT LATELY ......
Recently you've begun making tunes for famous artists as well.
SINGERS AND STUFF SEEM TO BE SUPER-POPULAR. I'VE ONLY READ ABOUT THEM ON THE NET, BUT MAYBE THIS P GUY'S POPULAR TOO.
THERE WAS THE ONE WHO GOT ARRESTED FOR HITTING ON A HIGH SCHOOL GIRL, THOUGH......
WELL... I GUESS ANYONE CAN BE POPULAR IF THEY GET FAMOUS...
YOU KNOW, THERE AREN'T A LOT OF WOMEN COMPOSERS...
IF A HIGH SCHOOL GIRL WROTE A SONG, WOULDN'T THAT ATTRACT ATTENTION?
ONE YEAR AGO
I'VE DONE EDITING BEFORE, SO IT MIGHT ACTUALLY BE A PIECE OF CAKE...
Does it feel good? (monotone)
Aah! Aaah! Tomo... Tomoko...
SFX: KACHI (CLICK) KACHI
With the overwhelming support of youth everywhere for her work as a high school girl, here's Roki-P!
......
TO BUILD A CHARACTER
THE HOT TOPIC OF NIGONIGO VIDEO! CURRENT HIGH SCHOOL GIRL-P, ROKI-P!

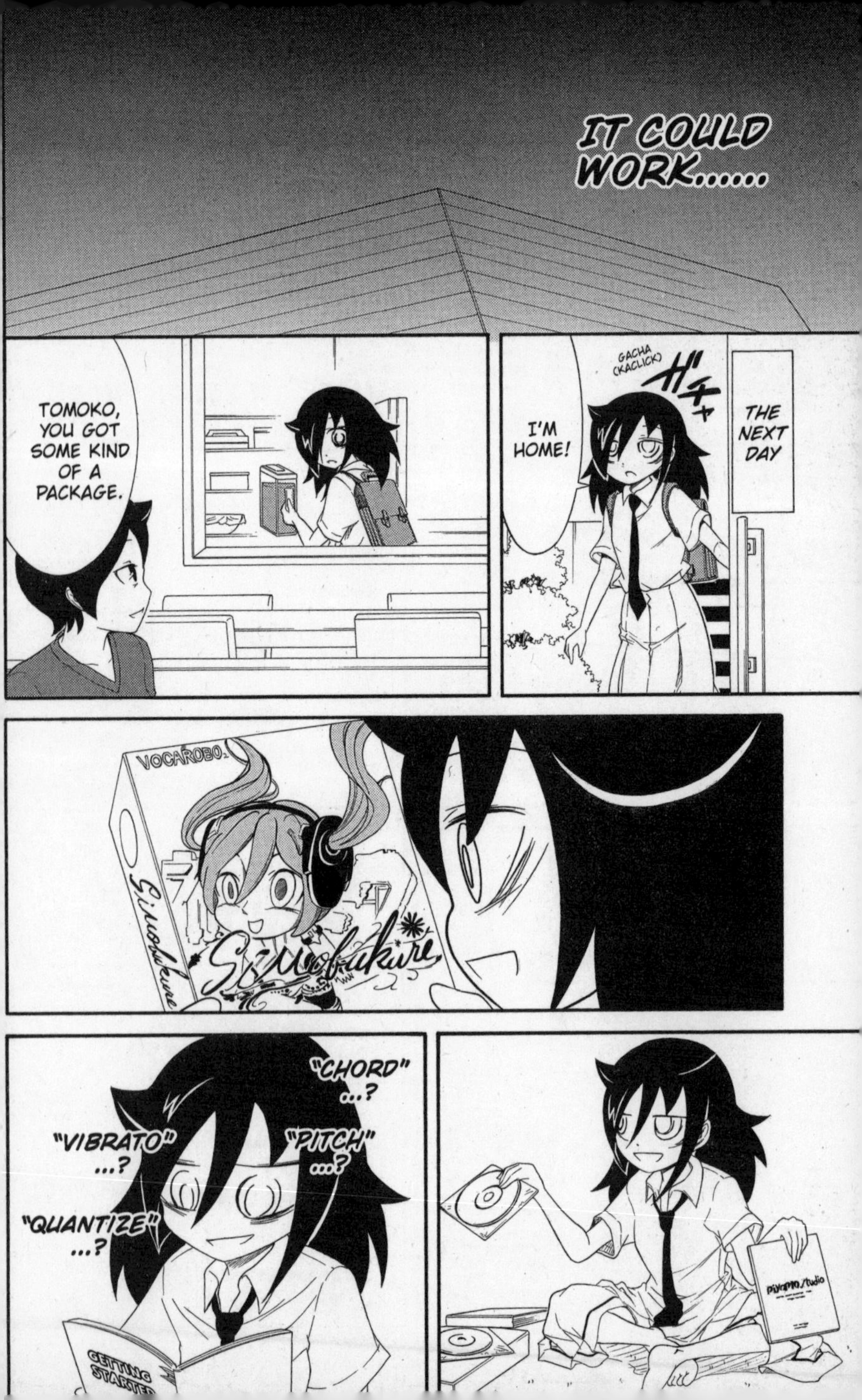
IT COULD WORK......
THE NEXT DAY
GACHA (KACLICK)
ガチャ
I'M HOME!
TOMOKO, YOU GOT SOME KIND OF A PACKAGE.
VOCAROBO
Siimofukure
"CHORD" ...?
"PITCH" ...?
"VIBRATO" ...?
"QUANTIZE" ...?
GETTING STARTED
PiyoPiyo Studio

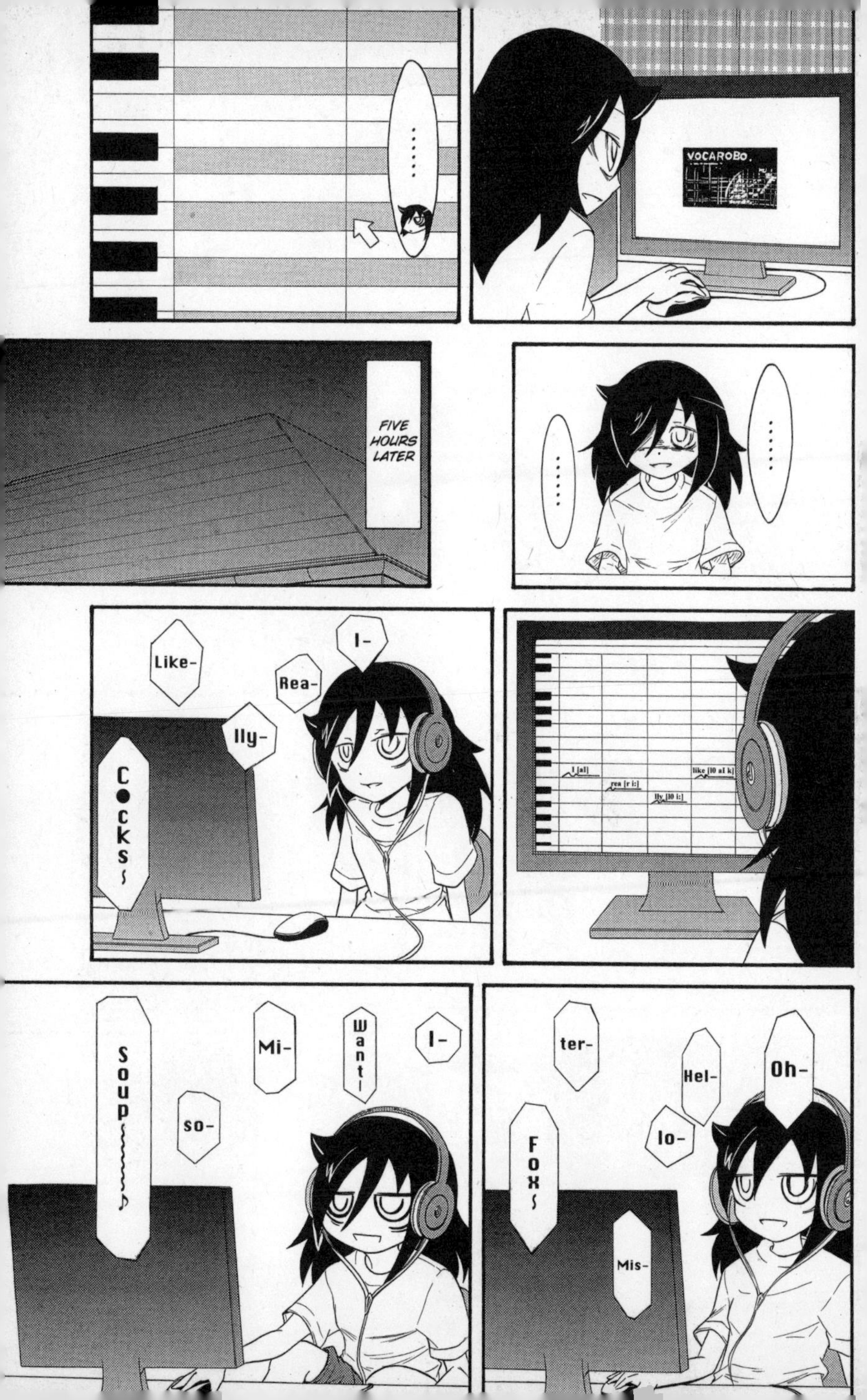
VOCAROBO.
......
......
......
FIVE HOURS LATER
I-
Rea-
lly-
Like-
C●cks~
Oh-
Hel-
lo-
Mis-
ter-
Fox~
I-
Want
Mi-
so-
Soup~~~♪

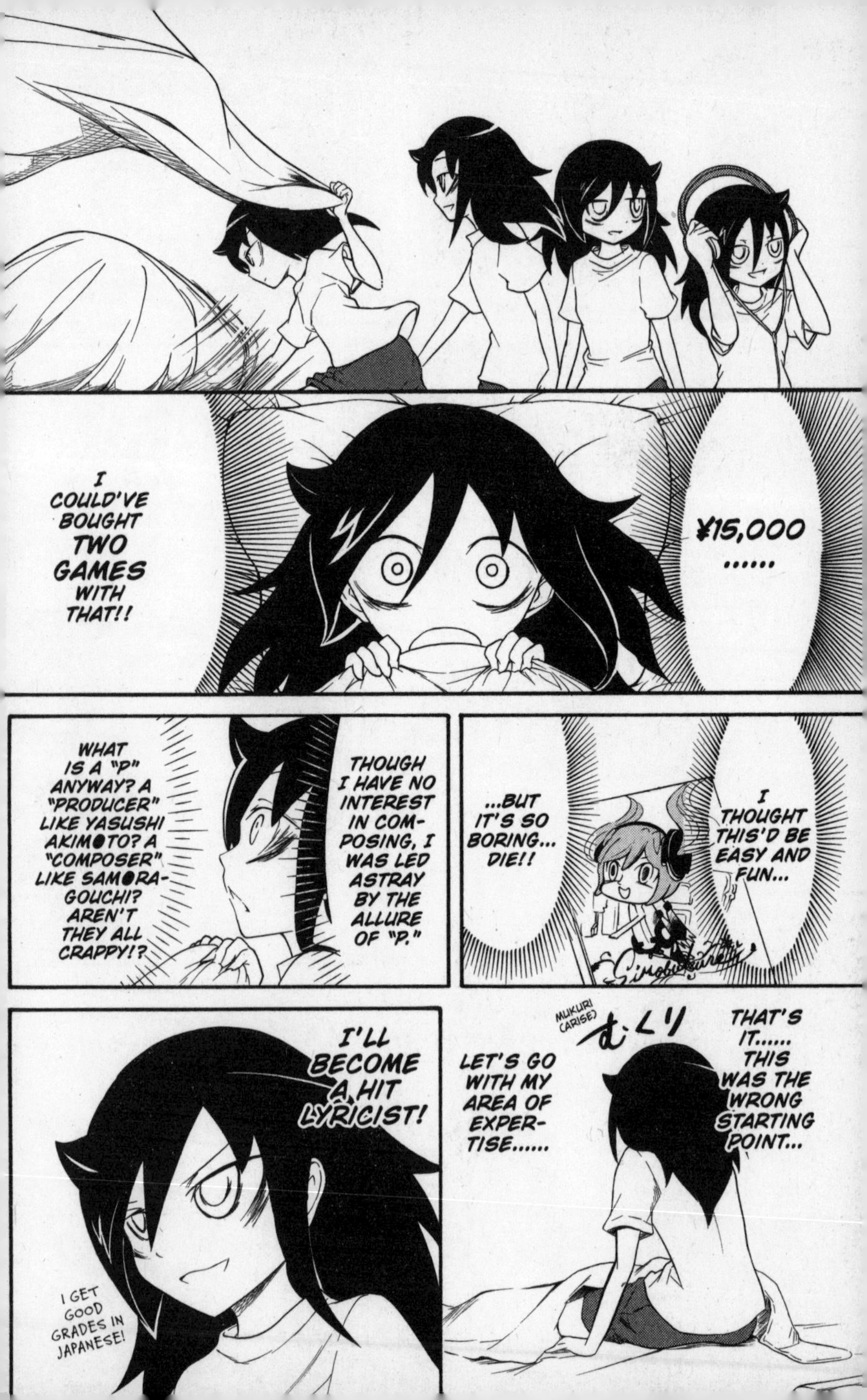
¥15,000 ......
I COULD'VE BOUGHT TWO GAMES WITH THAT!!
I THOUGHT THIS'D BE EASY AND FUN...
...BUT IT'S SO BORING... DIE!!
THOUGH I HAVE NO INTEREST IN COMPOSING, I WAS LED ASTRAY BY THE ALLURE OF "P."
WHAT IS A "P" ANYWAY? A "PRODUCER" LIKE YASUSHI AKIMOTO? A "COMPOSER" LIKE SAMORAGOUCHI? AREN'T THEY ALL CRAPPY!?
THAT'S IT...... THIS WAS THE WRONG STARTING POINT...
むくり
MUKURI (ARISE)
LET'S GO WITH MY AREA OF EXPERTISE......
I'LL BECOME A HIT LYRICIST!
I GET GOOD GRADES IN JAPANESE!

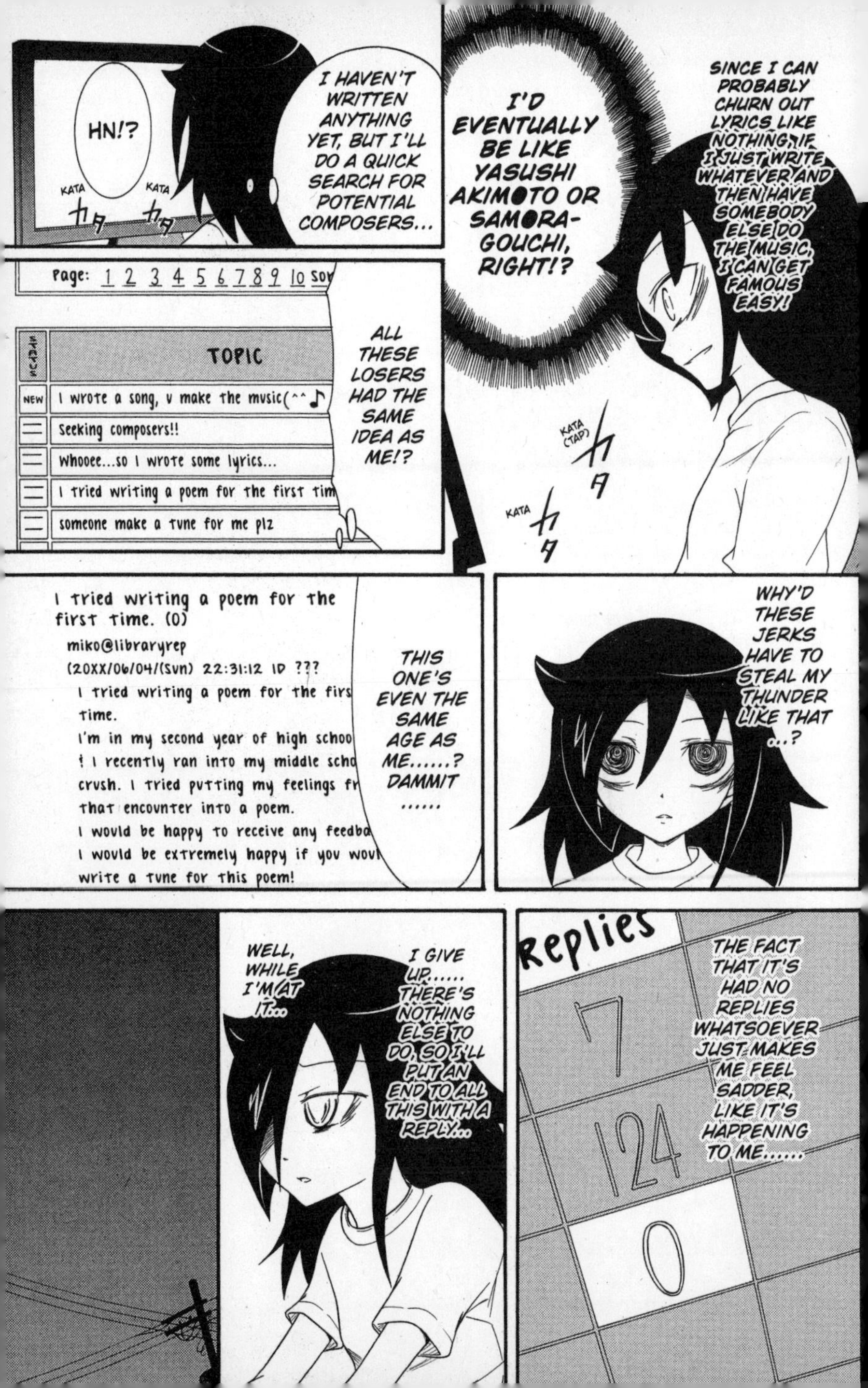
SINCE I CAN PROBABLY CHURN OUT LYRICS LIKE NOTHING IF I JUST WRITE WHATEVER AND THEN HAVE SOMEBODY ELSE DO THE MUSIC, I CAN GET FAMOUS EASY!
I'D EVENTUALLY BE LIKE YASUSHI AKIMOTO OR SAMORA-GOUCHI, RIGHT!?
KATA (TAP)
KATA
I HAVEN'T WRITTEN ANYTHING YET, BUT I'LL DO A QUICK SEARCH FOR POTENTIAL COMPOSERS...
HN!?
KATA
KATA
Page: 1 2 3 4 5 6 7 8 9 10
STATUS
TOPIC
NEW
I wrote a song, u make the music(^^♪
Seeking composers!!
Whooee...so I wrote some lyrics...
I tried writing a poem for the first tim
someone make a tune for me plz
ALL THESE LOSERS HAD THE SAME IDEA AS ME!?
WHY'D THESE JERKS HAVE TO STEAL MY THUNDER LIKE THAT...?
I tried writing a poem for the first time. (0)
miko@libraryrep
(20XX/06/04/(Sun) 22:31:12 ID ???
I tried writing a poem for the firs time.
I'm in my second year of high schoo
& I recently ran into my middle scho crush. I tried putting my feelings fr that encounter into a poem.
I would be happy to receive any feedba
I would be extremely happy if you woul write a tune for this poem!
THIS ONE'S EVEN THE SAME AGE AS ME......? DAMMIT......
Replies
7
124
0
THE FACT THAT IT'S HAD NO REPLIES WHATSOEVER JUST MAKES ME FEEL SADDER, LIKE IT'S HAPPENING TO ME......
I GIVE UP...... THERE'S NOTHING ELSE TO DO, SO I'LL PUT AN END TO ALL THIS WITH A REPLY...
WELL, WHILE I'M AT IT...

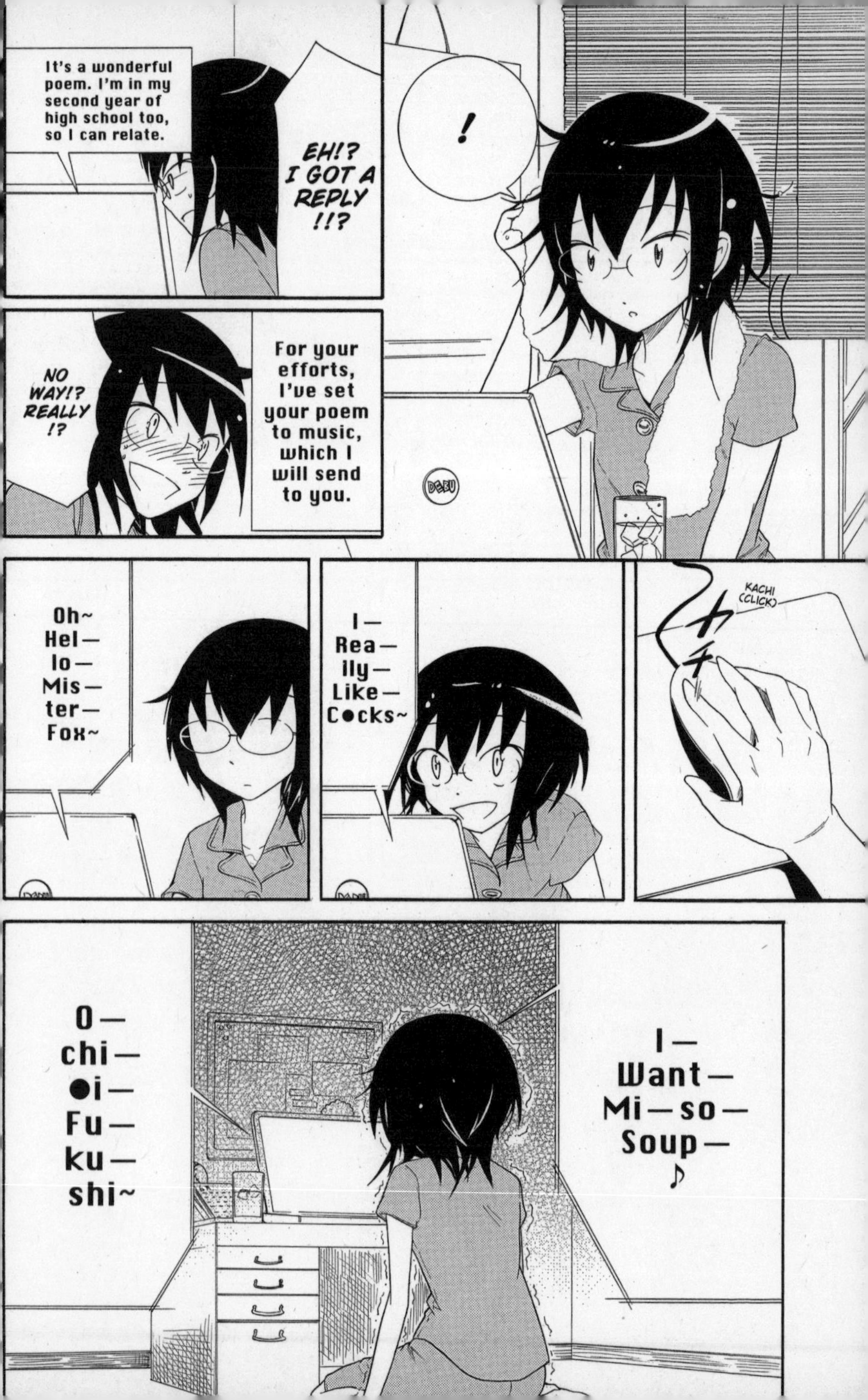
!
DEBU
EH!? I GOT A REPLY !!?
It's a wonderful poem. I'm in my second year of high school too, so I can relate.
For your efforts, I've set your poem to music, which I will send to you.
NO WAY!? REALLY !?
KACHI (CLICK)
I— Rea— lly— Like— C●cks~
Oh~ Hel— lo— Mis— ter— Fox~
I— Want— Mi—so— Soup— ♪
O— chi— ●i— Fu— ku— shi~

No Matter How I Look at It, It's You Guys' Fault I'm Not Popular!

FAIL 53: I'M NOT POPULAR, SO SOMETHING GOOD WILL HAPPEN.

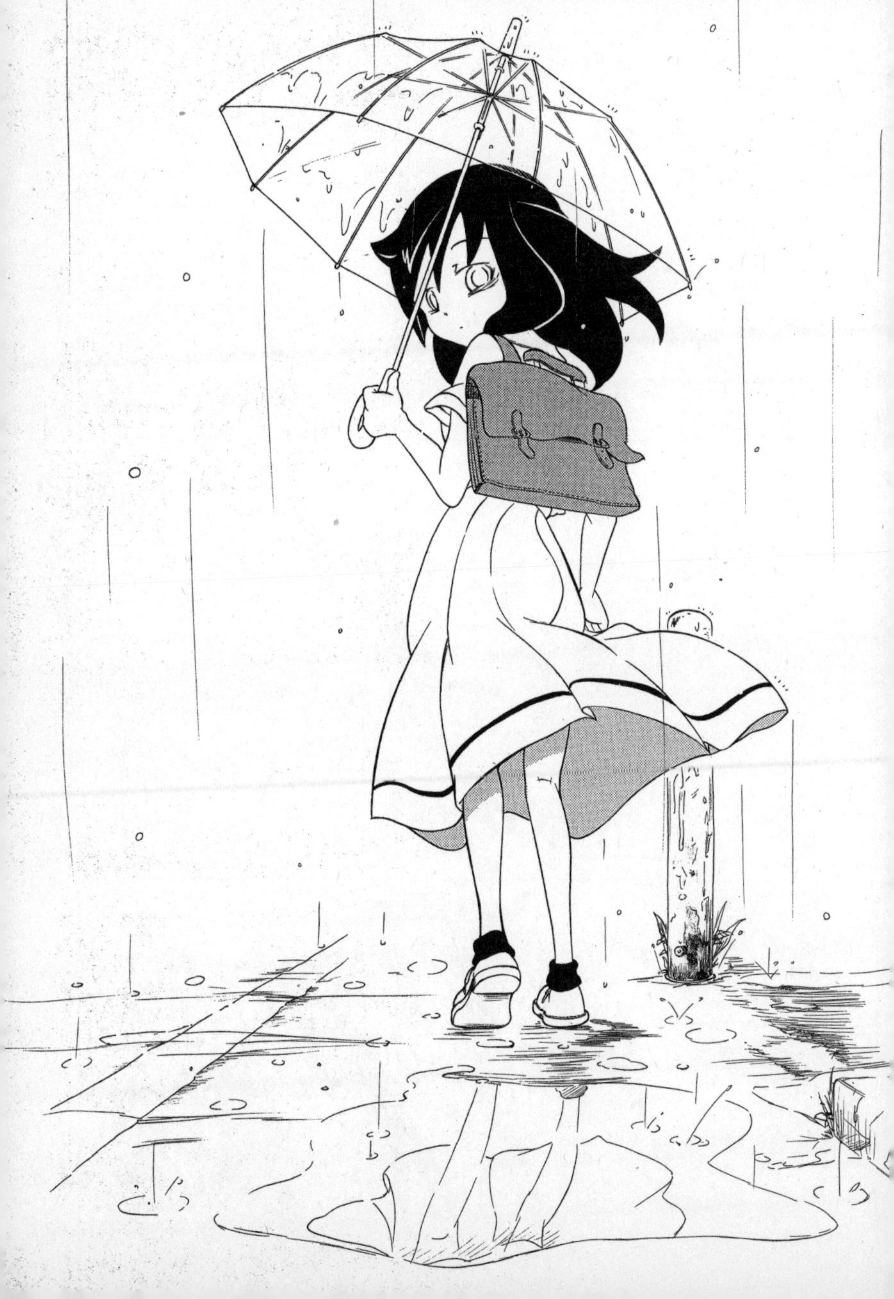

A PLEASANT MORNING

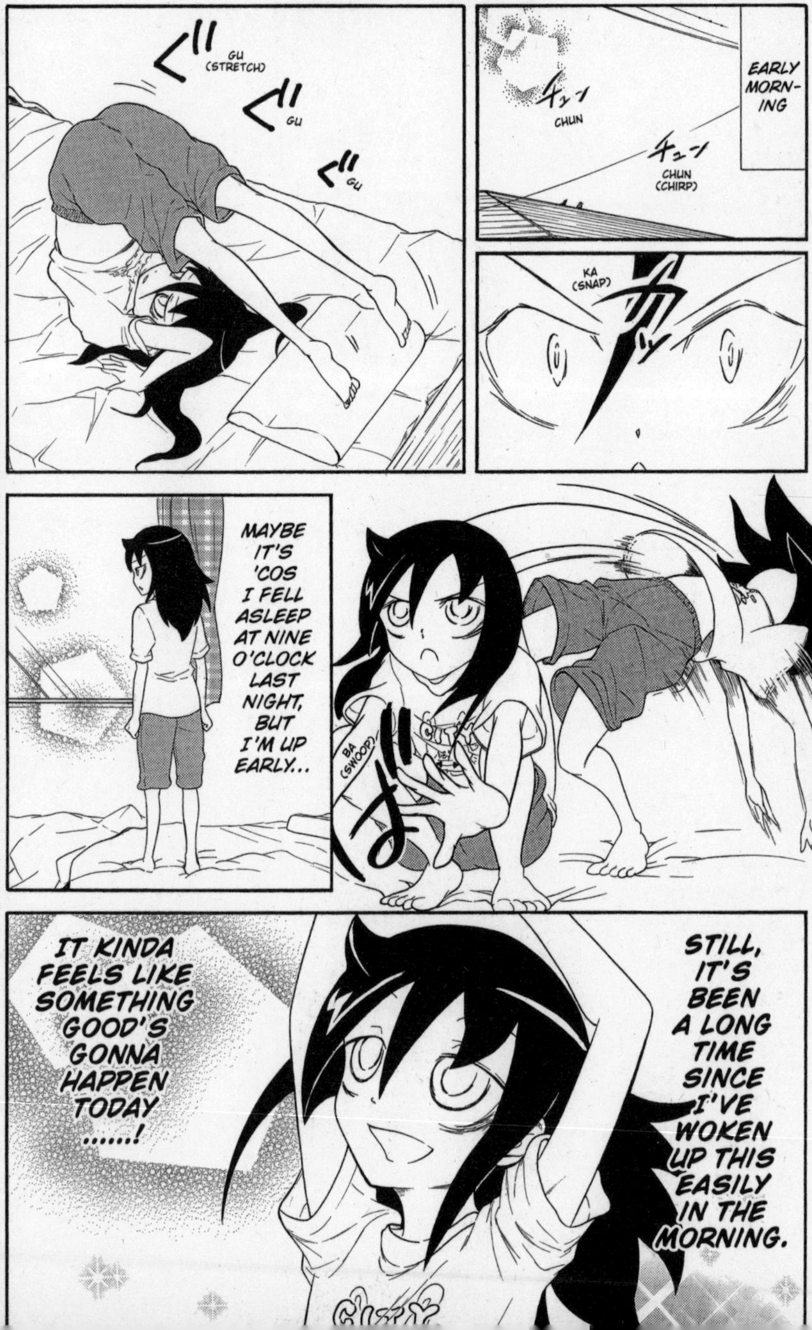

EARLY MORNING
CHUN
CHUN (CHIRP)
KA (SNAP)
GU (STRETCH)
GU
GU
BA (SWOOP)
MAYBE IT'S 'COS I FELL ASLEEP AT NINE O'CLOCK LAST NIGHT, BUT I'M UP EARLY...
STILL, IT'S BEEN A LONG TIME SINCE I'VE WOKEN UP THIS EASILY IN THE MORNING.
IT KINDA FEELS LIKE SOMETHING GOOD'S GONNA HAPPEN TODAY ......!

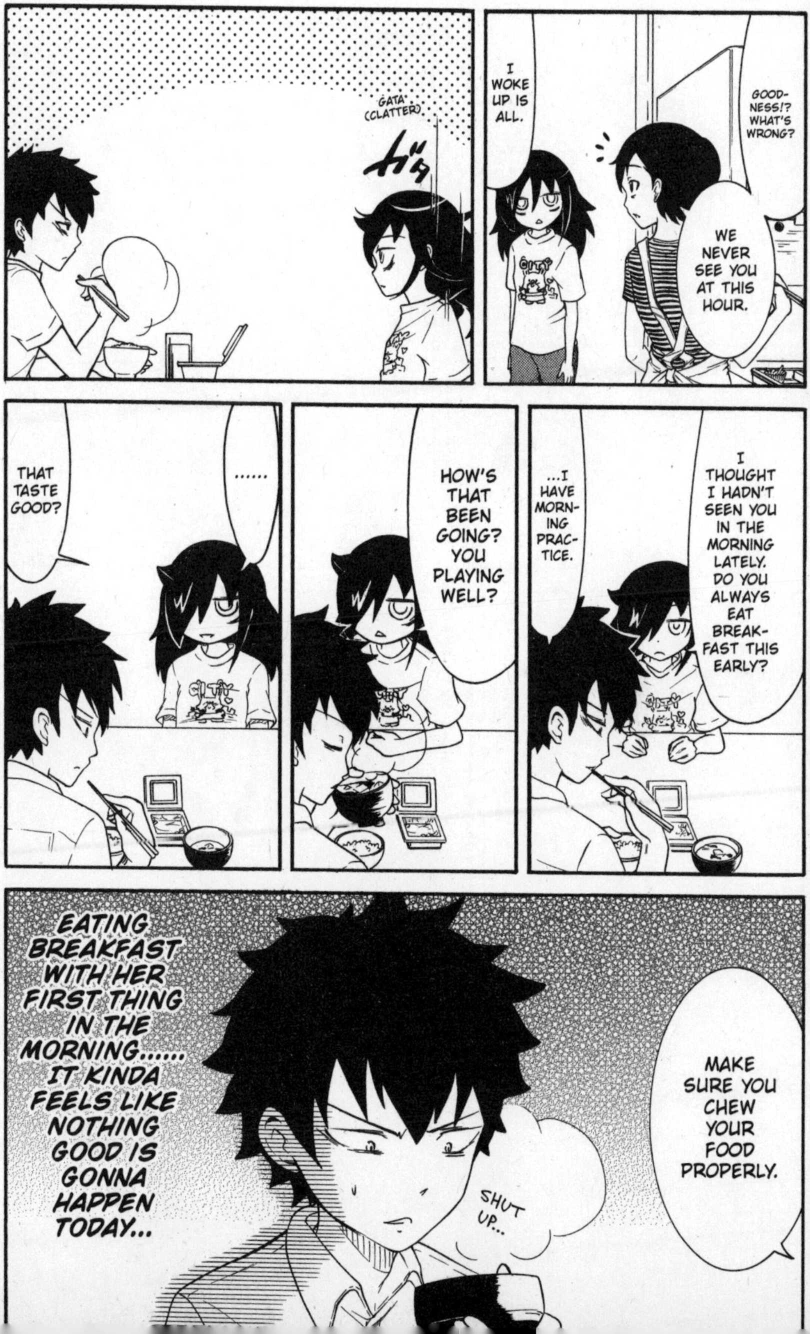
GOOD-NESS!? WHAT'S WRONG?
WE NEVER SEE YOU AT THIS HOUR.
I WOKE UP IS ALL.
GATA (CLATTER)
I THOUGHT I HADN'T SEEN YOU IN THE MORNING LATELY. DO YOU ALWAYS EAT BREAK-FAST THIS EARLY?
...I HAVE MORN-ING PRAC-TICE.
HOW'S THAT BEEN GOING? YOU PLAYING WELL?
......
THAT TASTE GOOD?
MAKE SURE YOU CHEW YOUR FOOD PROPERLY.
SHUT UP...
EATING BREAKFAST WITH HER FIRST THING IN THE MORNING...... IT KINDA FEELS LIKE NOTHING GOOD IS GONNA HAPPEN TODAY...

DUAL WIELDING

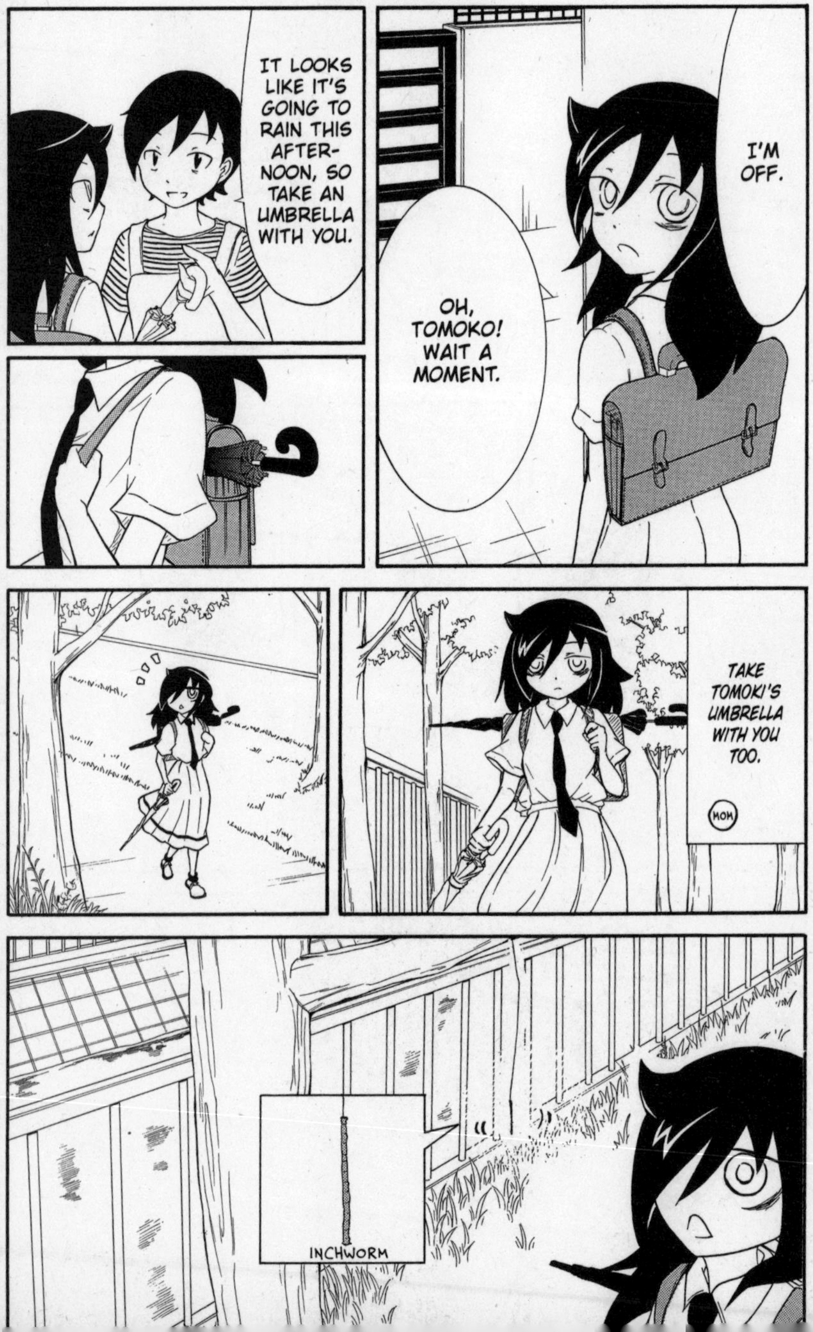
I'M OFF.
OH, TOMOKO! WAIT A MOMENT.
IT LOOKS LIKE IT'S GOING TO RAIN THIS AFTERNOON, SO TAKE AN UMBRELLA WITH YOU.
TAKE TOMOKI'S UMBRELLA WITH YOU TOO.
MOM
INCHWORM

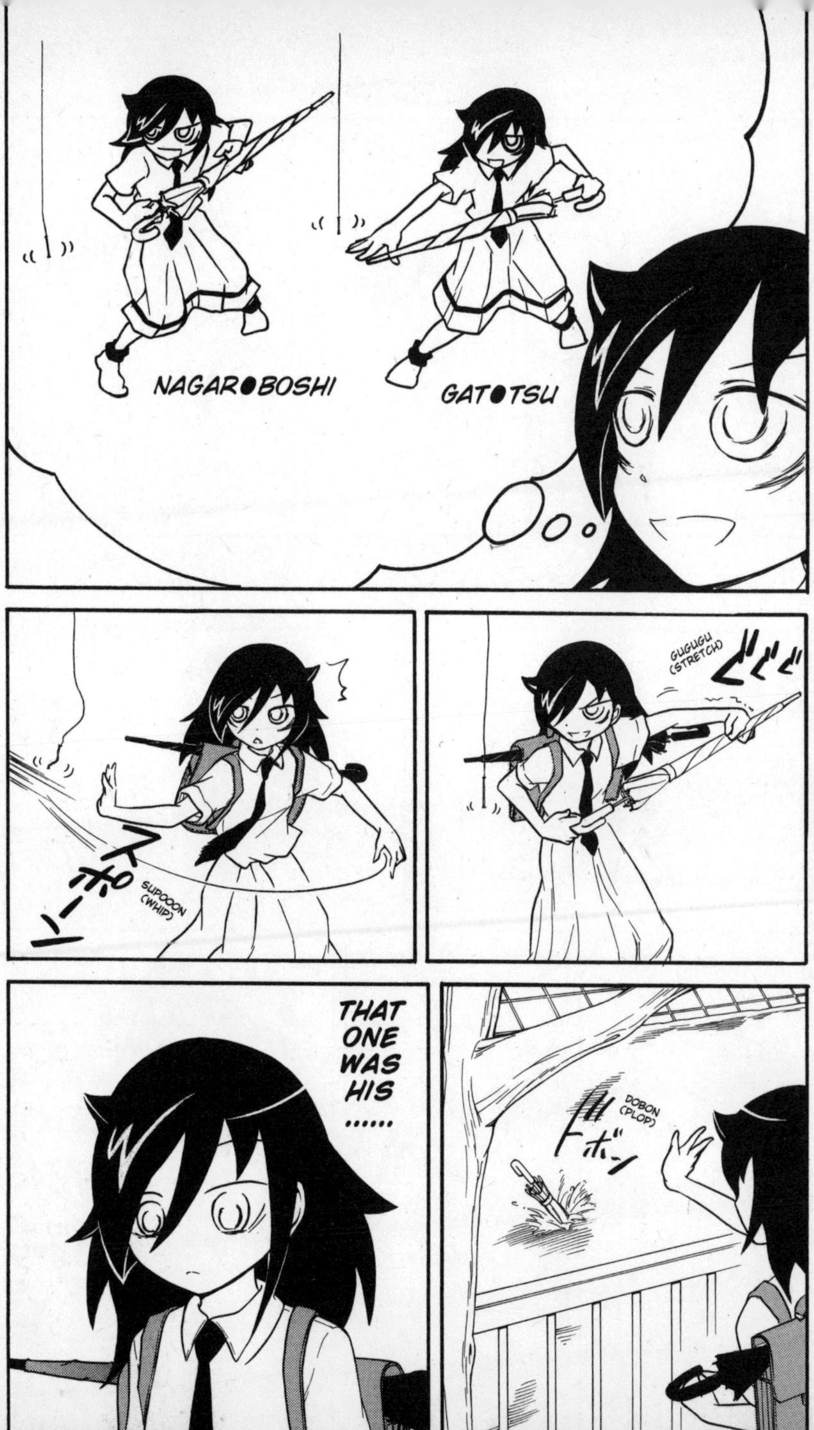
GATOTSU
NAGAROBOSHI
GUGUGU (STRETCH)
SUPOOON (WHIP)
DOBON (PLOP)
THAT ONE WAS HIS ......

ZEROSHIKI

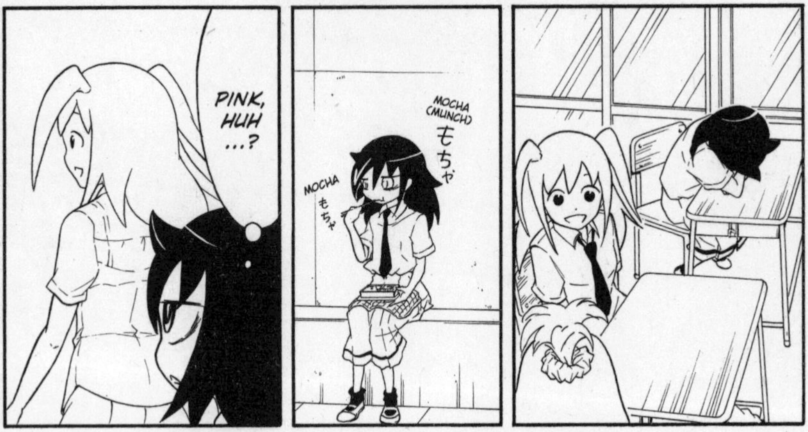
MOCHA (MUNCH)
もちゃ
MOCHA
もちゃ
PINK, HUH ...?

THE SCHOOL DAY GOES BY IN A FLASH...

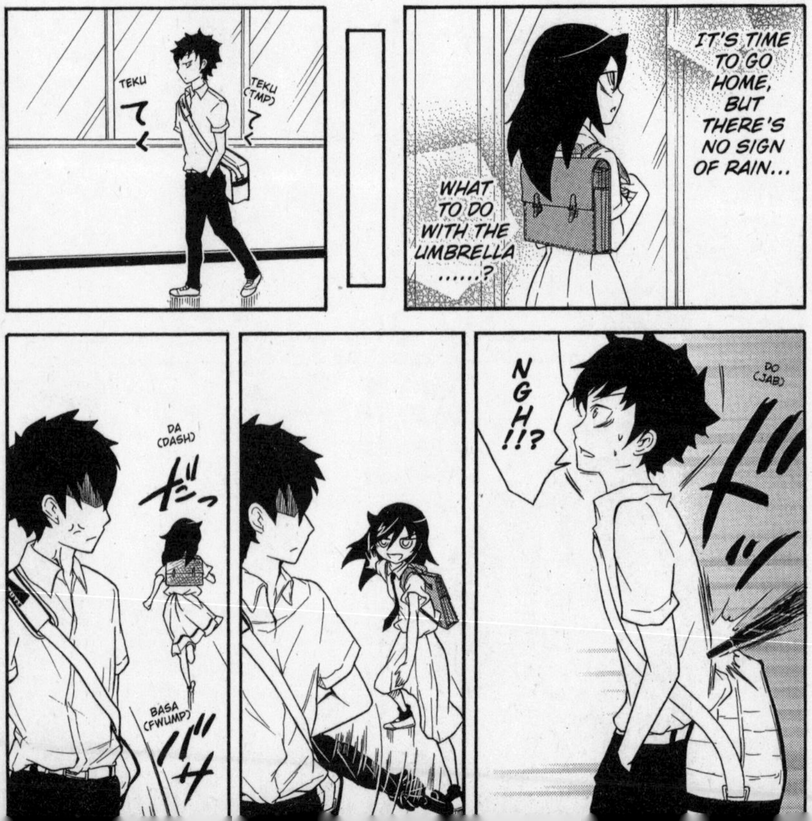
IT'S TIME TO GO HOME, BUT THERE'S NO SIGN OF RAIN...
WHAT TO DO WITH THE UMBRELLA ......?
TEKU (TMP)
てく
TEKU
てく
DO (JAB)
NGH!!?
DA (DASH)
BASA (FWUMP)

PRESENCE

5F	Kaikai CIUB Net Café
4F	Solebbia ソレッビア Italian
3F	UMA UMA Dining Bar

info

北口 NORTH EXIT

A BUNCH OF NEW ISSUES CAME OUT LAST WEEK...

GUESS I'LL DROP BY A MANGA CAFÉ...

EH!?

I SAID NO... LOOK... BEHIND US...

SOME-ONE'S STILL THERE...

!?

3

3

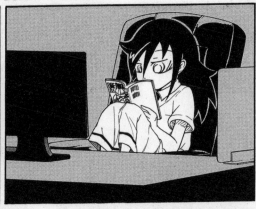

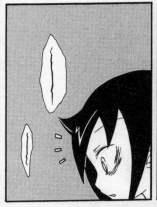

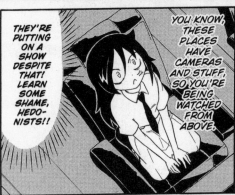

BEING WATCHED

C'MON, JUST A LITTLE ...
I SAID NO...
AH ...
EH!? THOSE TWO FROM BEFORE? GETTING IT ON IN A PLACE LIKE THIS?
YOU KNOW, THESE PLACES HAVE CAMERAS AND STUFF, SO YOU'RE BEING WATCHED FROM ABOVE.
THEY'RE PUTTING ON A SHOW DESPITE THAT! LEARN SOME SHAME, HEDO-NISTS!!
REC ●
00017:03

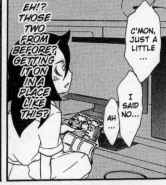

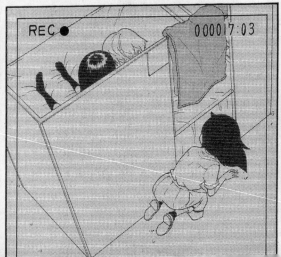

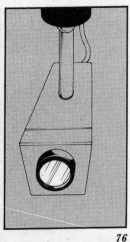

IGNORE

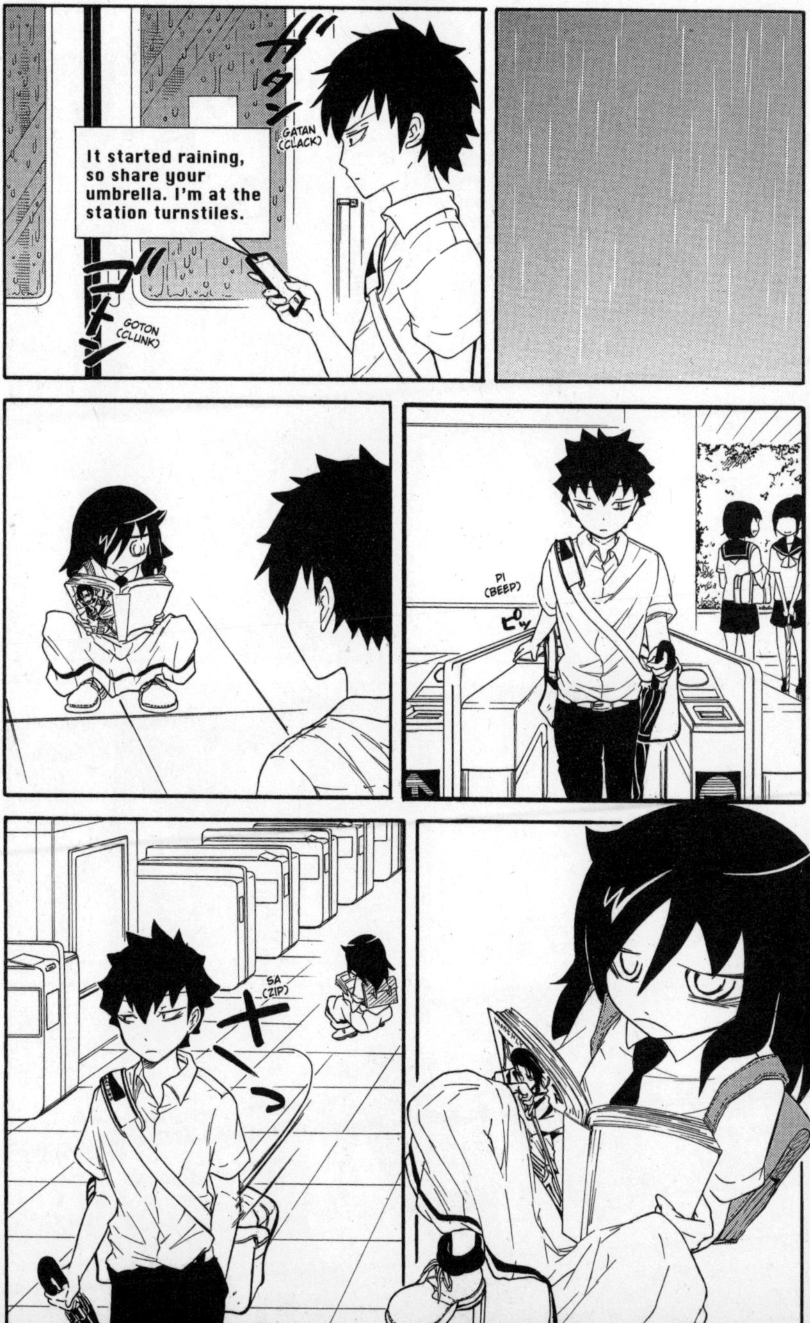
GATAN (CLACK)
It started raining, so share your umbrella. I'm at the station turnstiles.
GOTON (CLUNK)
PI (BEEP)
SA (ZIP)

ALL DAY TODAY

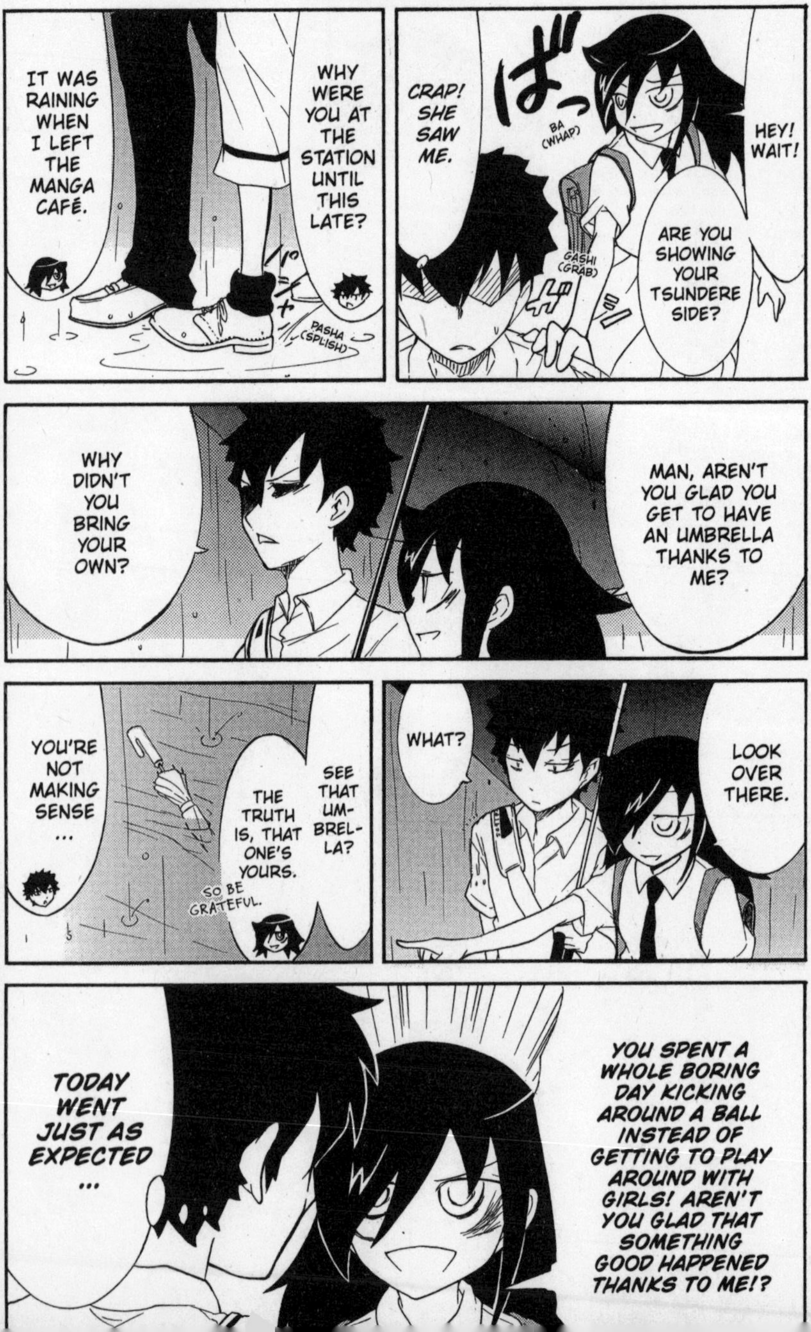
HEY! WAIT!
ARE YOU SHOWING YOUR TSUNDERE SIDE?
ばっ
BA (WHAP)
CRAP! SHE SAW ME.
GASHI (GRAB)
WHY WERE YOU AT THE STATION UNTIL THIS LATE?
PASHA (SPLISH)
IT WAS RAINING WHEN I LEFT THE MANGA CAFÉ.
MAN, AREN'T YOU GLAD YOU GET TO HAVE AN UMBRELLA THANKS TO ME?
WHY DIDN'T YOU BRING YOUR OWN?
LOOK OVER THERE.
WHAT?
SEE THAT UMBRELLA?
THE TRUTH IS, THAT ONE'S YOURS.
SO BE GRATEFUL.
YOU'RE NOT MAKING SENSE...
YOU SPENT A WHOLE BORING DAY KICKING AROUND A BALL INSTEAD OF GETTING TO PLAY AROUND WITH GIRLS! AREN'T YOU GLAD THAT SOMETHING GOOD HAPPENED THANKS TO ME!?
TODAY WENT JUST AS EXPECTED...

No Matter How I Look at It, It's You Guys' Fault I'm Not Popular!

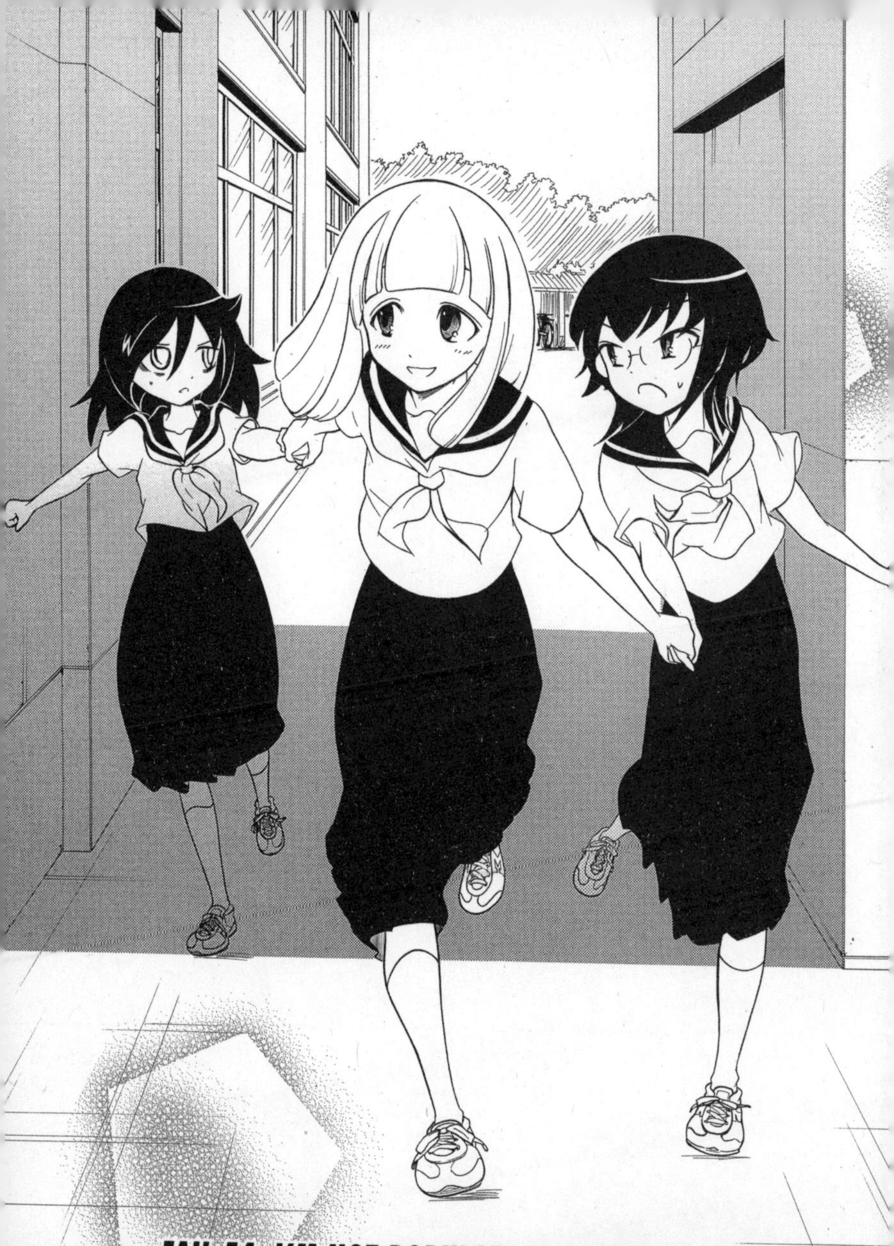

FAIL 54: I'M NOT POPULAR, SO I WON'T CHANGE.

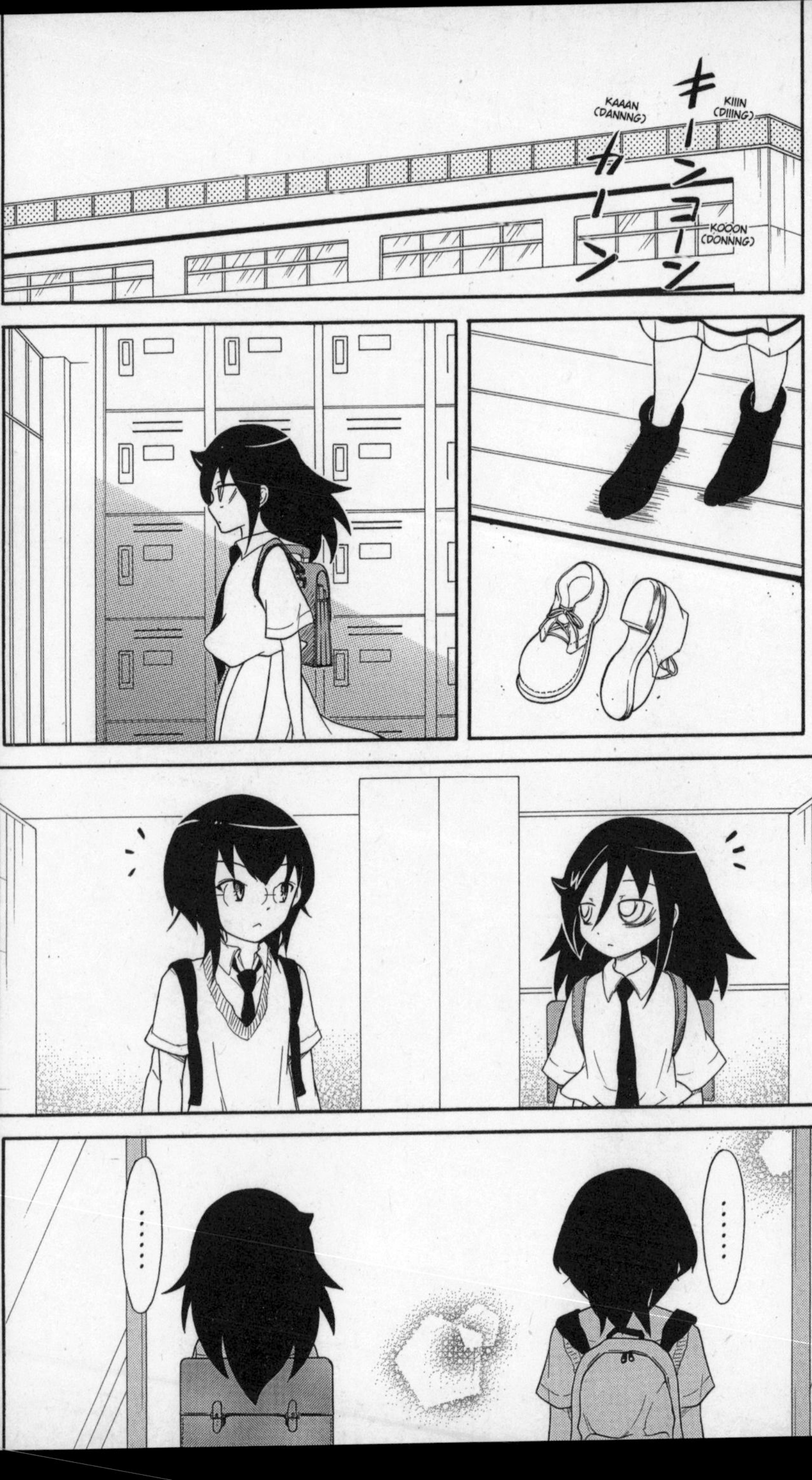
キーンコーン
KIIIN (DIIING)
KOOON (DONNNG)
カーン
KAAAN (DANNNG)
……
……

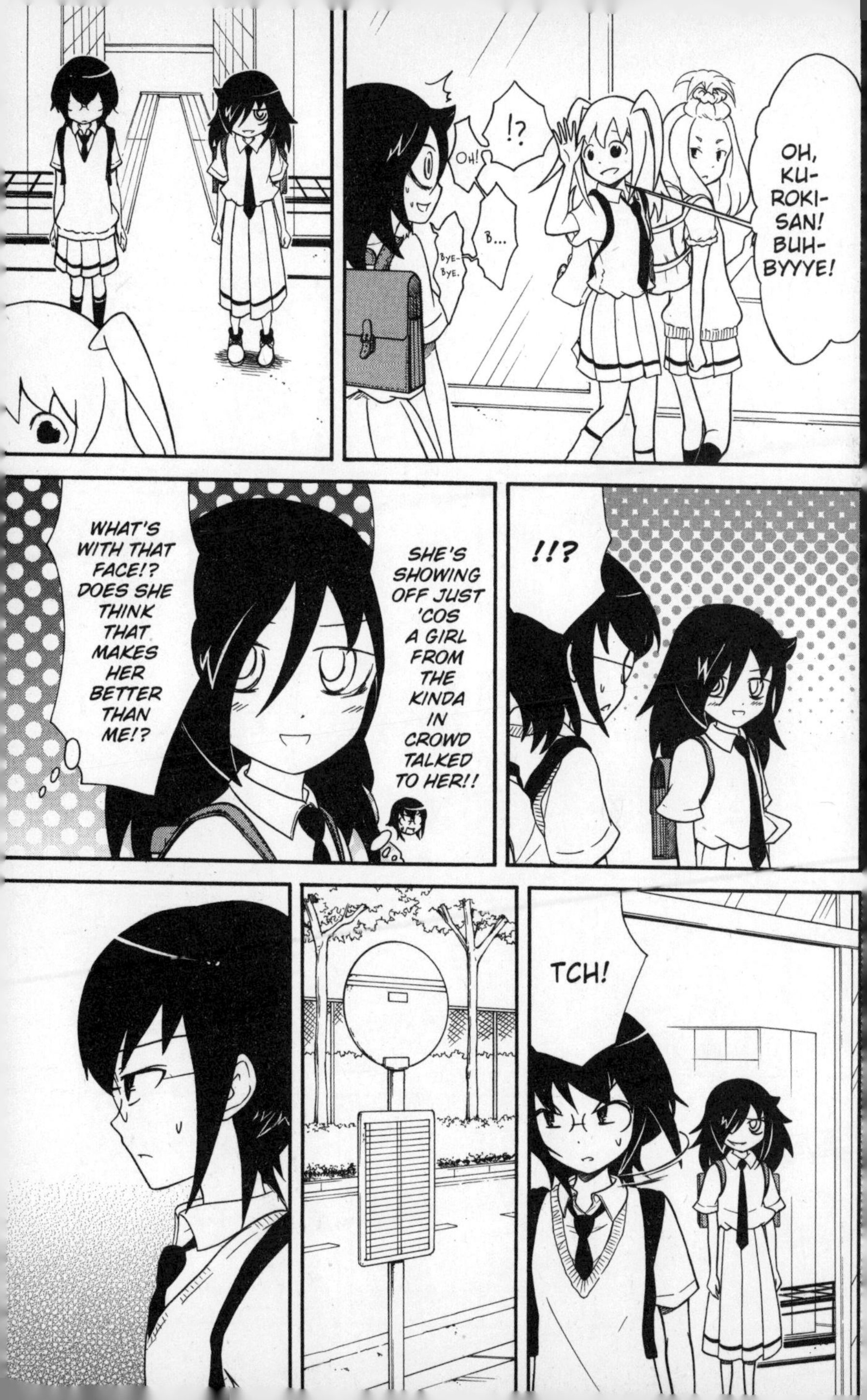
OH, KU-ROKI-SAN! BUH-BYYYE!
!?
OH!
B...
Bye-Bye.
!!?
SHE'S SHOWING OFF JUST 'COS A GIRL FROM THE KINDA IN CROWD TALKED TO HER!!
WHAT'S WITH THAT FACE!? DOES SHE THINK THAT MAKES HER BETTER THAN ME!?
TCH!

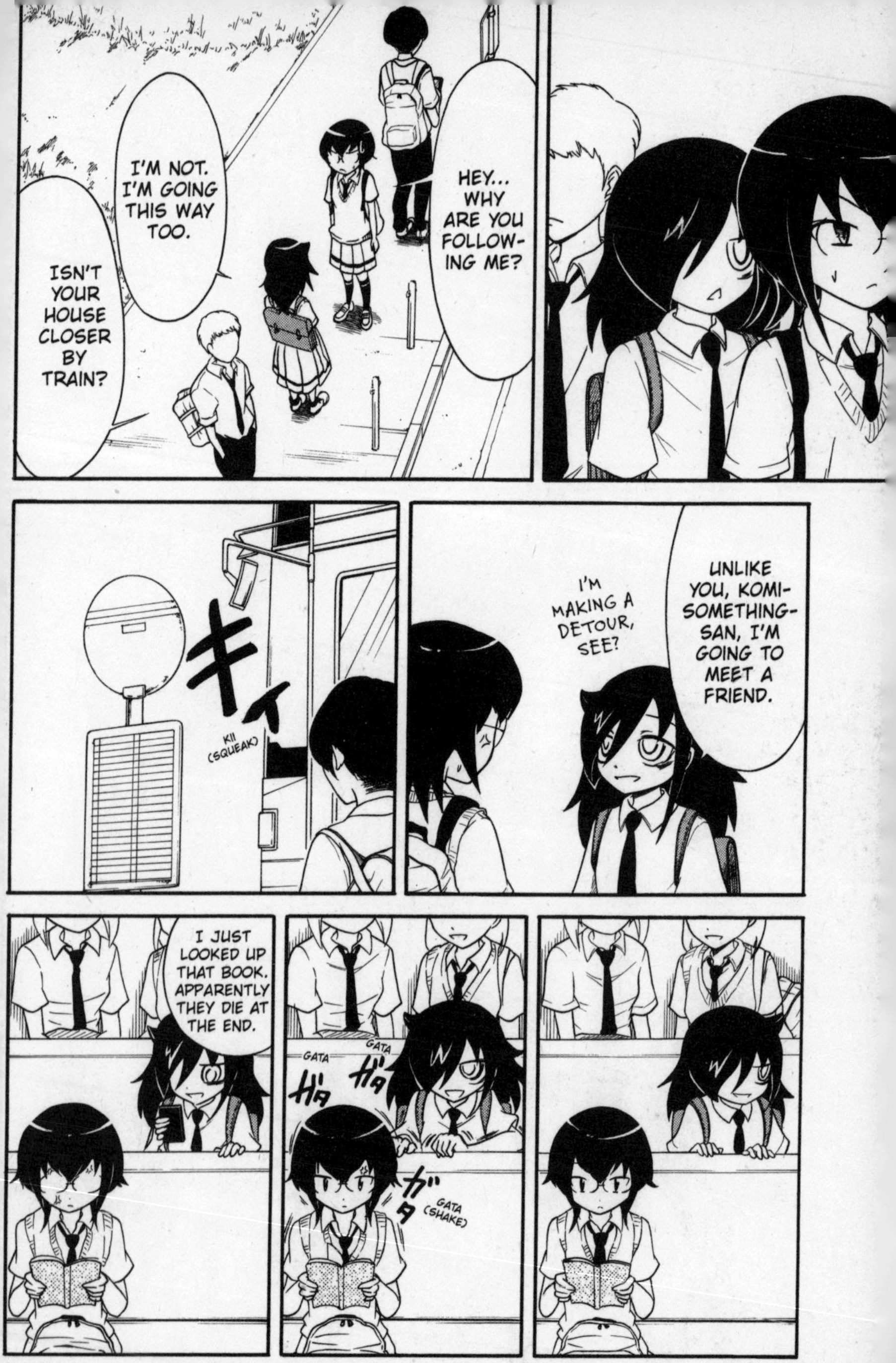
HEY... WHY ARE YOU FOLLOWING ME?
I'M NOT. I'M GOING THIS WAY TOO.
ISN'T YOUR HOUSE CLOSER BY TRAIN?
UNLIKE YOU, KOMI-SOMETHING-SAN, I'M GOING TO MEET A FRIEND.
I'M MAKING A DETOUR, SEE?
KII (SQUEAK)
GATA
GATA
GATA (SHAKE)
I JUST LOOKED UP THAT BOOK. APPARENTLY THEY DIE AT THE END.

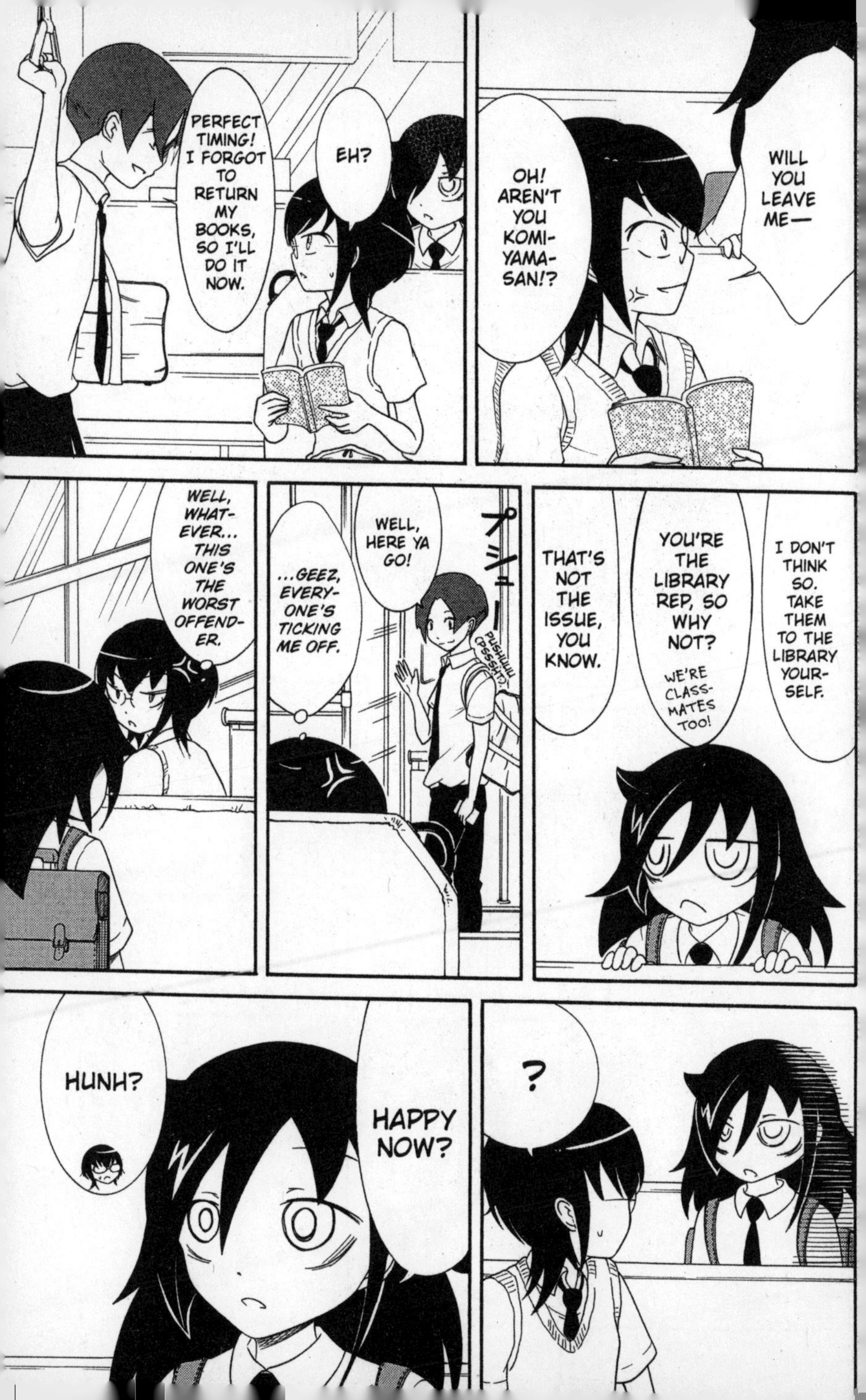

WILL YOU LEAVE ME—
OH! AREN'T YOU KOMI-YAMA-SAN!?
EH?
PERFECT TIMING! I FORGOT TO RETURN MY BOOKS, SO I'LL DO IT NOW.
I DON'T THINK SO. TAKE THEM TO THE LIBRARY YOUR-SELF.
YOU'RE THE LIBRARY REP, SO WHY NOT?
WE'RE CLASS-MATES TOO!
THAT'S NOT THE ISSUE, YOU KNOW.
PUSHUUU (PSSSHT).
WELL, HERE YA GO!
...GEEZ, EVERY-ONE'S TICKING ME OFF.
WELL, WHAT-EVER... THIS ONE'S THE WORST OFFEND-ER.
?
HAPPY NOW?
HUNH?

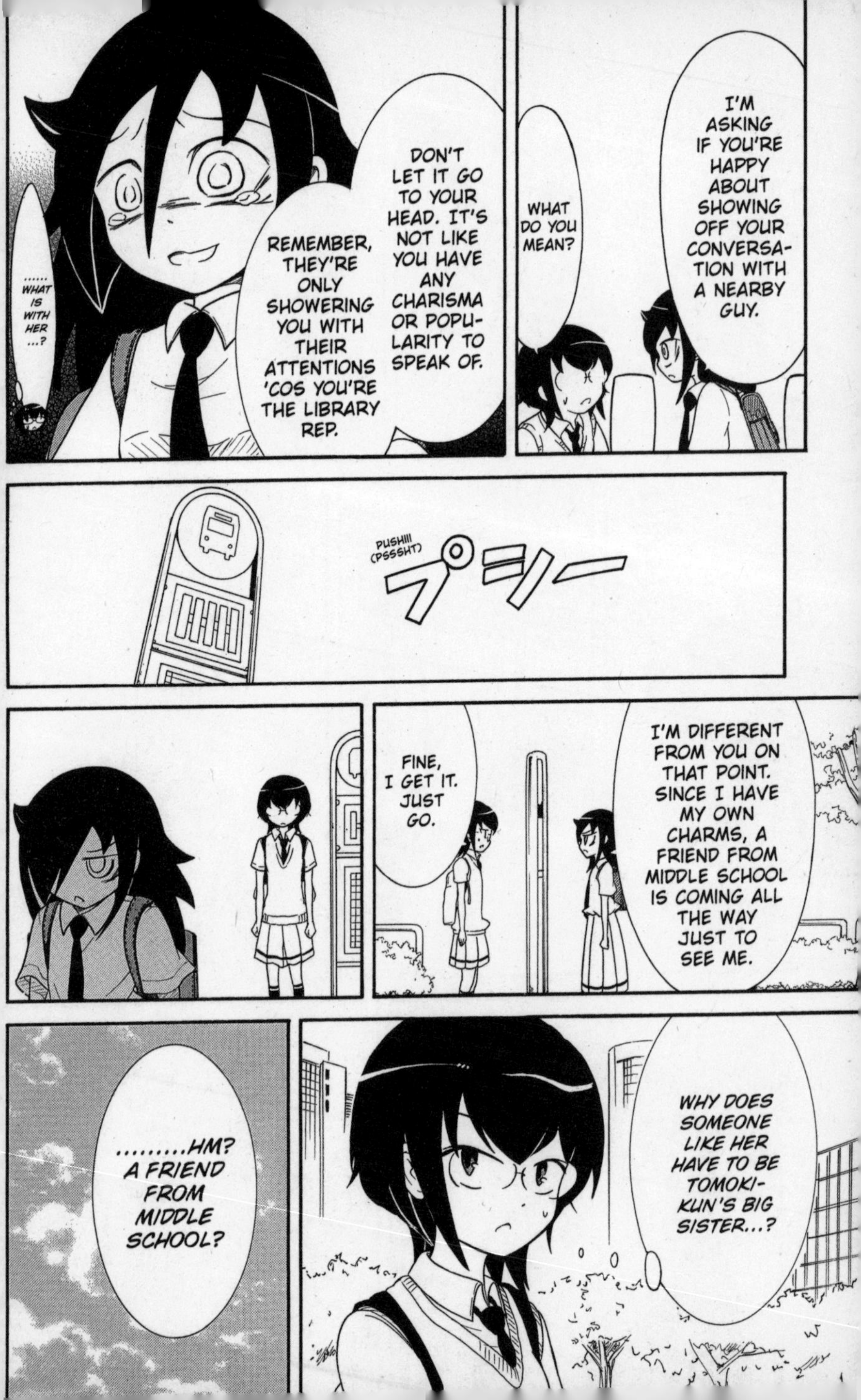
I'M ASKING IF YOU'RE HAPPY ABOUT SHOWING OFF YOUR CONVERSATION WITH A NEARBY GUY.
WHAT DO YOU MEAN?
DON'T LET IT GO TO YOUR HEAD. IT'S NOT LIKE YOU HAVE ANY CHARISMA OR POPULARITY TO SPEAK OF.
REMEMBER, THEY'RE ONLY SHOWERING YOU WITH THEIR ATTENTIONS 'COS YOU'RE THE LIBRARY REP.
......WHAT IS WITH HER ...?
PUSHIII (PSSSHT)
プシー
I'M DIFFERENT FROM YOU ON THAT POINT. SINCE I HAVE MY OWN CHARMS, A FRIEND FROM MIDDLE SCHOOL IS COMING ALL THE WAY JUST TO SEE ME.
FINE, I GET IT. JUST GO.
WHY DOES SOMEONE LIKE HER HAVE TO BE TOMOKI-KUN'S BIG SISTER...?
..........HM? A FRIEND FROM MIDDLE SCHOOL?

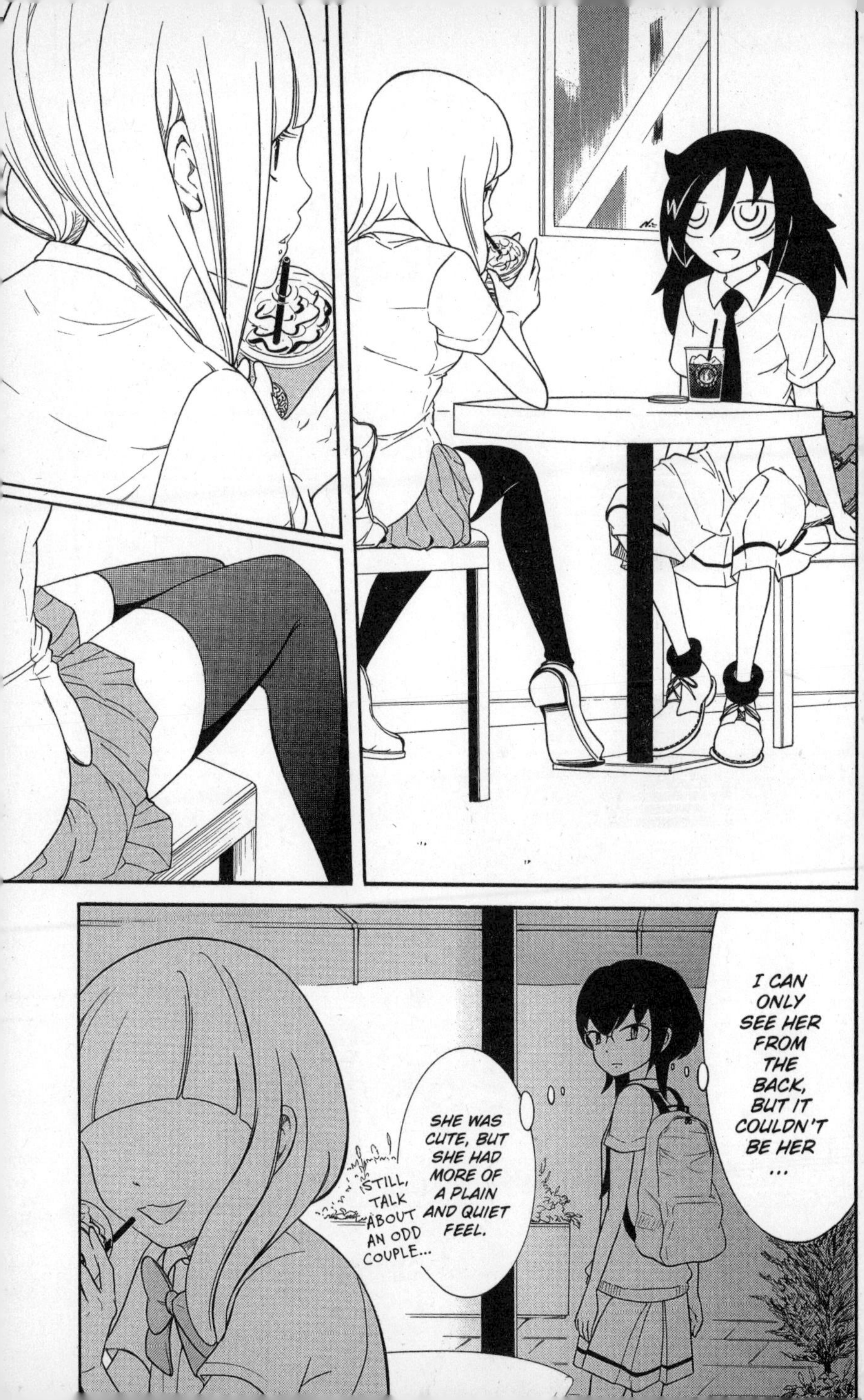
I CAN ONLY SEE HER FROM THE BACK, BUT IT COULDN'T BE HER ...
SHE WAS CUTE, BUT SHE HAD MORE OF A PLAIN AND QUIET FEEL.
STILL, TALK ABOUT AN ODD COUPLE...

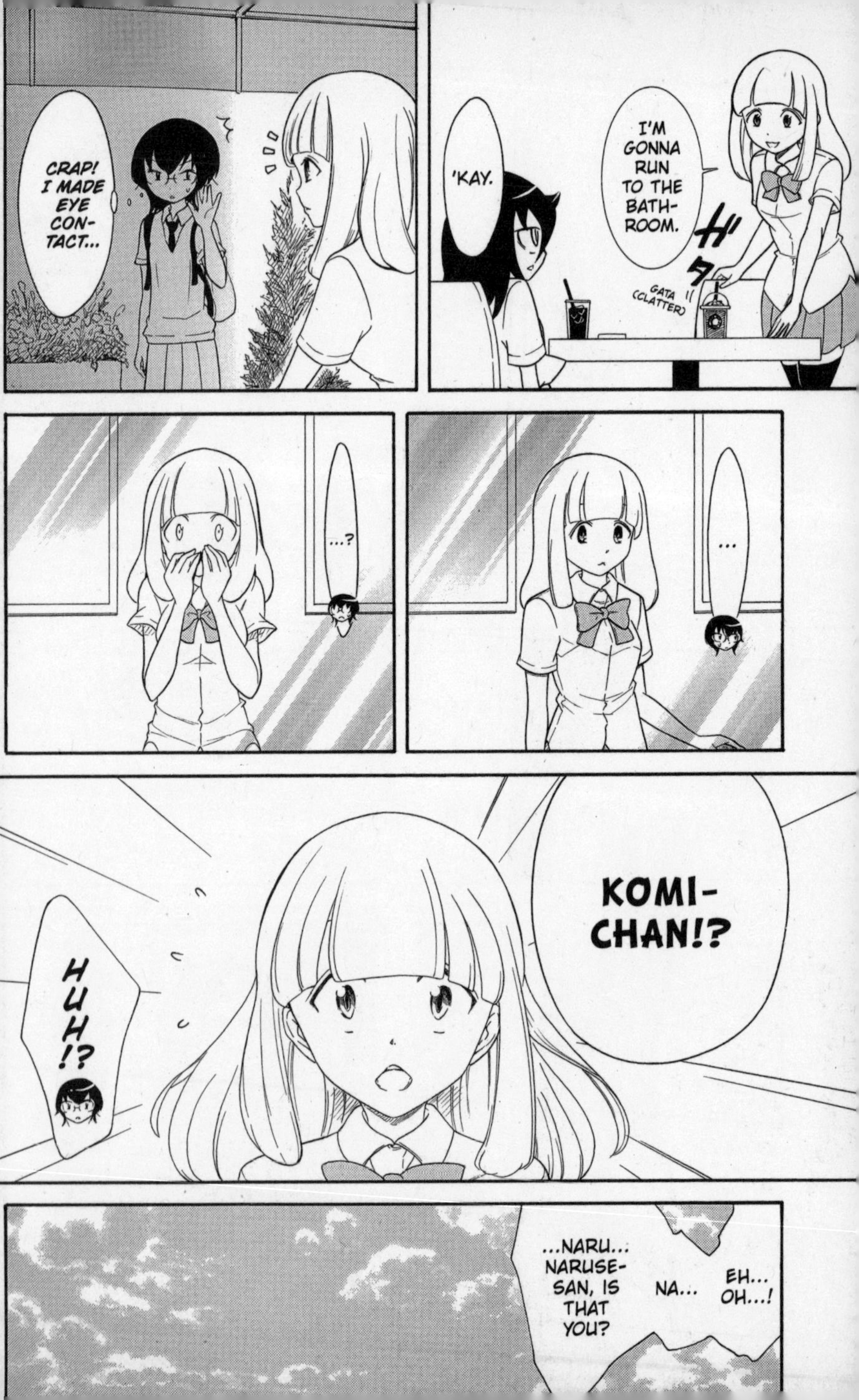
I'M GONNA RUN TO THE BATHROOM.
GATA (CLATTER)
'KAY.
CRAP! I MADE EYE CONTACT...
...
...?
KOMI-CHAN!?
HUH!?
EH... OH...!
NA...
...NARU... NARUSE-SAN, IS THAT YOU?

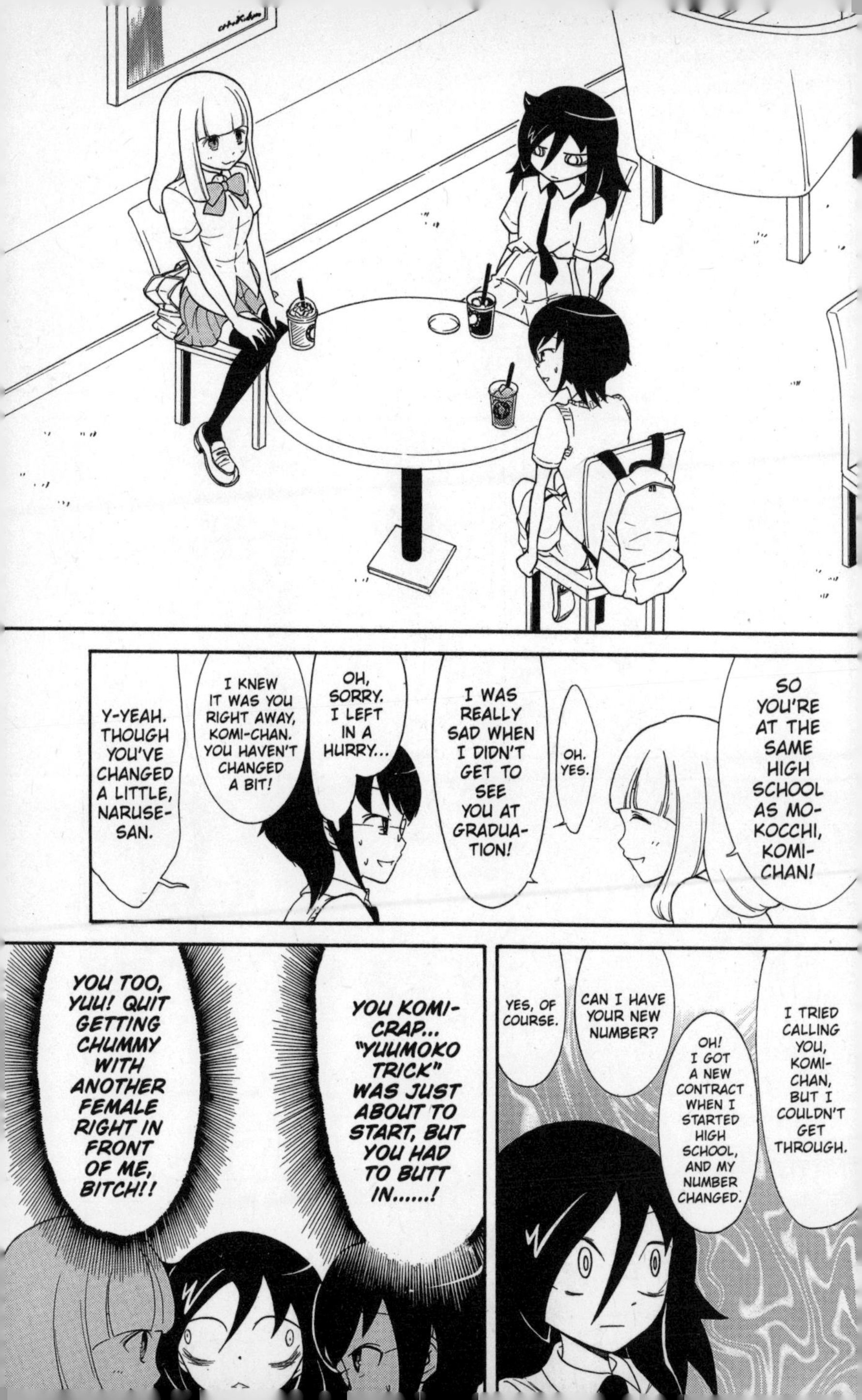
SO YOU'RE AT THE SAME HIGH SCHOOL AS MO-KOCCHI, KOMI-CHAN!
OH. YES.
I WAS REALLY SAD WHEN I DIDN'T GET TO SEE YOU AT GRADUATION!
OH, SORRY. I LEFT IN A HURRY...
I KNEW IT WAS YOU RIGHT AWAY, KOMI-CHAN. YOU HAVEN'T CHANGED A BIT!
Y-YEAH. THOUGH YOU'VE CHANGED A LITTLE, NARUSE-SAN.
I TRIED CALLING YOU, KOMI-CHAN, BUT I COULDN'T GET THROUGH.
OH! I GOT A NEW CONTRACT WHEN I STARTED HIGH SCHOOL, AND MY NUMBER CHANGED.
CAN I HAVE YOUR NEW NUMBER?
YES, OF COURSE.
YOU KOMI-CRAP... "YUUMOKO TRICK" WAS JUST ABOUT TO START, BUT YOU HAD TO BUTT IN......!
YOU TOO, YUU! QUIT GETTING CHUMMY WITH ANOTHER FEMALE RIGHT IN FRONT OF ME, BITCH!!

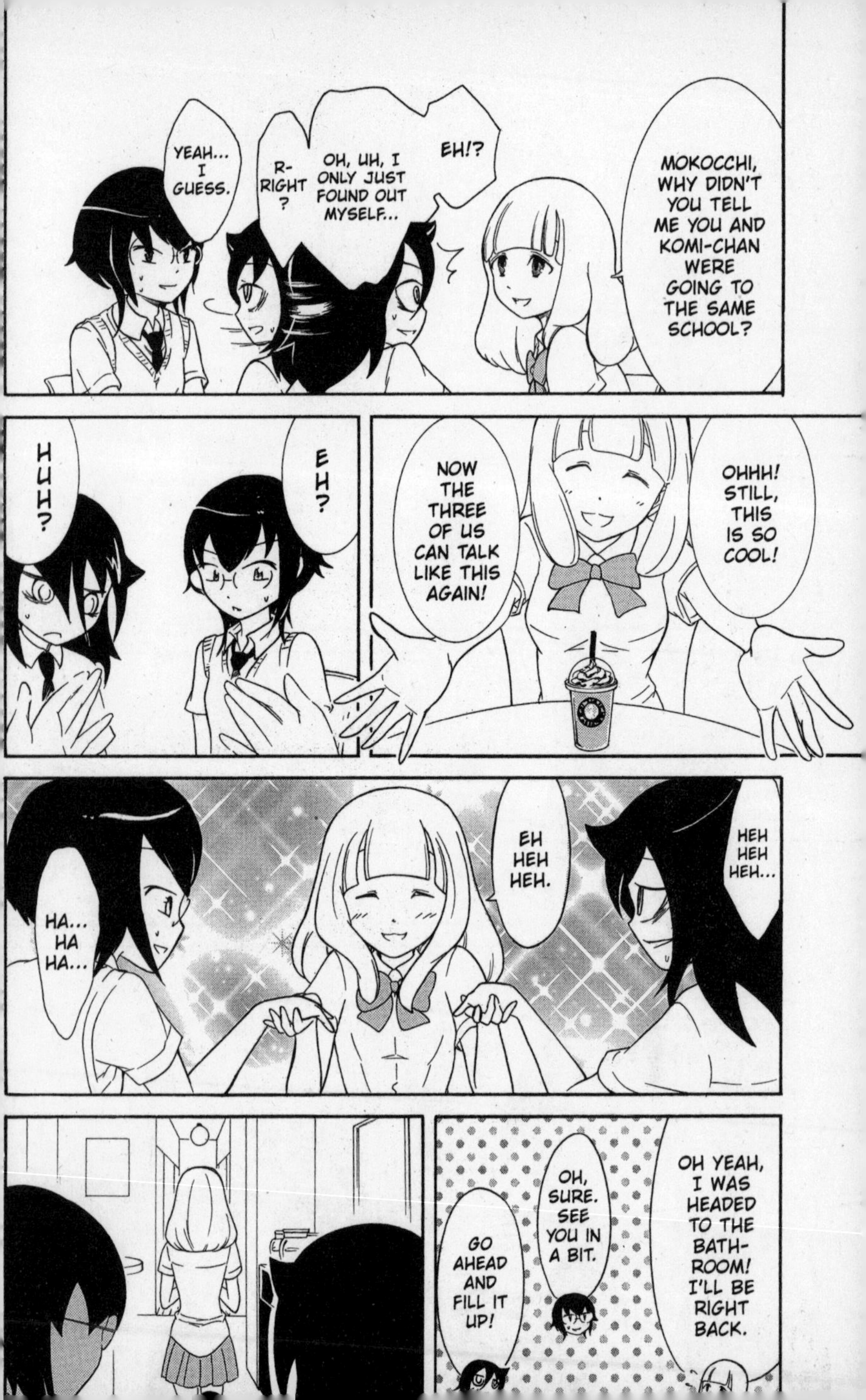
MOKOCCHI, WHY DIDN'T YOU TELL ME YOU AND KOMI-CHAN WERE GOING TO THE SAME SCHOOL?
EH!?
OH, UH, I ONLY JUST FOUND OUT MYSELF...
R-RIGHT?
YEAH... I GUESS.
OHHH! STILL, THIS IS SO COOL!
NOW THE THREE OF US CAN TALK LIKE THIS AGAIN!
EH?
HUH?
HEH HEH HEH...
EH HEH HEH.
HA... HA HA...
OH YEAH, I WAS HEADED TO THE BATH-ROOM! I'LL BE RIGHT BACK.
OH, SURE. SEE YOU IN A BIT.
GO AHEAD AND FILL IT UP!

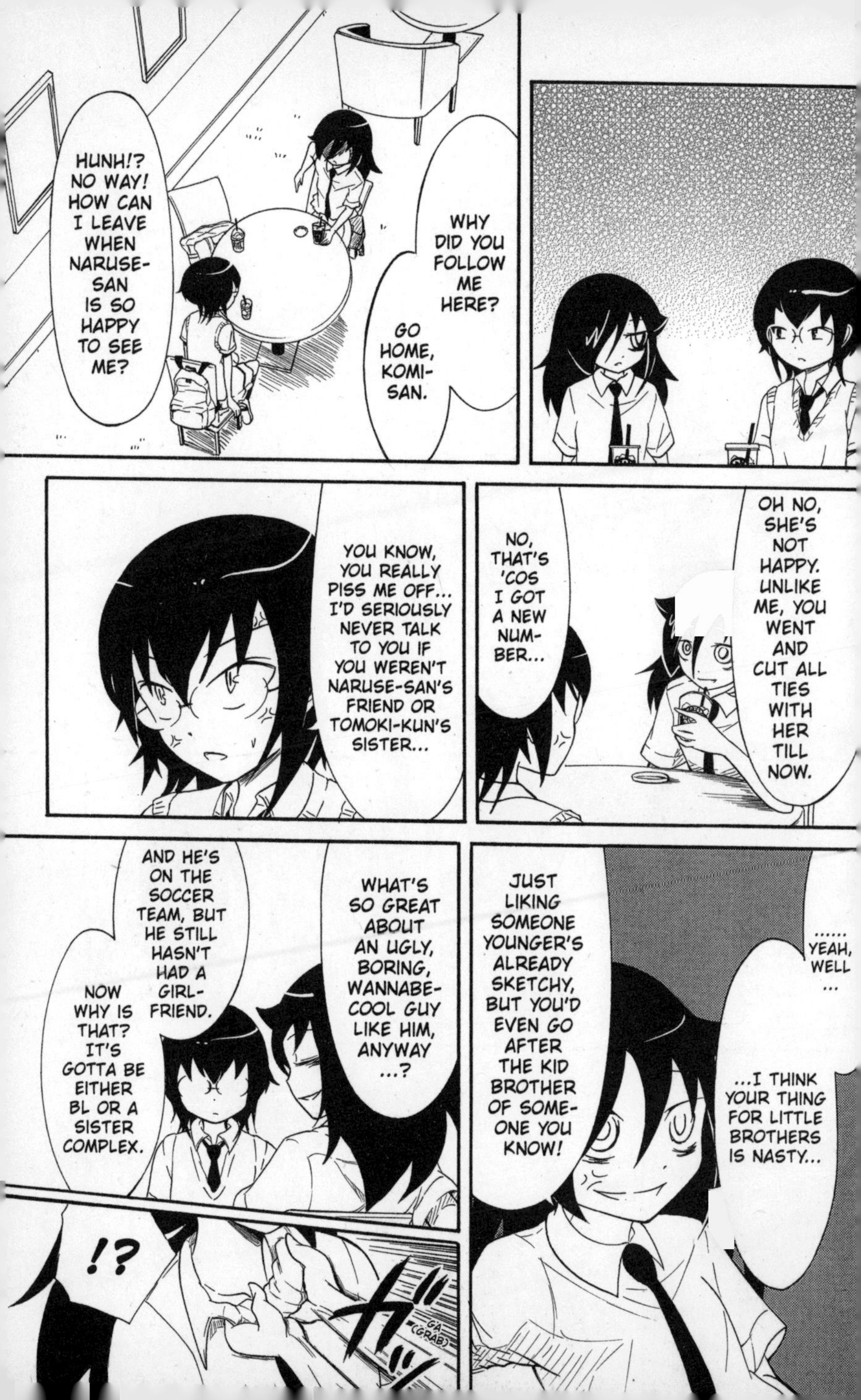
WHY DID YOU FOLLOW ME HERE?
GO HOME, KOMI-SAN.
HUNH!? NO WAY! HOW CAN I LEAVE WHEN NARUSE-SAN IS SO HAPPY TO SEE ME?
OH NO, SHE'S NOT HAPPY. UNLIKE ME, YOU WENT AND CUT ALL TIES WITH HER TILL NOW.
NO, THAT'S 'COS I GOT A NEW NUMBER...
YOU KNOW, YOU REALLY PISS ME OFF... I'D SERIOUSLY NEVER TALK TO YOU IF YOU WEREN'T NARUSE-SAN'S FRIEND OR TOMOKI-KUN'S SISTER...
...... YEAH, WELL ...
...I THINK YOUR THING FOR LITTLE BROTHERS IS NASTY...
JUST LIKING SOMEONE YOUNGER'S ALREADY SKETCHY, BUT YOU'D EVEN GO AFTER THE KID BROTHER OF SOMEONE YOU KNOW!
WHAT'S SO GREAT ABOUT AN UGLY, BORING, WANNABE-COOL GUY LIKE HIM, ANYWAY ...?
AND HE'S ON THE SOCCER TEAM, BUT HE STILL HASN'T HAD A GIRLFRIEND.
NOW WHY IS THAT? IT'S GOTTA BE EITHER BL OR A SISTER COMPLEX.
GA (GRAB)
!?

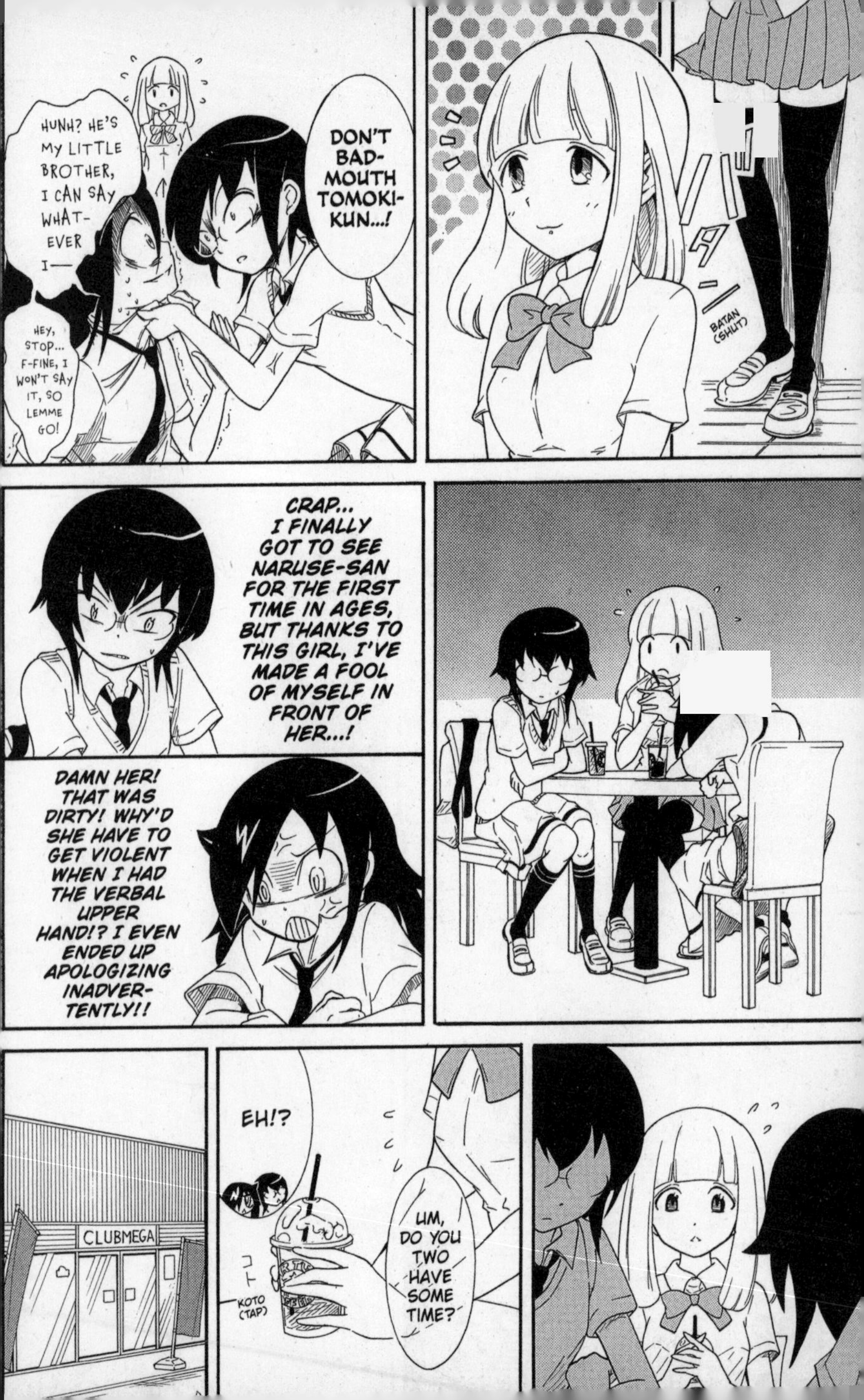
BATAN (SHUT)
DON'T BAD-MOUTH TOMOKI-KUN...!
HUNH? HE'S MY LITTLE BROTHER, I CAN SAY WHATEVER I—
HEY, STOP... F-FINE, I WON'T SAY IT, SO LEMME GO!
CRAP... I FINALLY GOT TO SEE NARUSE-SAN FOR THE FIRST TIME IN AGES, BUT THANKS TO THIS GIRL, I'VE MADE A FOOL OF MYSELF IN FRONT OF HER...!
DAMN HER! THAT WAS DIRTY! WHY'D SHE HAVE TO GET VIOLENT WHEN I HAD THE VERBAL UPPER HAND!? I EVEN ENDED UP APOLOGIZING INADVERTENTLY!!
KOTO (TAP)
UM, DO YOU TWO HAVE SOME TIME?
EH!?
CLUBMEGA

OH! YOU CAN PLAY THIS ONE TOGETHER!

AND SINCE YOU WERE BOTH GOOD AT GAMES...

YEAH. I CAME HERE WITH MOKOCCHI WHEN WE MET AGAIN LAST YEAR.

AN ARCADE?

UFO

LOSE

SHOOT, SHE'S TOO LOUSY TO PLAY AGAINST. WASTE OF MONEY...

AND I WAS ONLY PLAYING AT 30% OF MY POTENTIAL...

TASHI (MASH)

TASHI

TAN (THWAP)

TAN

TRUE. UNLIKE SOME PEOPLE, I'M TOO BUSY TO PLAY THE LATEST GAMES.

KOMI-CHAN, WEREN'T YOU BETTER AT STUFF LIKE QUIZZES?

TOMOKO	KOTOMI	YUU	CPU
2nd place	Champion	3rd place	4th place
59.80	84.08	49.50	24.37

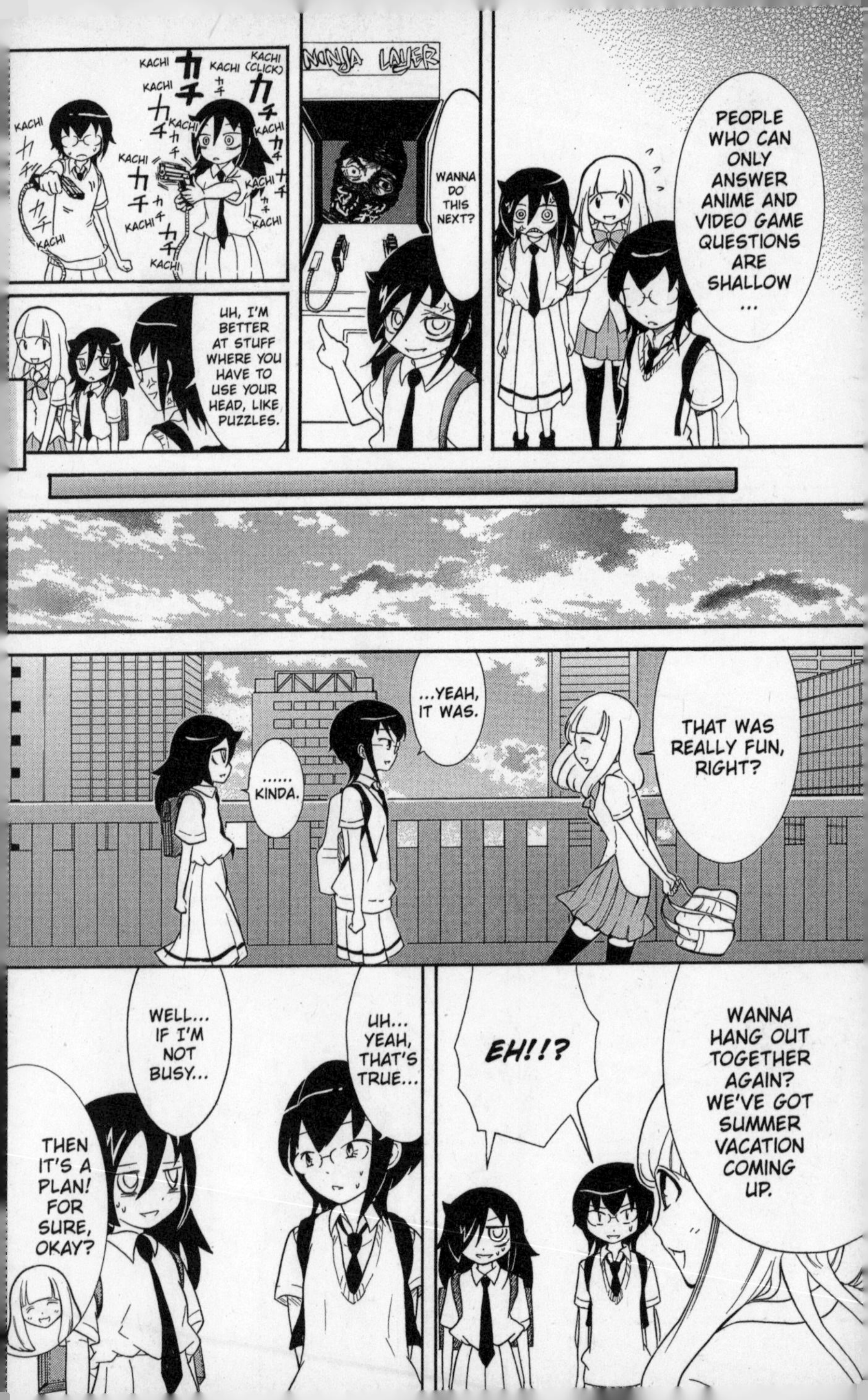
PEOPLE WHO CAN ONLY ANSWER ANIME AND VIDEO GAME QUESTIONS ARE SHALLOW ...
NINJA LAYER
WANNA DO THIS NEXT?
KACHI (CLICK)
カチ
KACHI
カチ
KACHI
カチ
KACHI
カチ
KACHI
カチ
KACHI
UH, I'M BETTER AT STUFF WHERE YOU HAVE TO USE YOUR HEAD, LIKE PUZZLES.
THAT WAS REALLY FUN, RIGHT?
...YEAH, IT WAS.
...... KINDA.
WANNA HANG OUT TOGETHER AGAIN? WE'VE GOT SUMMER VACATION COMING UP.
EH!!?
UH... YEAH, THAT'S TRUE...
WELL... IF I'M NOT BUSY...
THEN IT'S A PLAN! FOR SURE, OKAY?

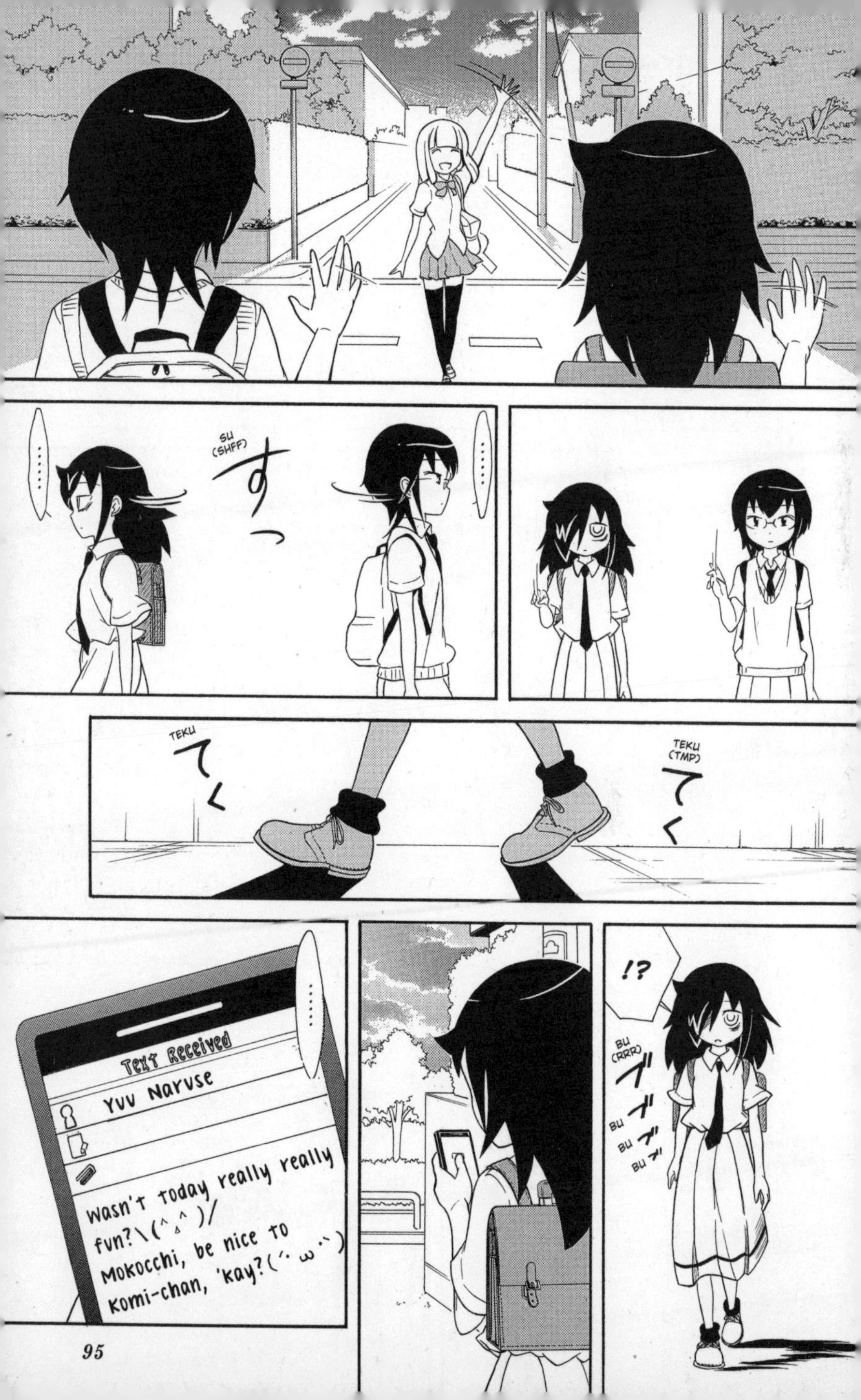

......
SU (SHFF)
すっ
......
TEKU (TMP)
てく
TEKU
てく
!?
BU (RRR)
ブ
BU
ブ
BU
ブ
BU
ブ
......
Text Received
Yuu Naruse
Wasn't today really really fun?\(^▵^)/
Mokocchi, be nice to Komi-chan, 'kay?(´・ω・`)

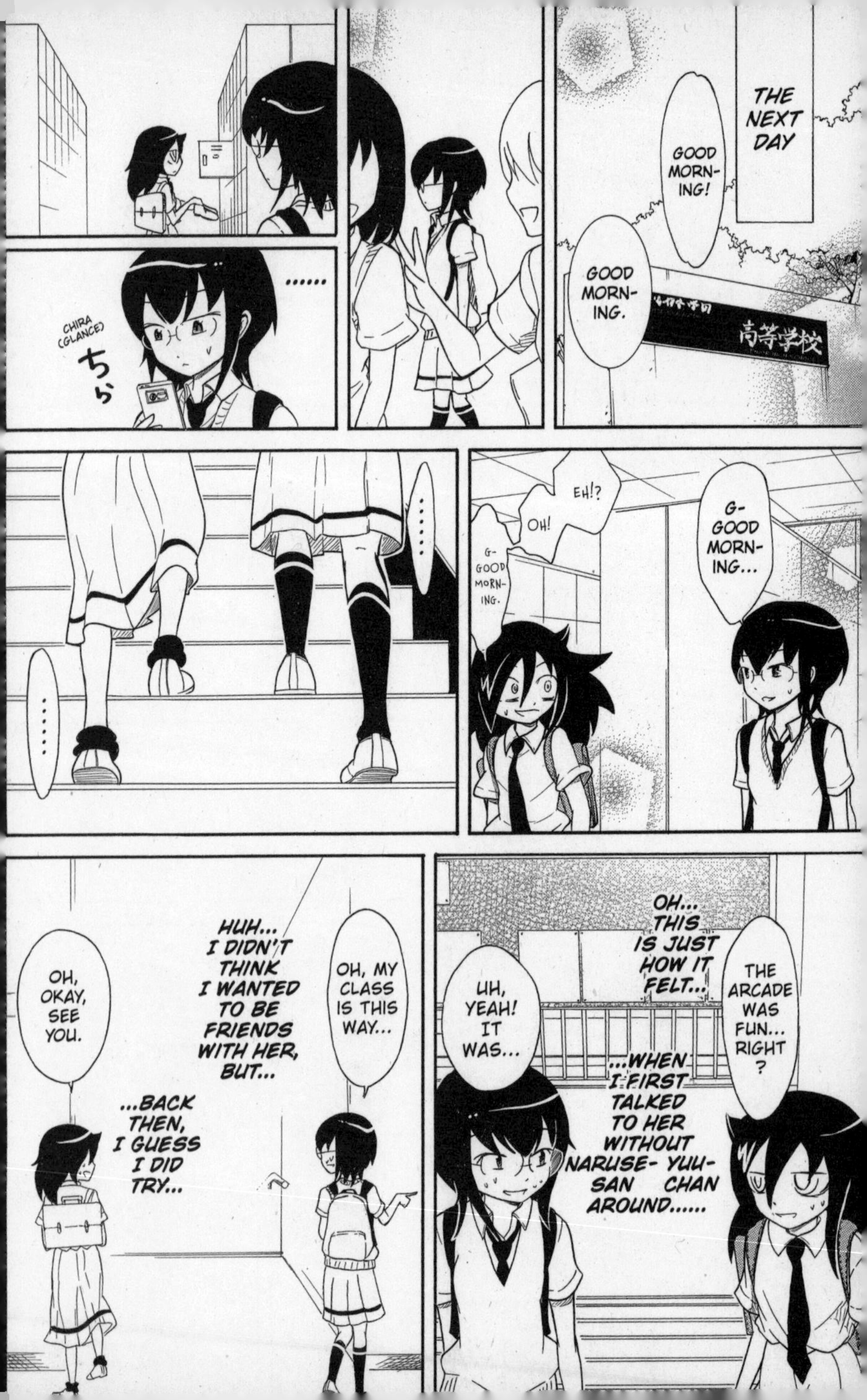
THE NEXT DAY
GOOD MORNING!
GOOD MORNING.
高等学校
......
CHIRA (GLANCE)
ちら
G-GOOD MORNING...
EH!?
OH!
G-GOOD MORNING.
......
......
THE ARCADE WAS FUN... RIGHT?
OH... THIS IS JUST HOW IT FELT...
UH, YEAH! IT WAS...
...WHEN I FIRST TALKED TO HER WITHOUT NARUSE-SAN YUU-CHAN AROUND......
OH, MY CLASS IS THIS WAY...
HUH... I DIDN'T THINK I WANTED TO BE FRIENDS WITH HER, BUT...
OH, OKAY, SEE YOU.
...BACK THEN, I GUESS I DID TRY...

No Matter How I Look at It, It's You Guys' Fault I'm Not Popular!

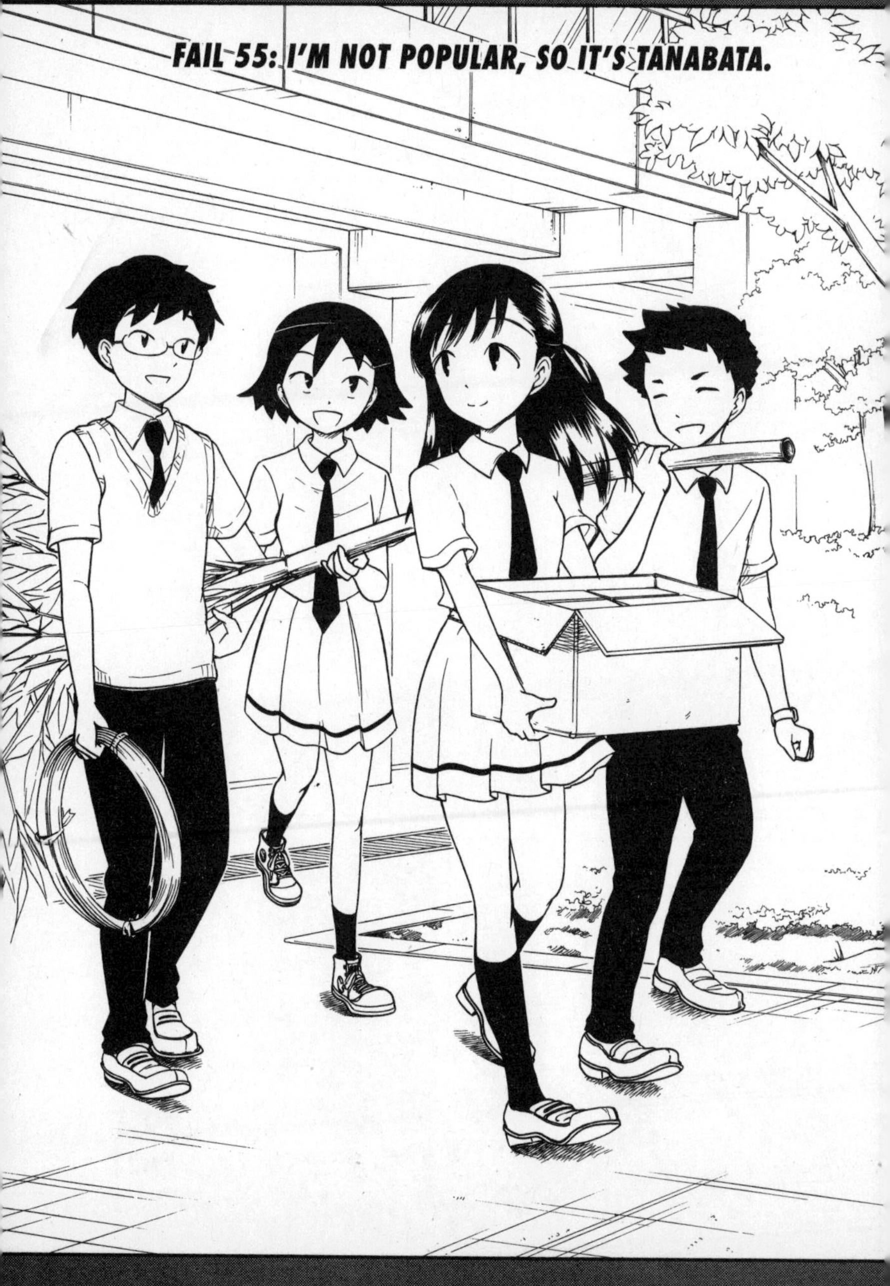
FAIL 55: I'M NOT POPULAR, SO IT'S TANABATA.

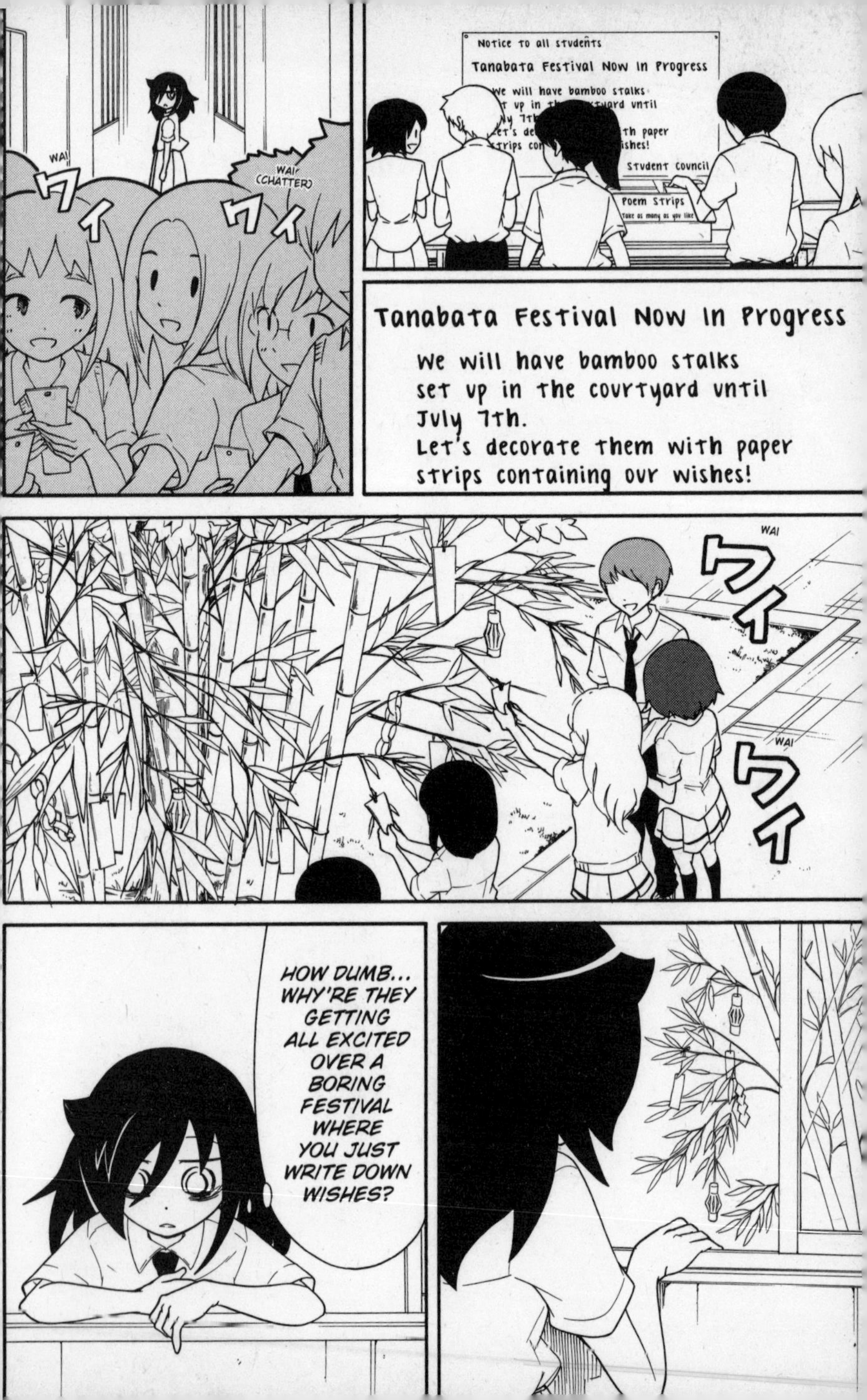
Notice to all students
Tanabata Festival Now In Progress
Student Council
Poem Strips
Take as many as you like
Tanabata Festival Now In Progress
We will have bamboo stalks set up in the courtyard until July 7th.
Let's decorate them with paper strips containing our wishes!
WAI
WAI (CHATTER)
WAI
WAI
HOW DUMB... WHY'RE THEY GETTING ALL EXCITED OVER A BORING FESTIVAL WHERE YOU JUST WRITE DOWN WISHES?

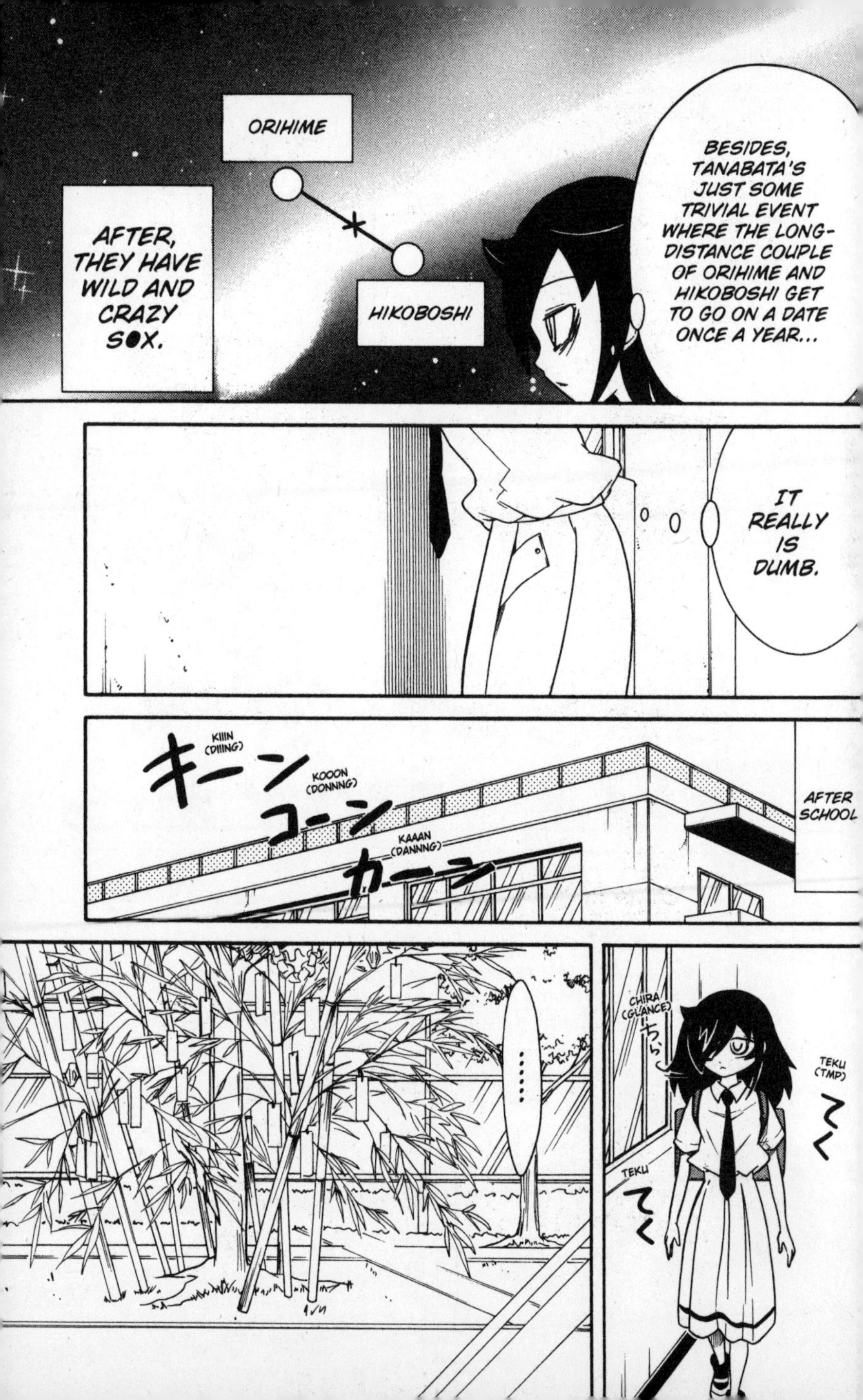
BESIDES, TANABATA'S JUST SOME TRIVIAL EVENT WHERE THE LONG-DISTANCE COUPLE OF ORIHIME AND HIKOBOSHI GET TO GO ON A DATE ONCE A YEAR...
ORIHIME
HIKOBOSHI
AFTER, THEY HAVE WILD AND CRAZY S●X.
IT REALLY IS DUMB.
AFTER SCHOOL
KIIIN (DIIING)
キーン
KOOON (DONNNG)
コーン
KAAAN (DANNNG)
カーン
TEKU (TMP)
てく
CHIRA (GLANCE)
ちら
TEKU
てく
......

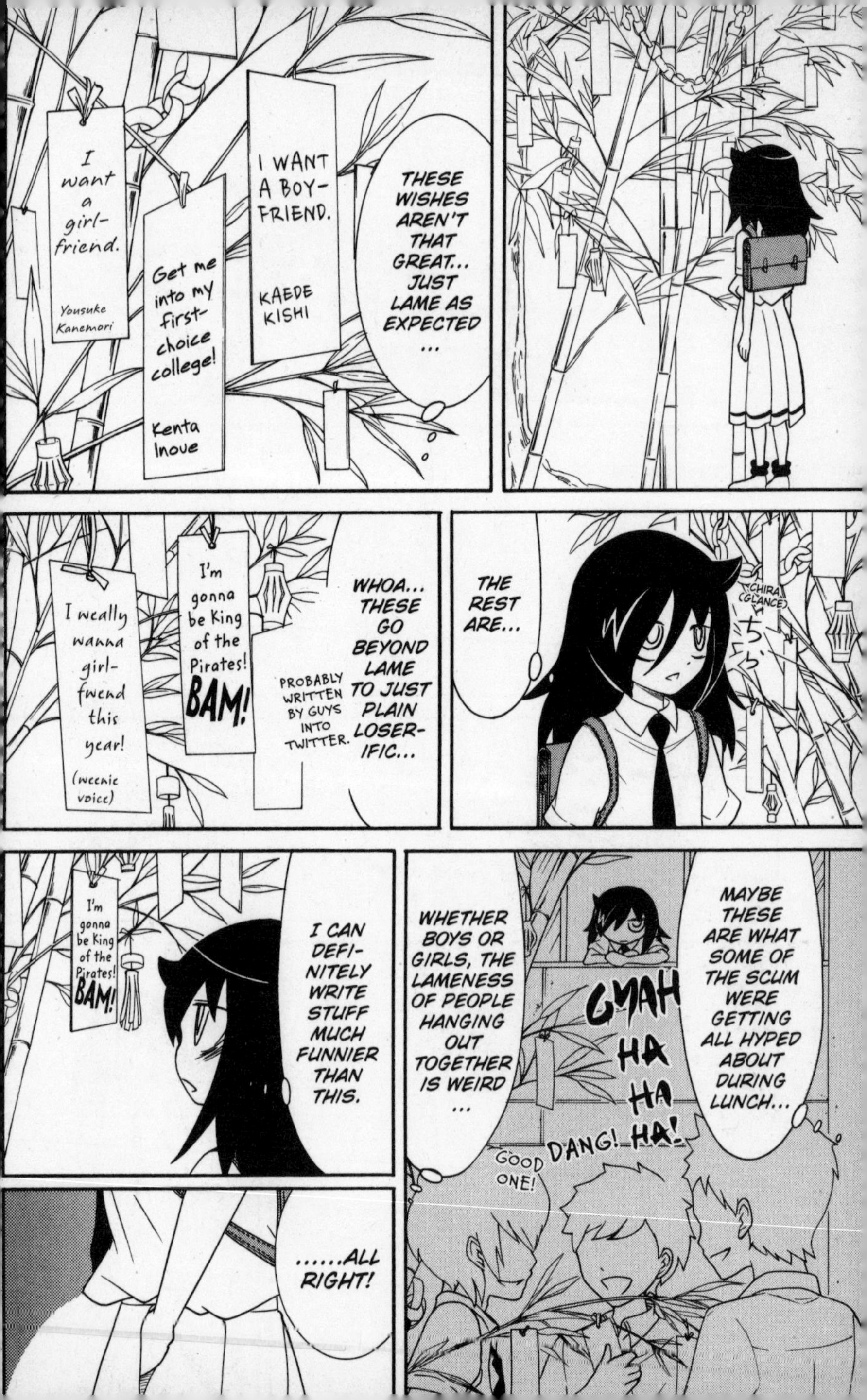
THESE WISHES AREN'T THAT GREAT... JUST LAME AS EXPECTED...
I WANT A BOY-FRIEND.
KAEDE KISHI
Get me into my first-choice college!
Kenta Inoue
I want a girl-friend.
Yousuke Kanemori
CHIRA (GLANCE)
ちら
THE REST ARE...
WHOA... THESE GO BEYOND LAME TO JUST PLAIN LOSER-IFIC...
PROBABLY WRITTEN BY GUYS INTO TWITTER.
I'm gonna be King of the Pirates! BAM!
I weally wanna girl-fwend this year!
(weenie voice)
MAYBE THESE ARE WHAT SOME OF THE SCUM WERE GETTING ALL HYPED ABOUT DURING LUNCH...
GYAH HA HA HA!
WHETHER BOYS OR GIRLS, THE LAMENESS OF PEOPLE HANGING OUT TOGETHER IS WEIRD...
DANG!
GOOD ONE!
I CAN DEFI-NITELY WRITE STUFF MUCH FUNNIER THAN THIS.
I'm gonna be King of the Pirates! BAM!
......ALL RIGHT!

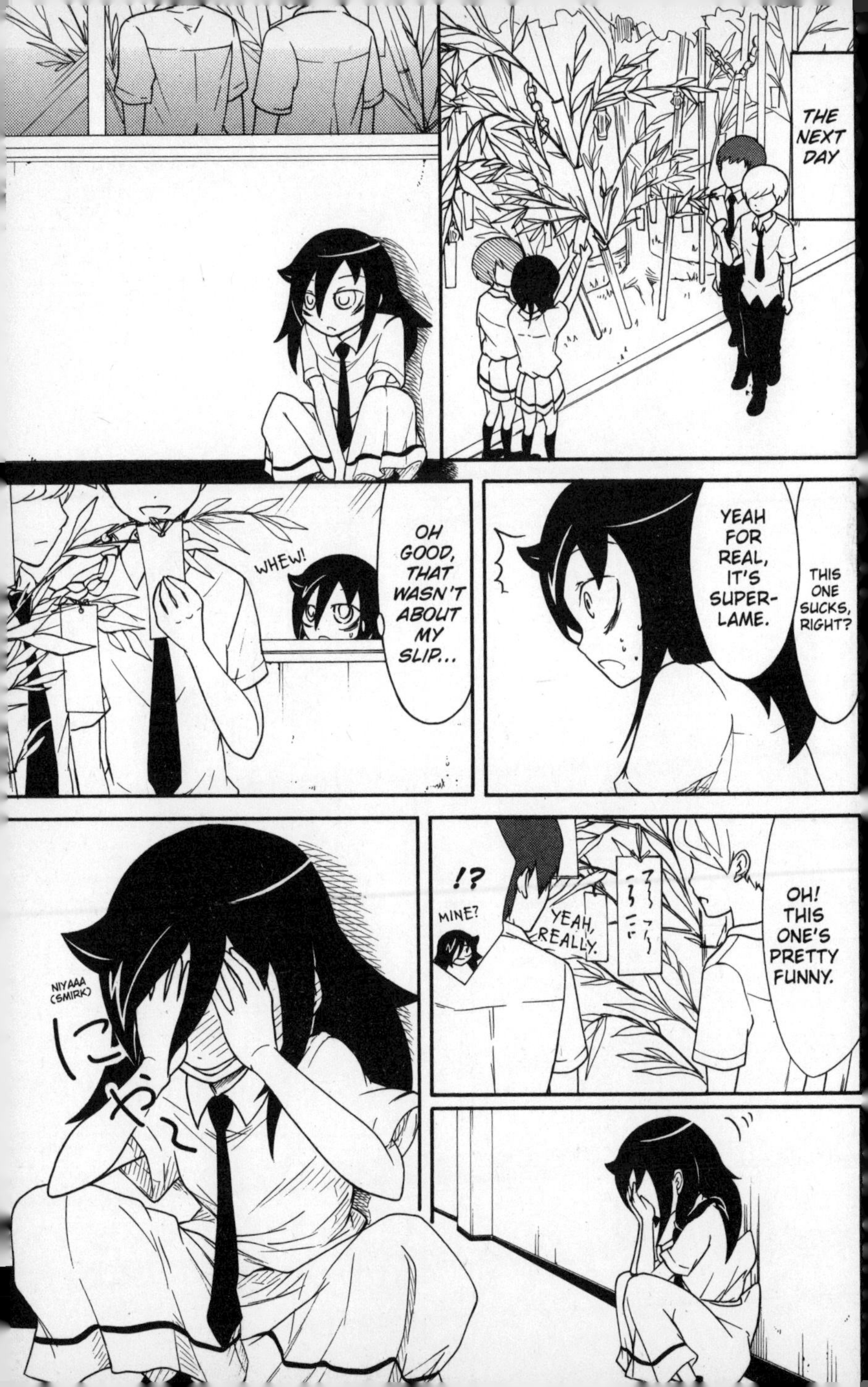

THE NEXT DAY
THIS ONE SUCKS, RIGHT?
YEAH FOR REAL, IT'S SUPER-LAME.
OH GOOD, THAT WASN'T ABOUT MY SLIP...
WHEW!
OH! THIS ONE'S PRETTY FUNNY.
YEAH, REALLY.
!?
MINE?
NIYAAA (SMIRK)

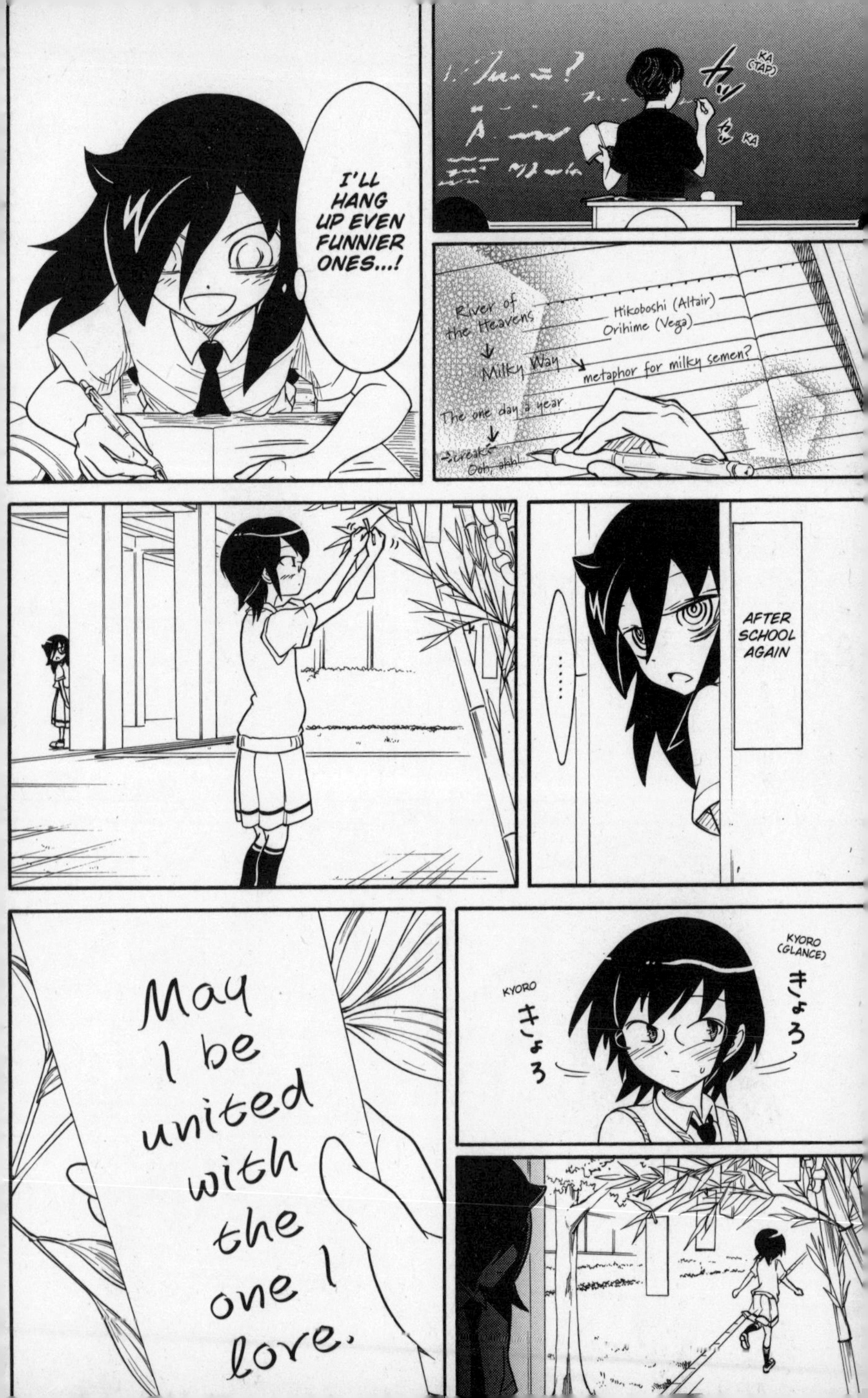
KA (TAP)
KA
River of the Heavens
Hikoboshi (Altair)
Orihime (Vega)
Milky Way
metaphor for milky semen?
The one day a year
creak
Ooh, ahh!
I'LL HANG UP EVEN FUNNIER ONES...!
AFTER SCHOOL AGAIN
......
KYORO (GLANCE)
KYORO
May I be united with the one I love.

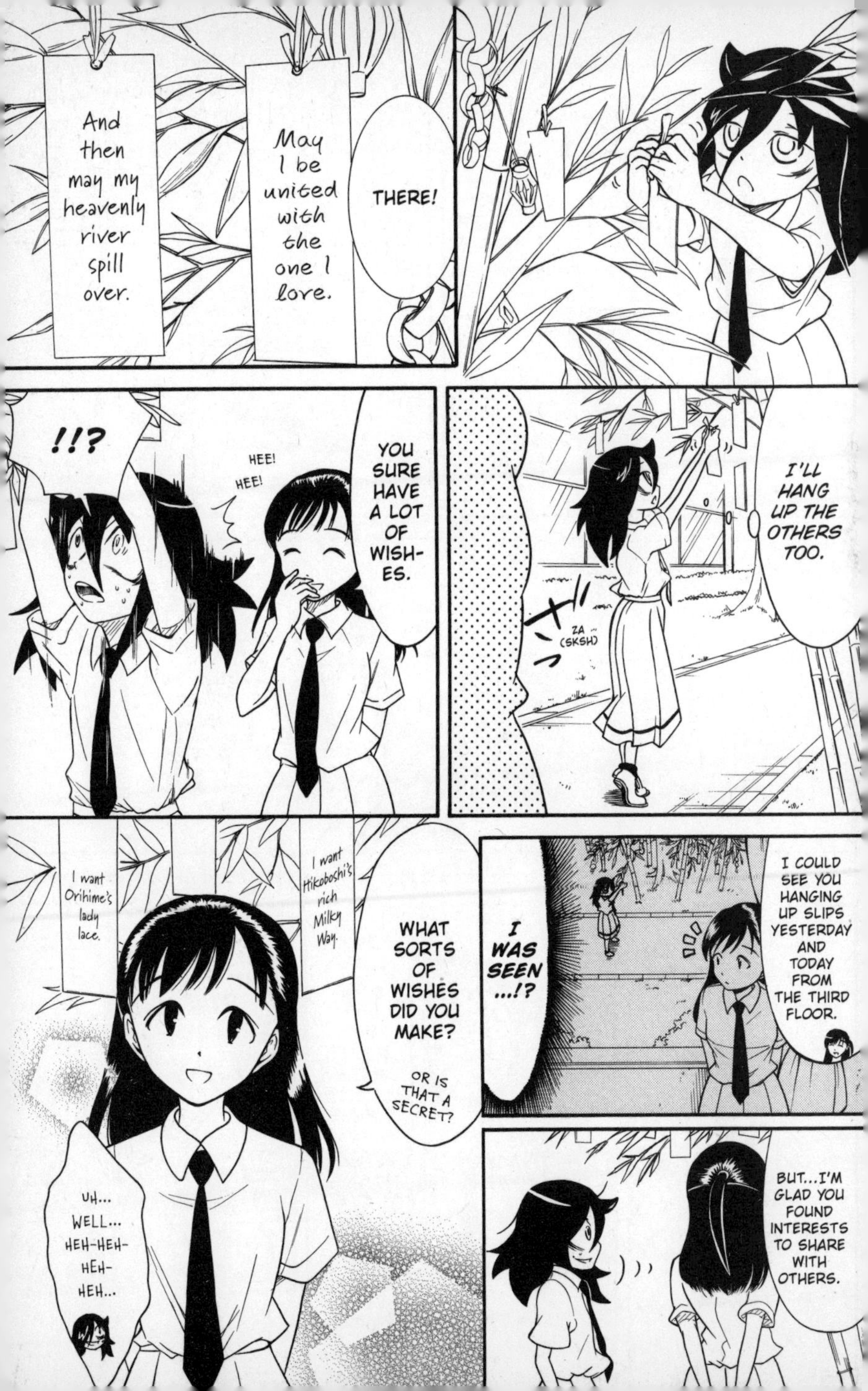
THERE!
May I be united with the one I love.
And then may my heavenly river spill over.
I'LL HANG UP THE OTHERS TOO.
ZA (SKSH)
YOU SURE HAVE A LOT OF WISH-ES.
HEE! HEE!
!!?
I COULD SEE YOU HANGING UP SLIPS YESTERDAY AND TODAY FROM THE THIRD FLOOR.
I WAS SEEN ...!?
BUT...I'M GLAD YOU FOUND INTERESTS TO SHARE WITH OTHERS.
WHAT SORTS OF WISHES DID YOU MAKE?
OR IS THAT A SECRET?
I want Hikoboshi's rich Milky Way.
I want Orihime's lady lace.
UH... WELL... HEH-HEH-HEH-HEH...

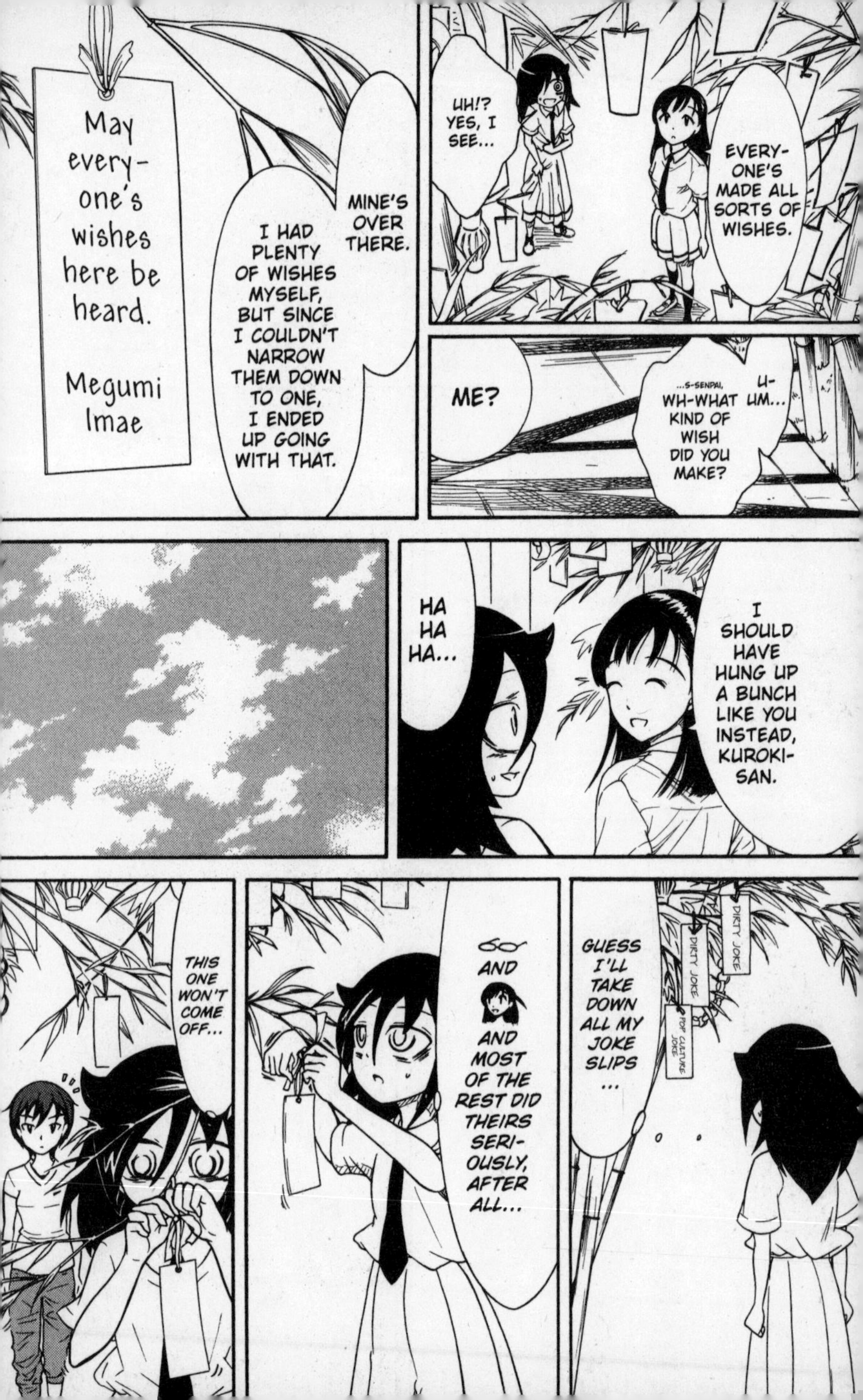
EVERYONE'S MADE ALL SORTS OF WISHES.
UH!? YES, I SEE...
U-UM... ...S-SENPAI, WH-WHAT KIND OF WISH DID YOU MAKE?
ME?
MINE'S OVER THERE.
I HAD PLENTY OF WISHES MYSELF, BUT SINCE I COULDN'T NARROW THEM DOWN TO ONE, I ENDED UP GOING WITH THAT.
May everyone's wishes here be heard.
Megumi Imae
I SHOULD HAVE HUNG UP A BUNCH LIKE YOU INSTEAD, KUROKI-SAN.
HA HA HA...
DIRTY JOKE
DIRTY JOKE
POP CULTURE JOKE
GUESS I'LL TAKE DOWN ALL MY JOKE SLIPS...
AND
AND MOST OF THE REST DID THEIRS SERIOUSLY, AFTER ALL...
THIS ONE WON'T COME OFF...

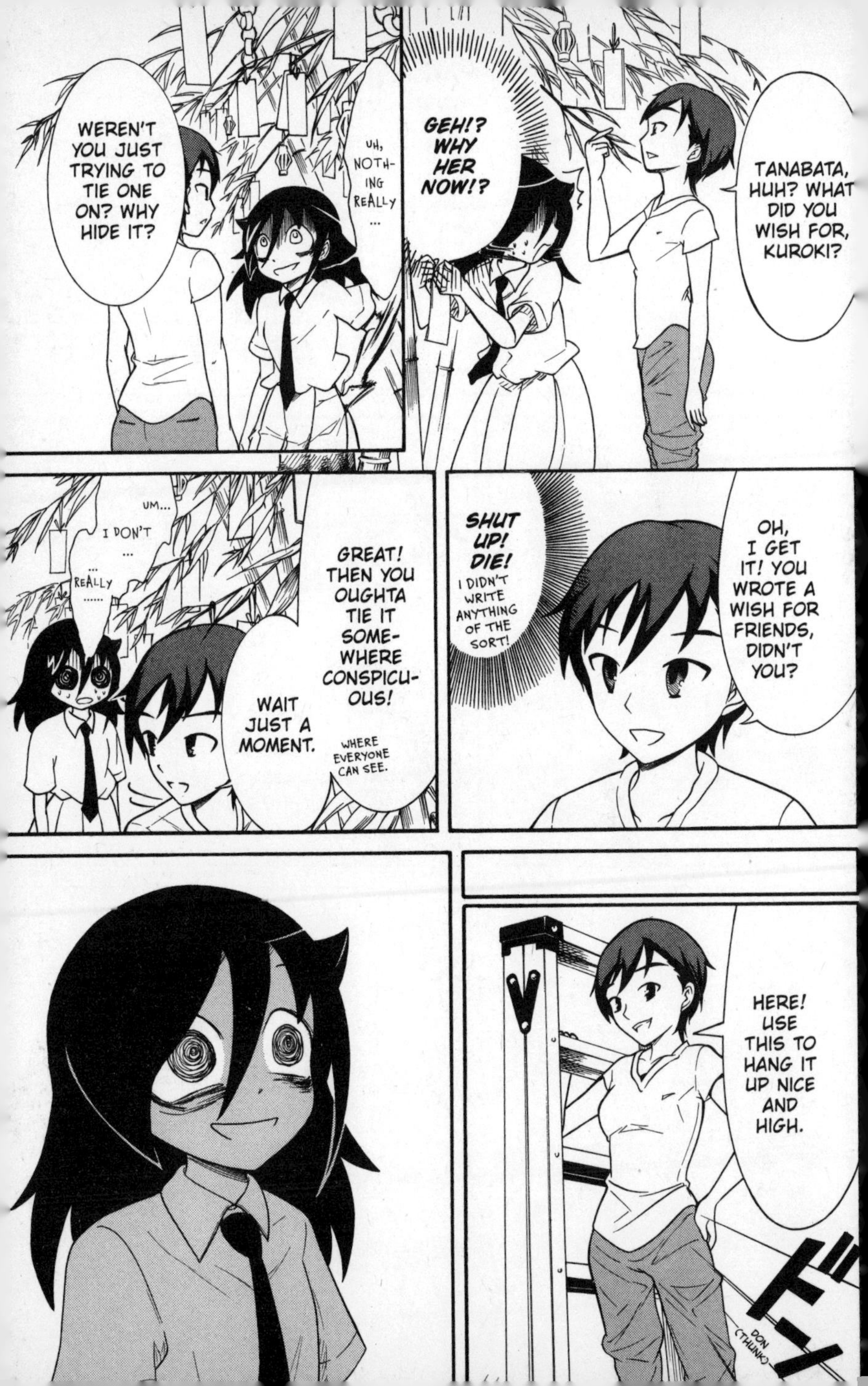
TANABATA, HUH? WHAT DID YOU WISH FOR, KUROKI?
GEH!? WHY HER NOW!?
UH, NOTHING REALLY ...
WEREN'T YOU JUST TRYING TO TIE ONE ON? WHY HIDE IT?
OH, I GET IT! YOU WROTE A WISH FOR FRIENDS, DIDN'T YOU?
SHUT UP! DIE!
I DIDN'T WRITE ANYTHING OF THE SORT!
GREAT! THEN YOU OUGHTA TIE IT SOMEWHERE CONSPICUOUS!
WHERE EVERYONE CAN SEE.
UM... I DON'T ... ... REALLY ......
WAIT JUST A MOMENT.
HERE! USE THIS TO HANG IT UP NICE AND HIGH.
ドン
DON (THUNK)

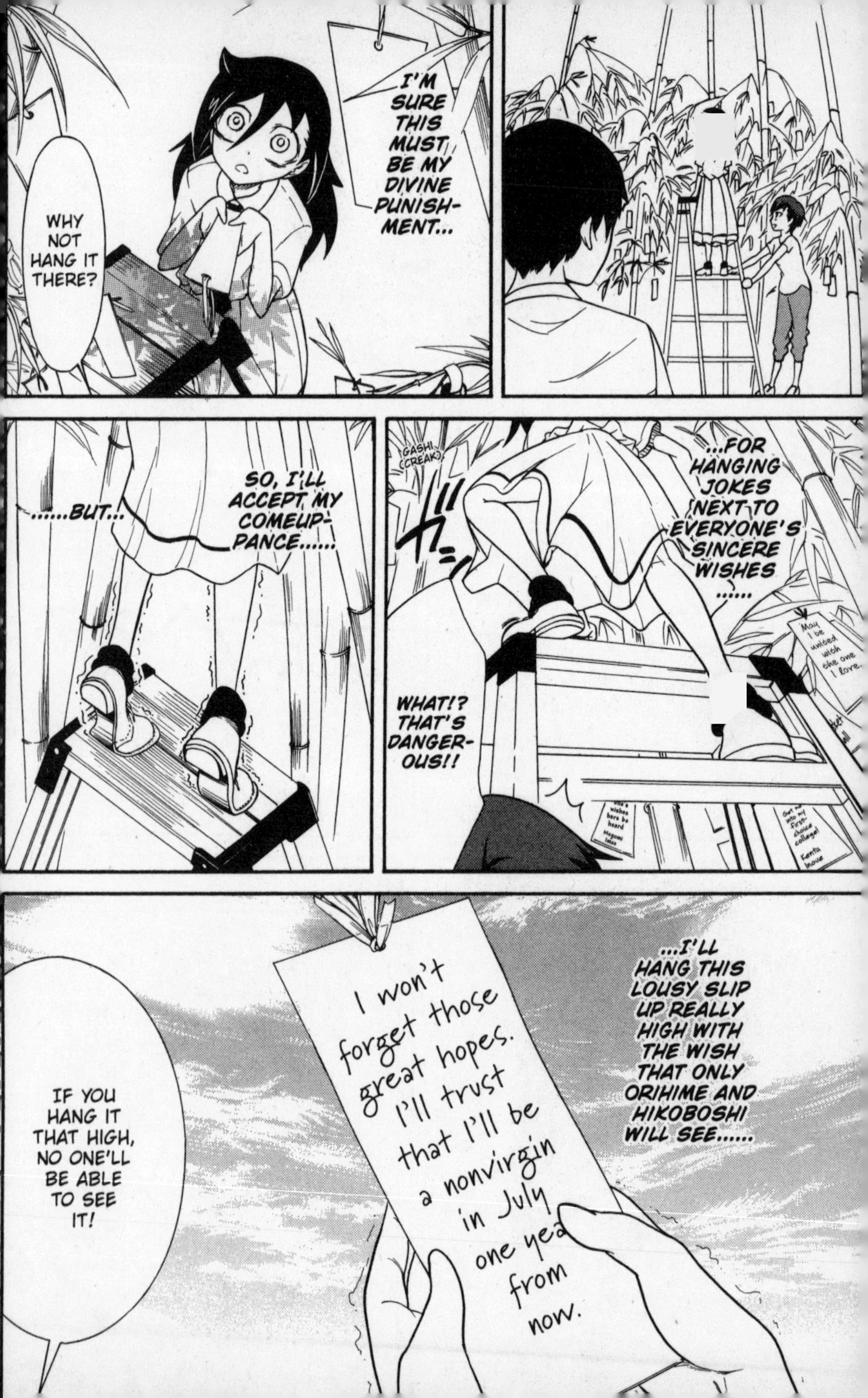
I'M SURE THIS MUST BE MY DIVINE PUNISHMENT...
WHY NOT HANG IT THERE?
...FOR HANGING JOKES NEXT TO EVERYONE'S SINCERE WISHES......
GASHI (CREAK)
May I be united with the one I love.
WHAT!? THAT'S DANGEROUS!!
SO, I'LL ACCEPT MY COMEUPPANCE......
......BUT...
...I'LL HANG THIS LOUSY SLIP UP REALLY HIGH WITH THE WISH THAT ONLY ORIHIME AND HIKOBOSHI WILL SEE......
I won't forget those great hopes. I'll trust that I'll be a nonvirgin in July one yea from now.
IF YOU HANG IT THAT HIGH, NO ONE'LL BE ABLE TO SEE IT!

No Matter How I Look at It, It's You Guys' Fault I'm Not Popular!

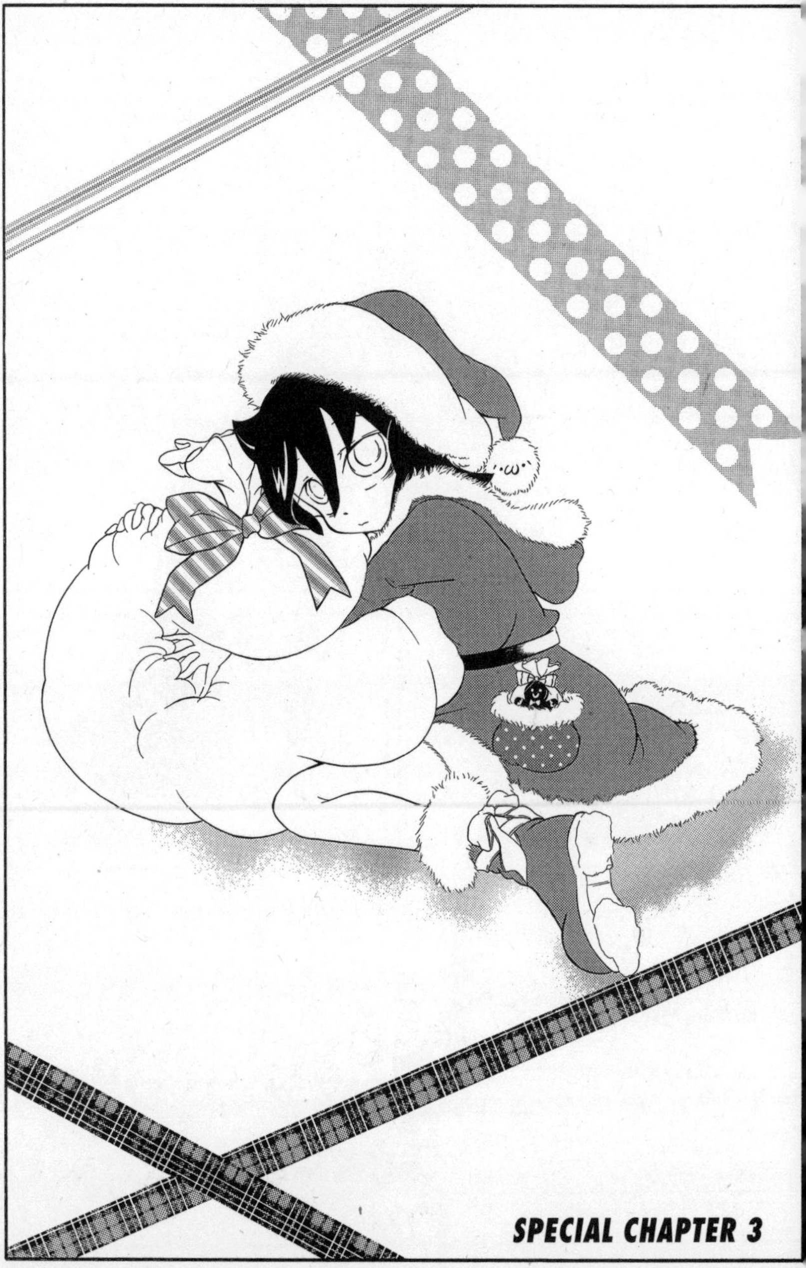

SPECIAL CHAPTER 3

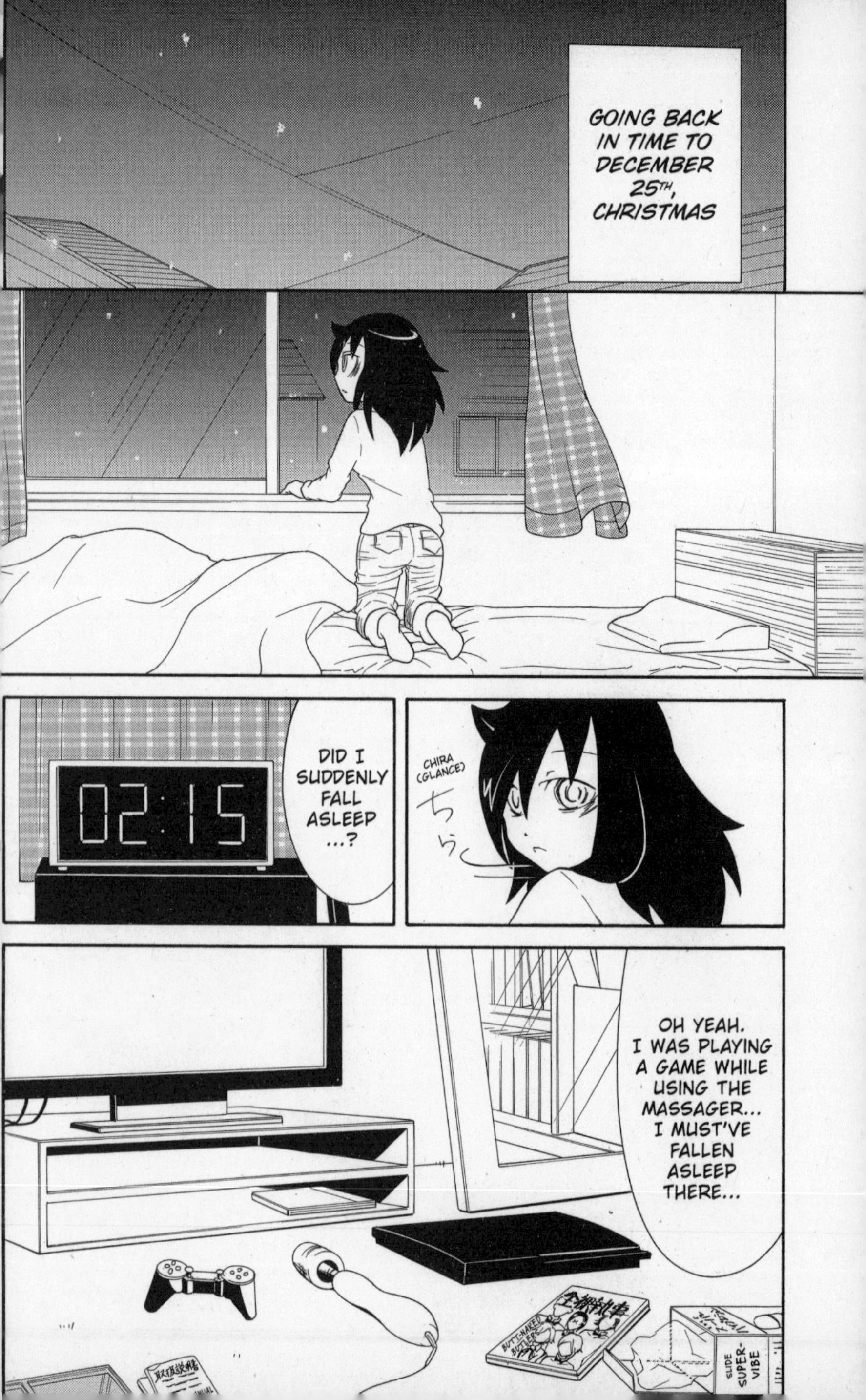
GOING BACK IN TIME TO DECEMBER 25TH, CHRISTMAS
CHIRA (GLANCE)
02:15
DID I SUDDENLY FALL ASLEEP ...?
OH YEAH. I WAS PLAYING A GAME WHILE USING THE MASSAGER... I MUST'VE FALLEN ASLEEP THERE...
SLIDE SUPER-VIBE
BUTT-NAKED BUTLERS

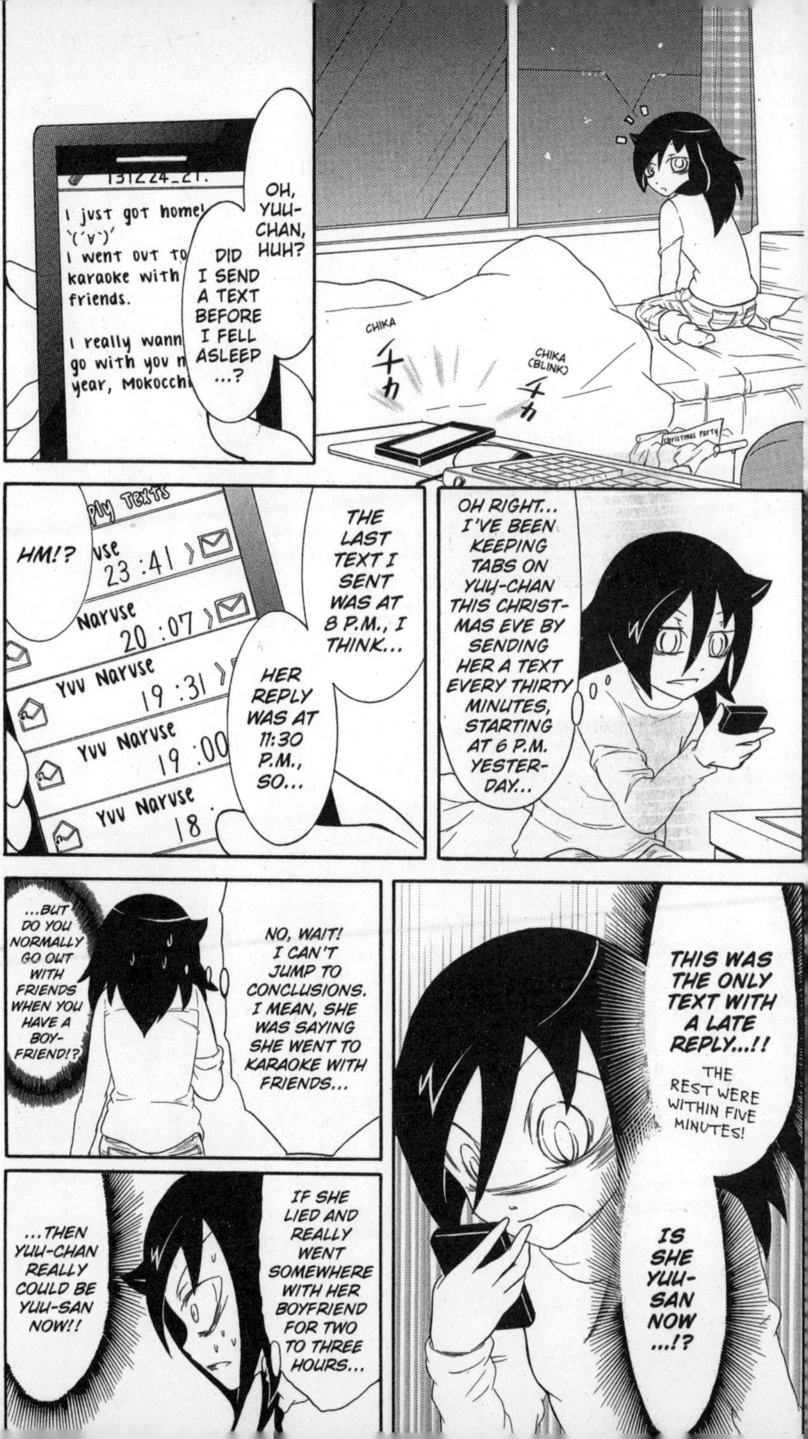

CHIKA
チカ
CHIKA (BLINK)
チカ
Christmas Party
131224_21.
I just got home! `(´∀`)´
I went out to karaoke with friends.
I really wann go with you n year, Mokocch
OH, YUU-CHAN, HUH?
DID I SEND A TEXT BEFORE I FELL ASLEEP ...?
OH RIGHT... I'VE BEEN KEEPING TABS ON YUU-CHAN THIS CHRISTMAS EVE BY SENDING HER A TEXT EVERY THIRTY MINUTES, STARTING AT 6 P.M. YESTERDAY...
THE LAST TEXT I SENT WAS AT 8 P.M., I THINK...
HER REPLY WAS AT 11:30 P.M., SO...
ply Texts
HM!?
use 23:41
Naruse 20:07
Yuu Naruse 19:31
Yuu Naruse 19:00
Yuu Naruse 18
THIS WAS THE ONLY TEXT WITH A LATE REPLY...!!
THE REST WERE WITHIN FIVE MINUTES!
IS SHE YUU-SAN NOW ...!?
NO, WAIT! I CAN'T JUMP TO CONCLUSIONS. I MEAN, SHE WAS SAYING SHE WENT TO KARAOKE WITH FRIENDS...
...BUT DO YOU NORMALLY GO OUT WITH FRIENDS WHEN YOU HAVE A BOY-FRIEND!?
IF SHE LIED AND REALLY WENT SOMEWHERE WITH HER BOYFRIEND FOR TWO TO THREE HOURS...
...THEN YUU-CHAN REALLY COULD BE YUU-SAN NOW!!

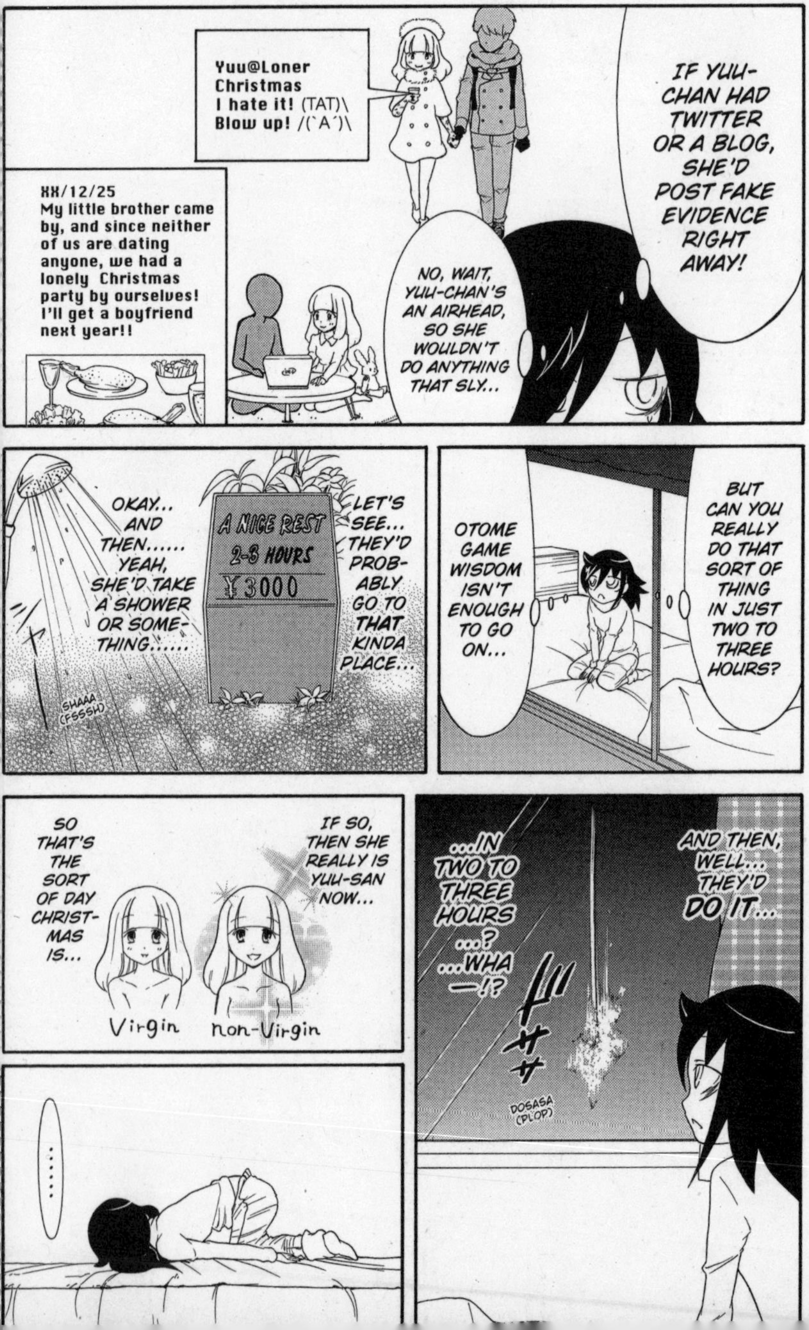
IF YUU-CHAN HAD TWITTER OR A BLOG, SHE'D POST FAKE EVIDENCE RIGHT AWAY!
Yuu@Loner
Christmas
I hate it! (TAT)\
Blow up! /(`A´)\
XX/12/25
My little brother came by, and since neither of us are dating anyone, we had a lonely Christmas party by ourselves! I'll get a boyfriend next year!!
NO, WAIT, YUU-CHAN'S AN AIRHEAD, SO SHE WOULDN'T DO ANYTHING THAT SLY...
BUT CAN YOU REALLY DO THAT SORT OF THING IN JUST TWO TO THREE HOURS?
OTOME GAME WISDOM ISN'T ENOUGH TO GO ON...
LET'S SEE... THEY'D PROBABLY GO TO THAT KINDA PLACE...
A NICE REST
2-3 HOURS
¥3000
OKAY... AND THEN...... YEAH, SHE'D TAKE A SHOWER OR SOMETHING......
SHAAA (FSSSH)
AND THEN, WELL... THEY'D DO IT...
...IN TWO TO THREE HOURS ...? ...WHA—!?
DOSASA (PLOP)
IF SO, THEN SHE REALLY IS YUU-SAN NOW...
SO THAT'S THE SORT OF DAY CHRISTMAS IS...
Virgin
non-Virgin
......

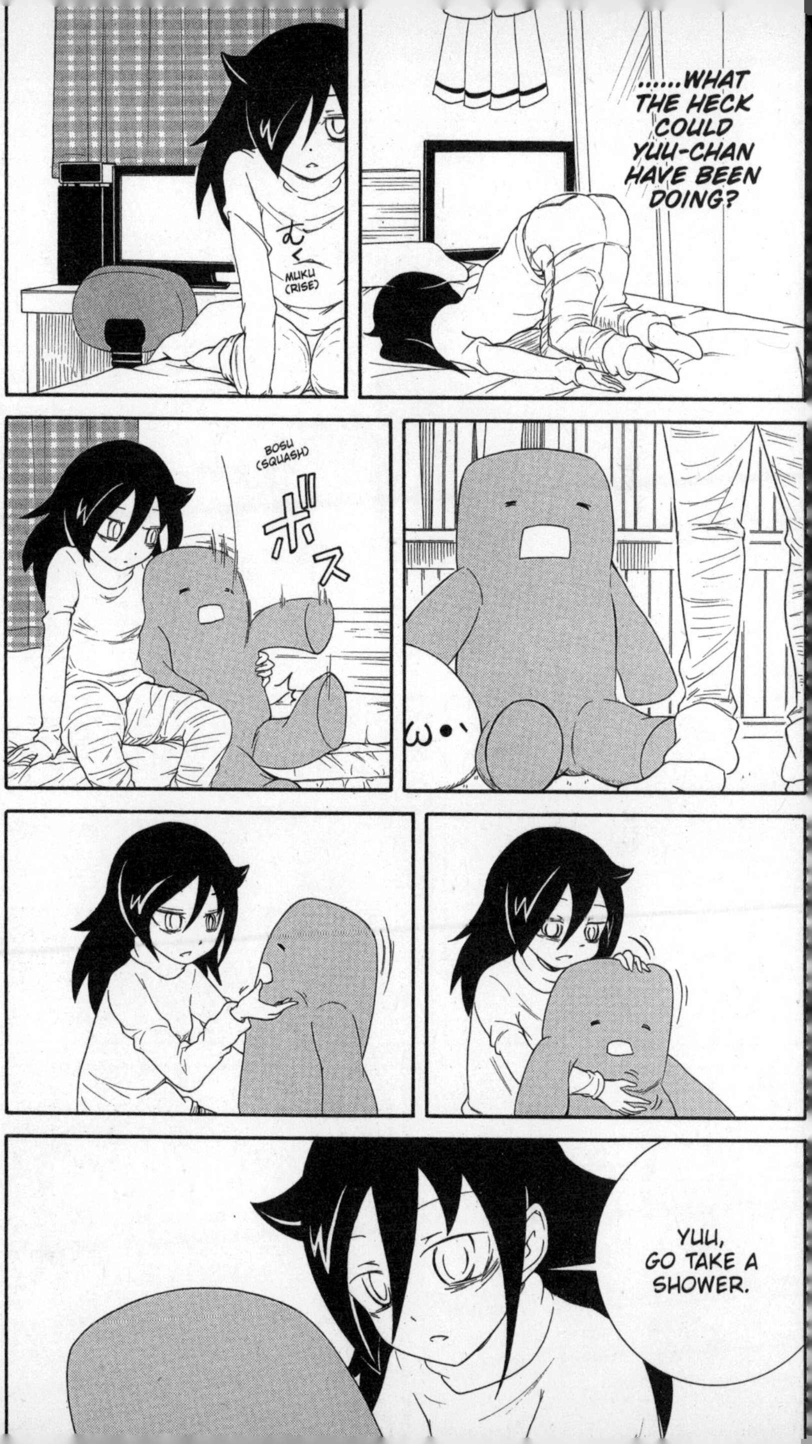
......WHAT THE HECK COULD YUU-CHAN HAVE BEEN DOING?
むく
MUKU (RISE)
ボス
BOSU (SQUASH)
YUU, GO TAKE A SHOWER.

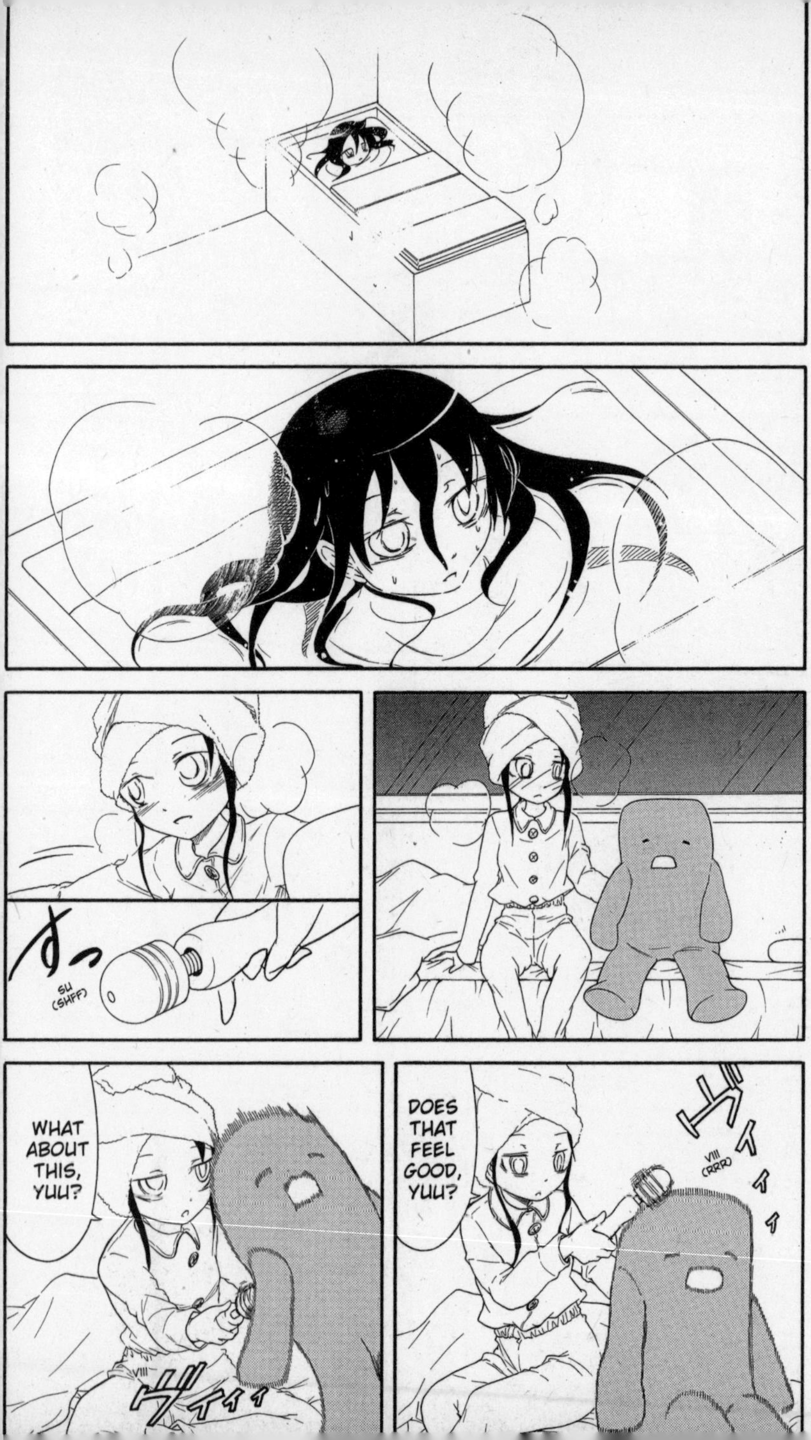
すっ
SU (SHFF)
DOES THAT FEEL GOOD, YUU?
ヴィィィ
VIII (RRR)
WHAT ABOUT THIS, YUU?
ヴィィィ
VIII

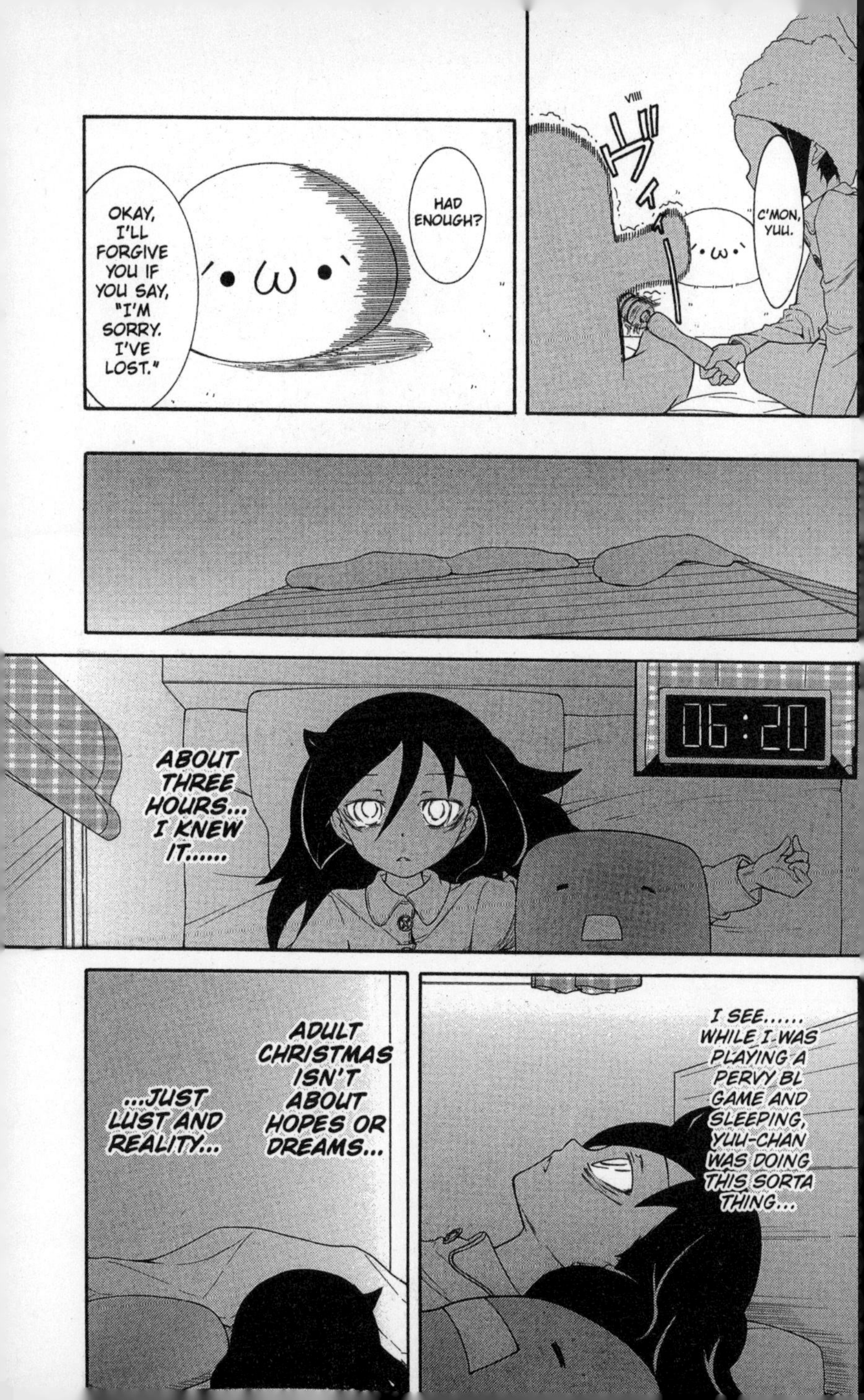
VIIII
C'MON, YUU.
HAD ENOUGH?
OKAY, I'LL FORGIVE YOU IF YOU SAY, "I'M SORRY. I'VE LOST."
ABOUT THREE HOURS... I KNEW IT......
I SEE...... WHILE I WAS PLAYING A PERVY BL GAME AND SLEEPING, YUU-CHAN WAS DOING THIS SORTA THING...
ADULT CHRISTMAS ISN'T ABOUT HOPES OR DREAMS...
...JUST LUST AND REALITY...

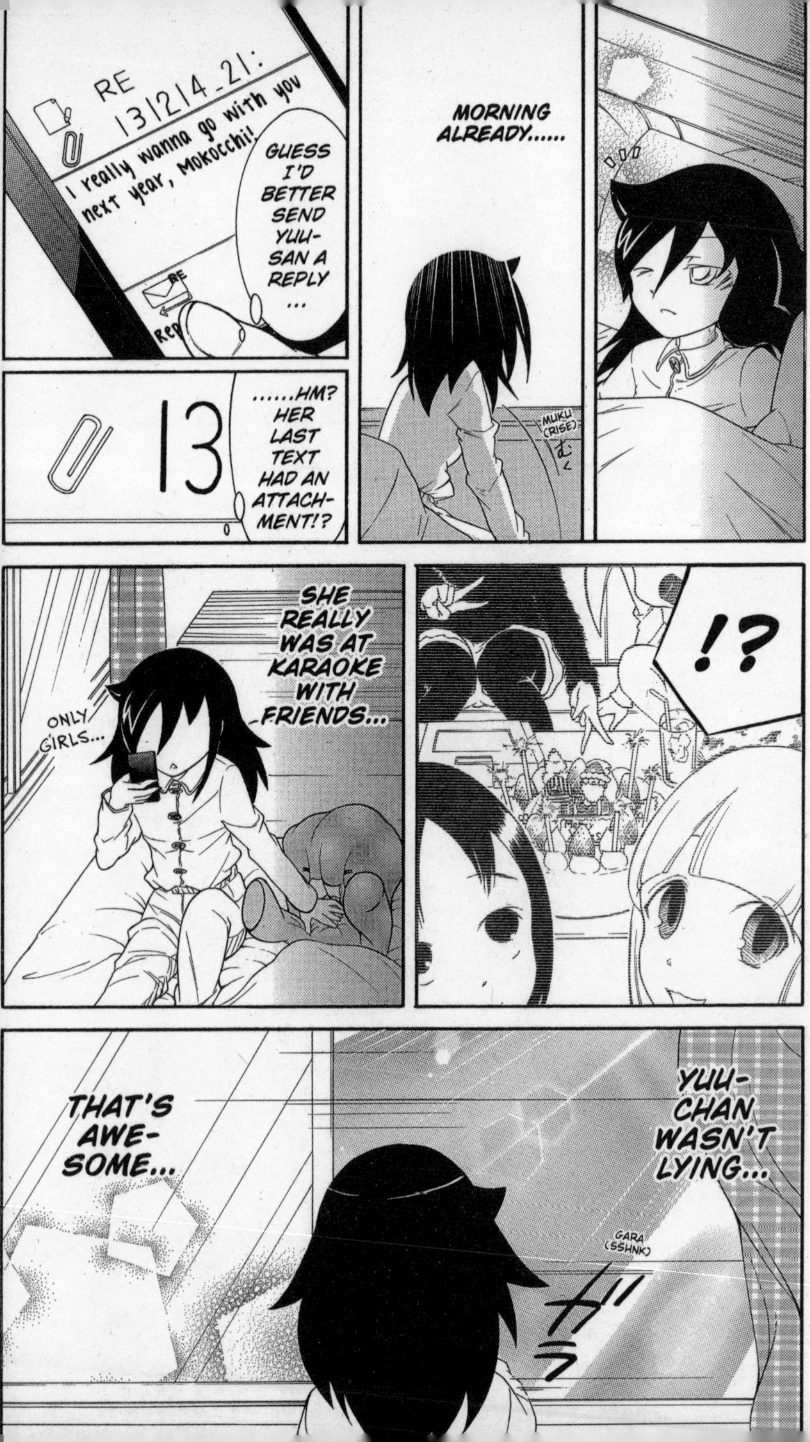

MORNING ALREADY......
MUKU (RISE)
RE
13|2|4_21:
I really wanna go with you next year, Mokocchi!
GUESS I'D BETTER SEND YUU-SAN A REPLY...
13
......HM? HER LAST TEXT HAD AN ATTACHMENT!?
!?
SHE REALLY WAS AT KARAOKE WITH FRIENDS...
ONLY GIRLS...
YUU-CHAN WASN'T LYING...
THAT'S AWE-SOME...
GARA (SSHNK)

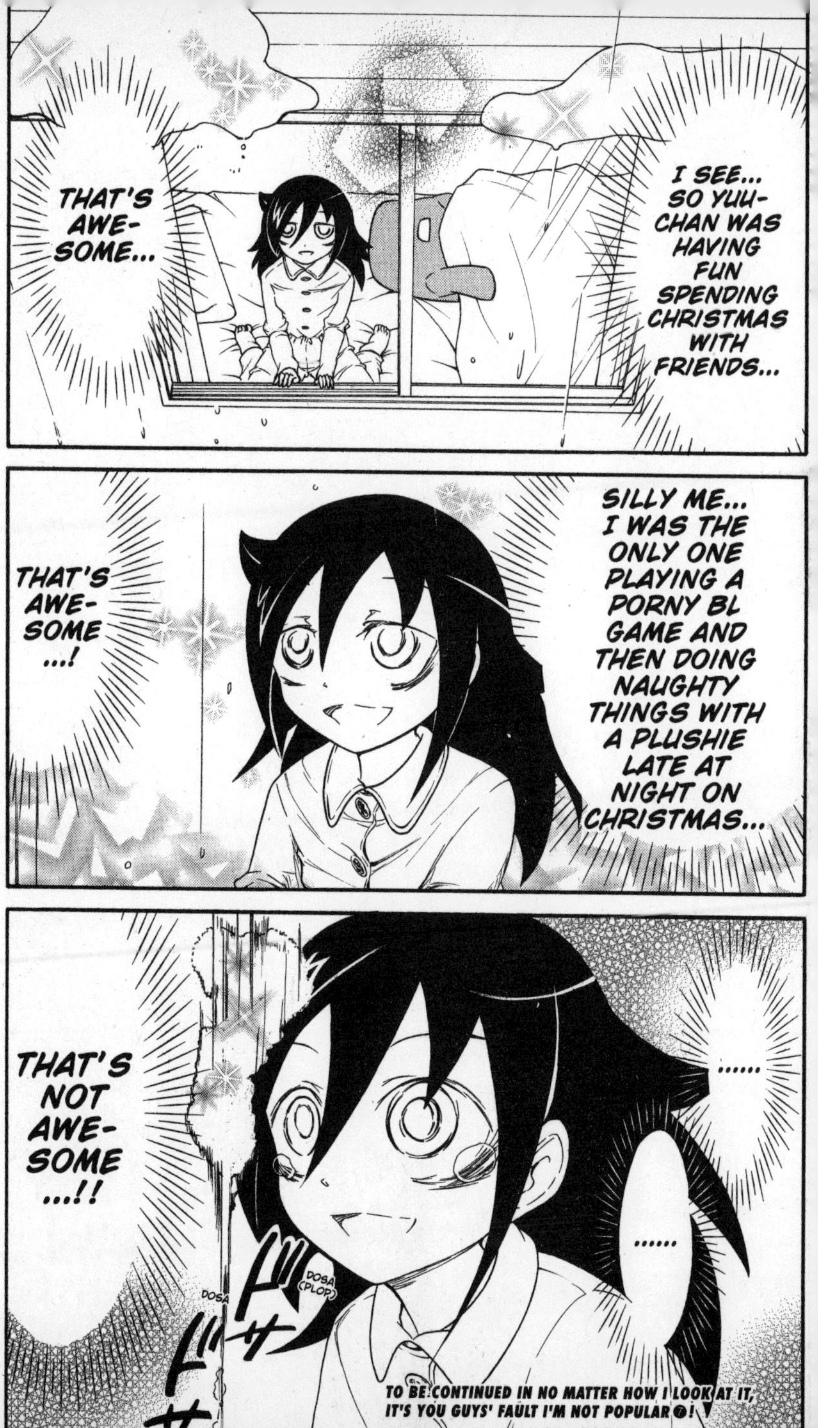
I SEE... SO YUU-CHAN WAS HAVING FUN SPENDING CHRISTMAS WITH FRIENDS...
THAT'S AWE-SOME...
SILLY ME... I WAS THE ONLY ONE PLAYING A PORNY BL GAME AND THEN DOING NAUGHTY THINGS WITH A PLUSHIE LATE AT NIGHT ON CHRISTMAS...
THAT'S AWE-SOME ...!
......
......
DOSA (PLOP)
DOSA
THAT'S NOT AWE-SOME ...!!
TO BE CONTINUED IN NO MATTER HOW I LOOK AT IT, IT'S YOU GUYS' FAULT I'M NOT POPULAR 7!

No Matter How I Look at It, It's You Guys' Fault I'm Not Popular!

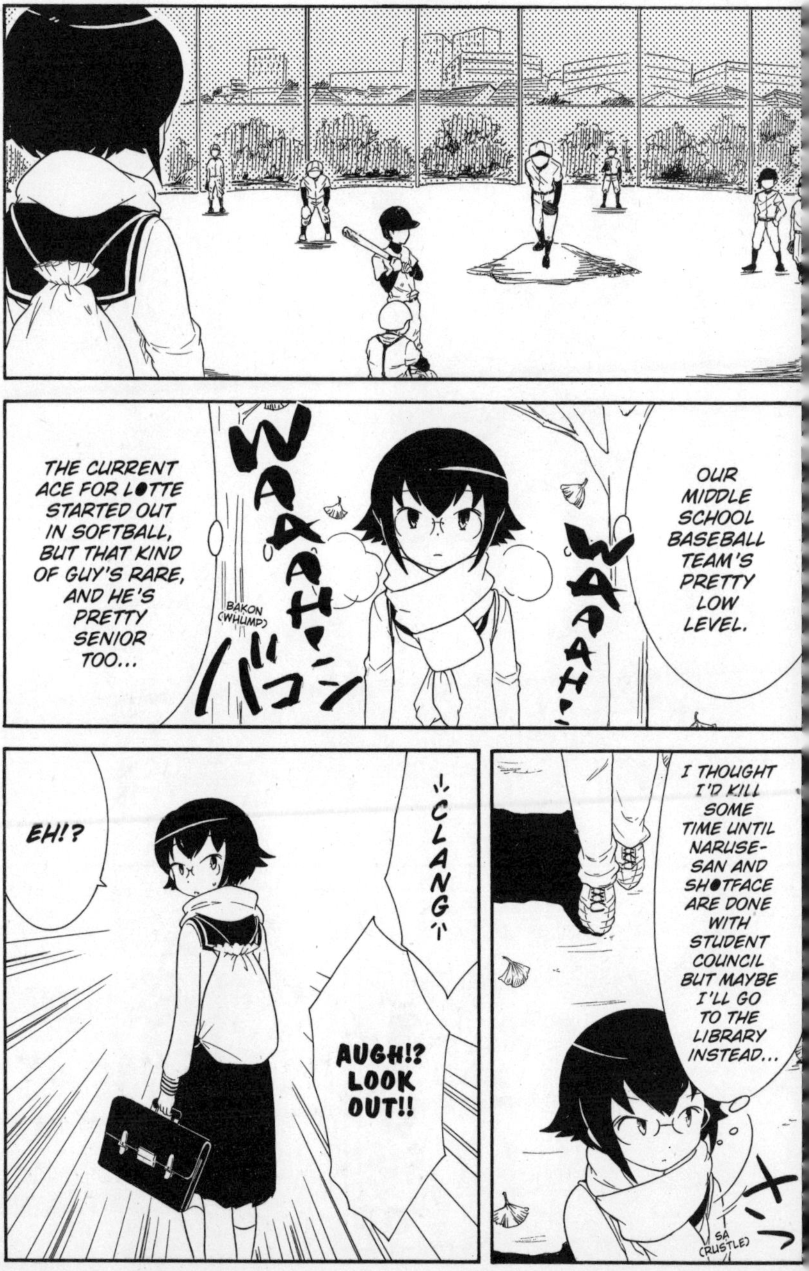
OUR MIDDLE SCHOOL BASEBALL TEAM'S PRETTY LOW LEVEL.
WAAAH!
WAAAH!
BAKON (WHUMP)
THE CURRENT ACE FOR LOTTE STARTED OUT IN SOFTBALL, BUT THAT KIND OF GUY'S RARE, AND HE'S PRETTY SENIOR TOO...
I THOUGHT I'D KILL SOME TIME UNTIL NARUSE-SAN AND SHOTFACE ARE DONE WITH STUDENT COUNCIL BUT MAYBE I'LL GO TO THE LIBRARY INSTEAD...
SA (RUSTLE)
CLANG
AUGH!? LOOK OUT!!
EH!?

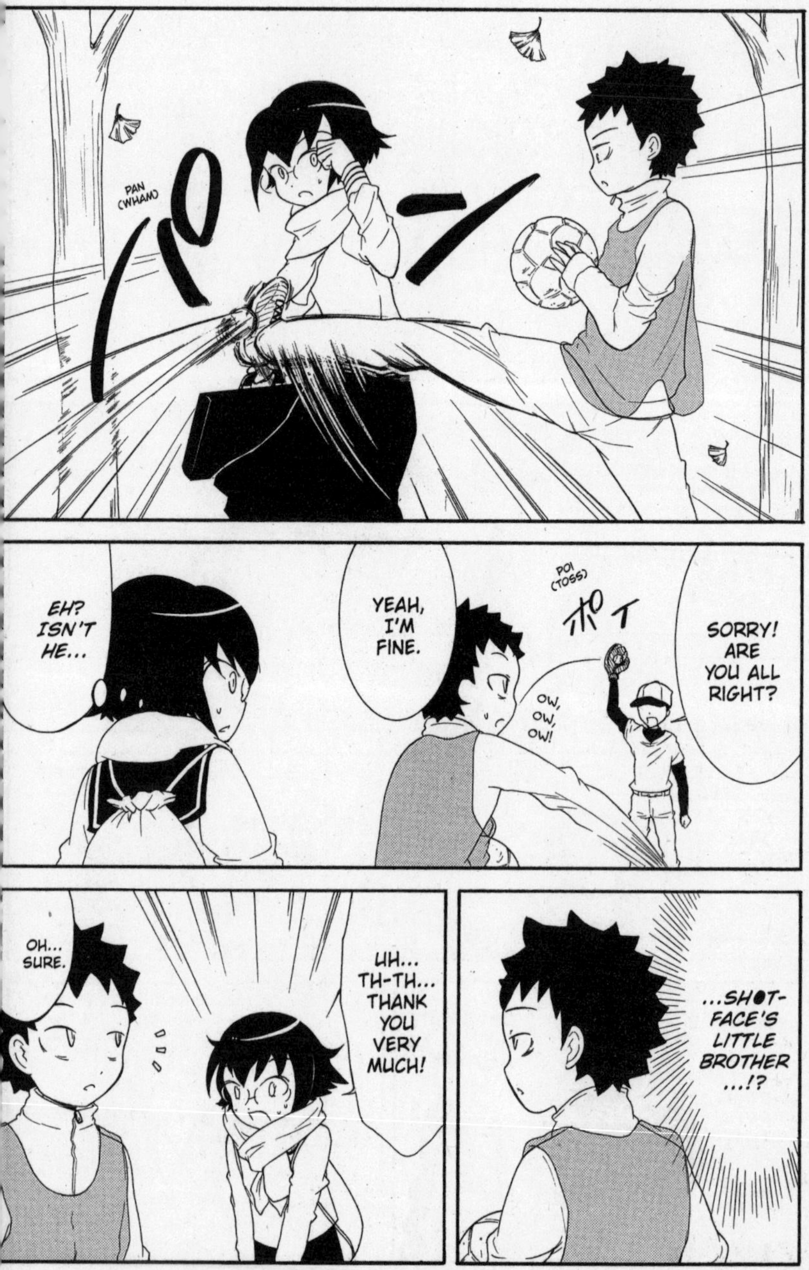
パーン
PAN (WHAM)
SORRY! ARE YOU ALL RIGHT?
ポイ
POI (TOSS)
OW, OW, OW!
YEAH, I'M FINE.
EH? ISN'T HE...
...SHOT-FACE'S LITTLE BROTHER ...!?
UH... TH-TH... THANK YOU VERY MUCH!
OH... SURE.

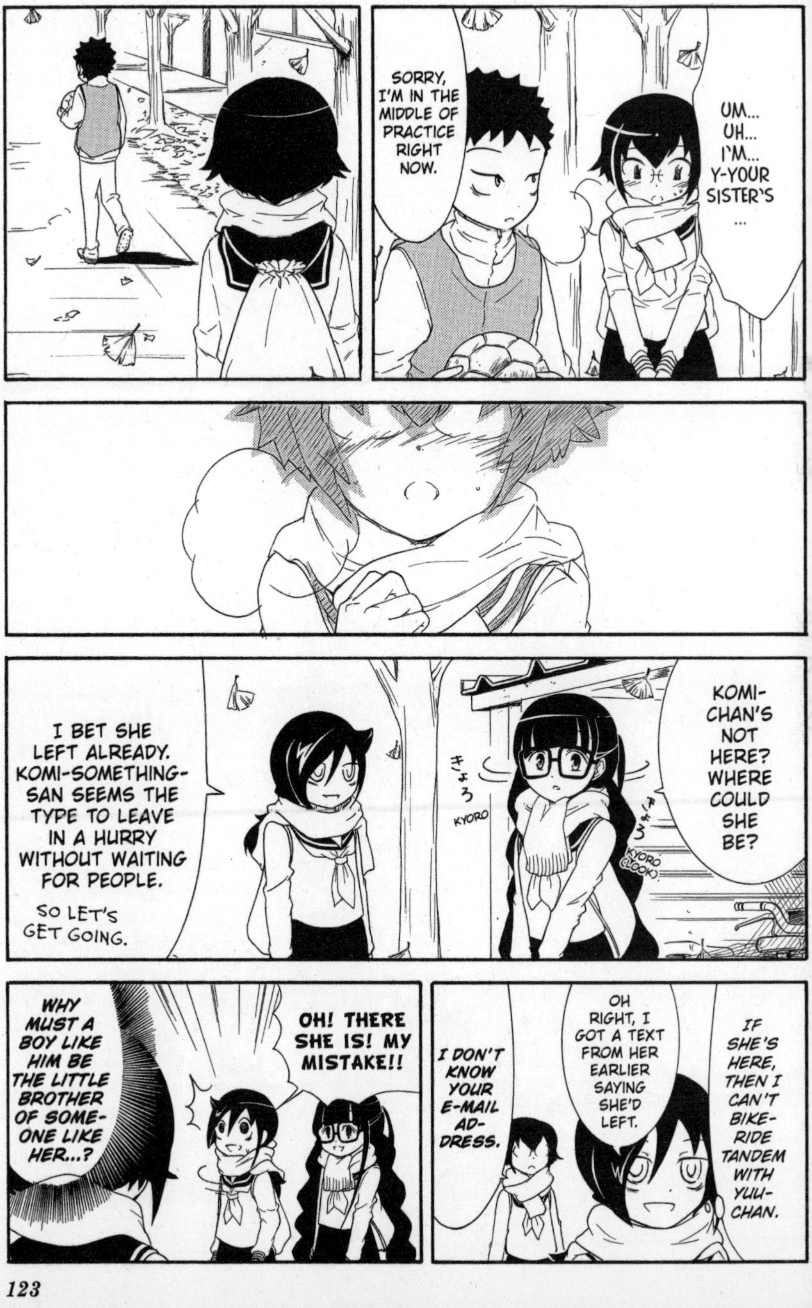
UM... UH... I'M... Y-YOUR SISTER'S ...
SORRY, I'M IN THE MIDDLE OF PRACTICE RIGHT NOW.
KOMI-CHAN'S NOT HERE? WHERE COULD SHE BE?
きょろ
KYORO (LOOK)
きょろ
KYORO
I BET SHE LEFT ALREADY. KOMI-SOMETHING-SAN SEEMS THE TYPE TO LEAVE IN A HURRY WITHOUT WAITING FOR PEOPLE.
SO LET'S GET GOING.
IF SHE'S HERE, THEN I CAN'T BIKE-RIDE TANDEM WITH YUU-CHAN.
OH RIGHT, I GOT A TEXT FROM HER EARLIER SAYING SHE'D LEFT.
I DON'T KNOW YOUR E-MAIL AD-DRESS.
OH! THERE SHE IS! MY MISTAKE!!
WHY MUST A BOY LIKE HIM BE THE LITTLE BROTHER OF SOME-ONE LIKE HER...?

No Matter How I Look at It, It's You Guys' Fault I'm Not Popular!

NEW ILLUSTRATION FOR THE
OVERSEAS EDITION OF VOLUME 1

AFTERWORD

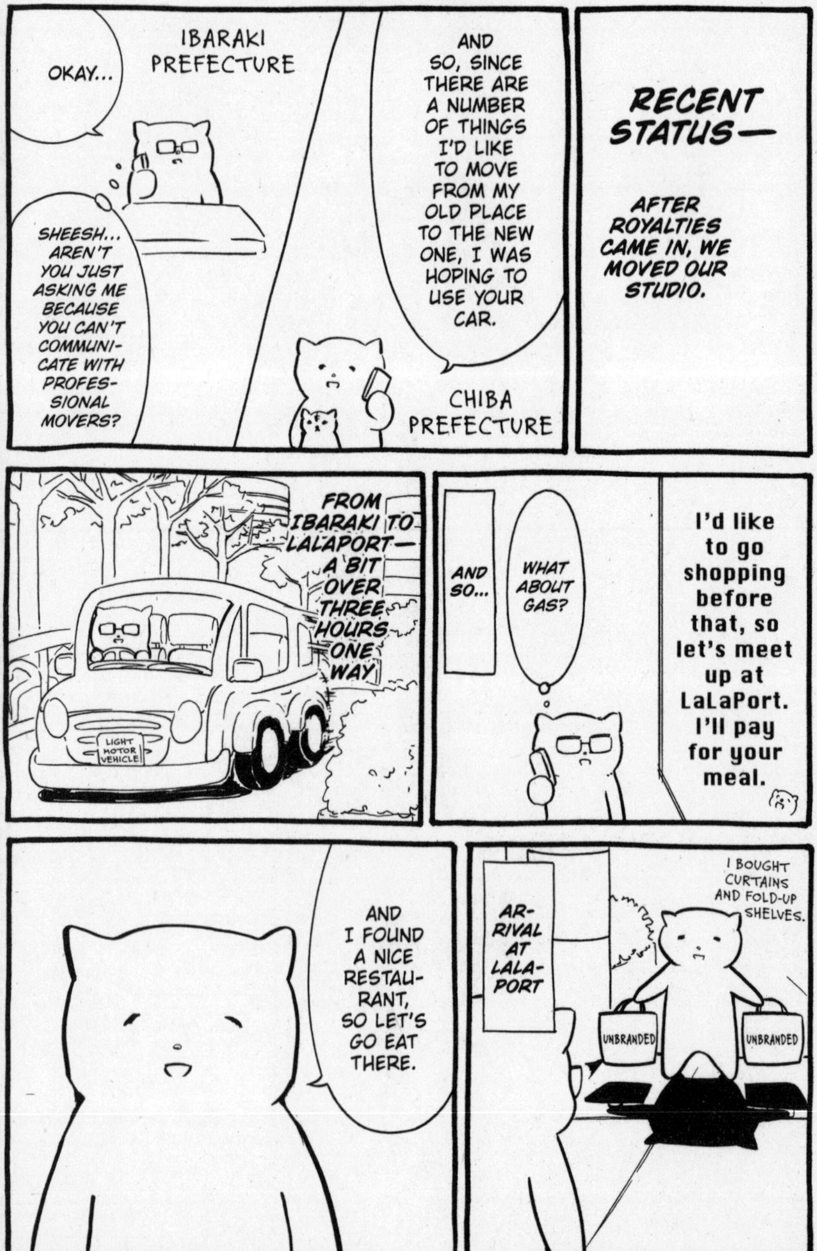
RECENT STATUS—
AFTER ROYALTIES CAME IN, WE MOVED OUR STUDIO.
AND SO, SINCE THERE ARE A NUMBER OF THINGS I'D LIKE TO MOVE FROM MY OLD PLACE TO THE NEW ONE, I WAS HOPING TO USE YOUR CAR.
CHIBA PREFECTURE
IBARAKI PREFECTURE
OKAY...
SHEESH... AREN'T YOU JUST ASKING ME BECAUSE YOU CAN'T COMMUNICATE WITH PROFESSIONAL MOVERS?
I'd like to go shopping before that, so let's meet up at LaLaPort. I'll pay for your meal.
WHAT ABOUT GAS?
AND SO...
FROM IBARAKI TO LALAPORT— A BIT OVER THREE HOURS ONE WAY
LIGHT MOTOR VEHICLE
I BOUGHT CURTAINS AND FOLD-UP SHELVES.
ARRIVAL AT LALAPORT
UNBRANDED
UNBRANDED
AND I FOUND A NICE RESTAURANT, SO LET'S GO EAT THERE.

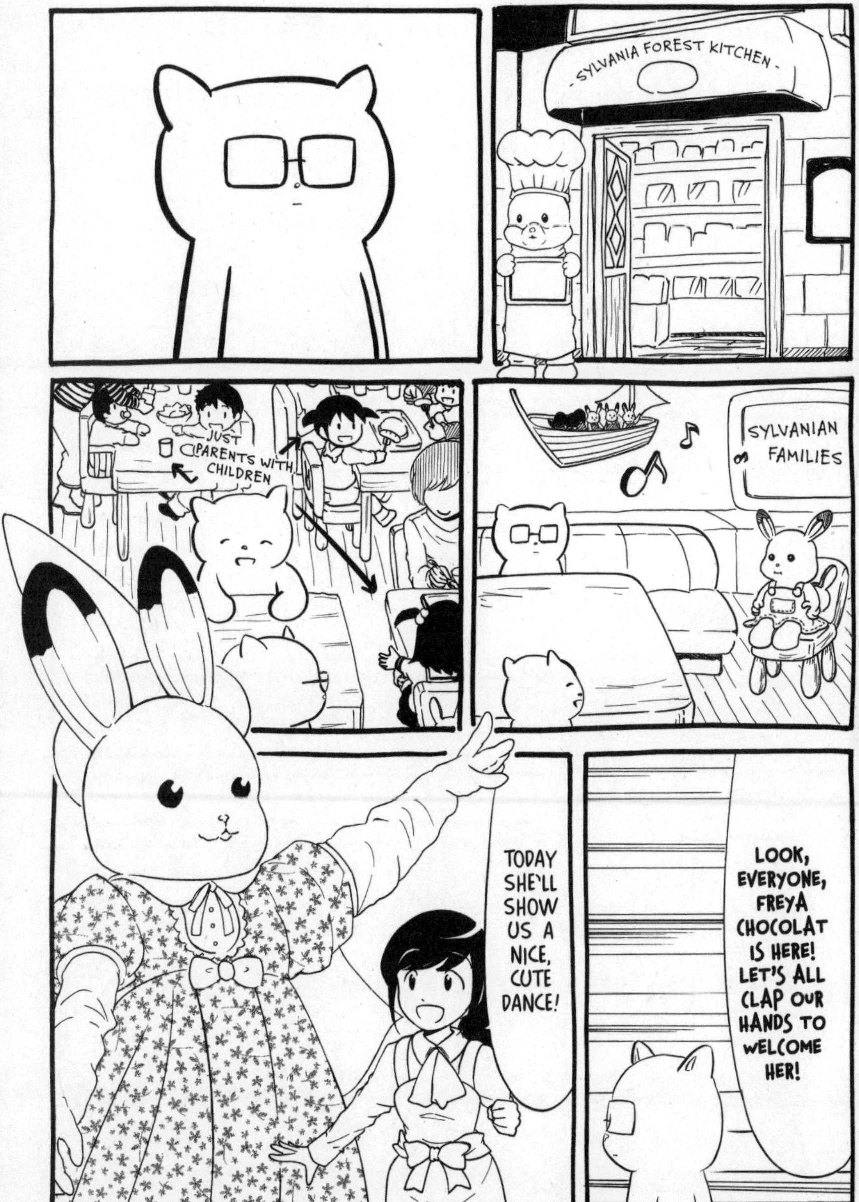
- SYLVANIA FOREST KITCHEN -
SYLVANIAN FAMILIES
JUST PARENTS WITH CHILDREN
LOOK, EVERYONE, FREYA CHOCOLAT IS HERE! LET'S ALL CLAP OUR HANDS TO WELCOME HER!
TODAY SHE'LL SHOW US A NICE, CUTE DANCE!

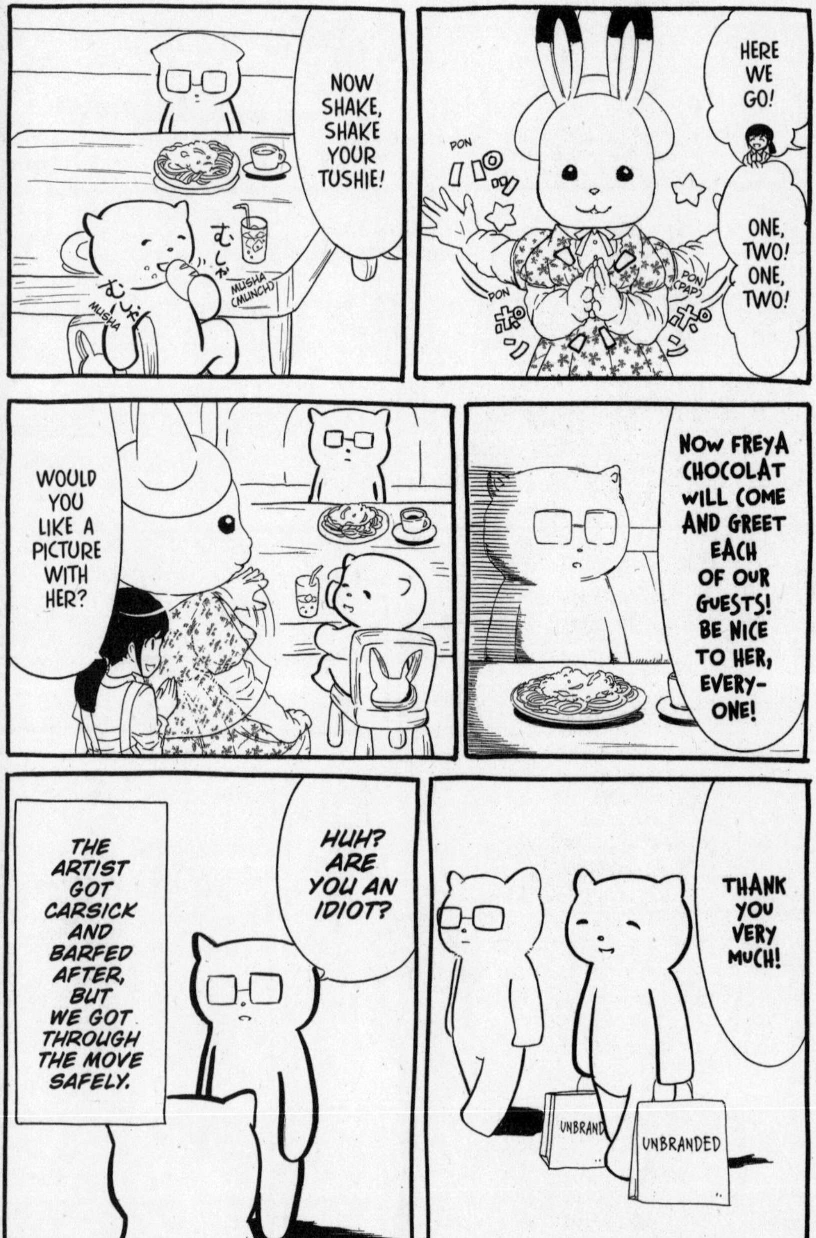
HERE WE GO!
PON
ポン
PON (PAP)
ポン
ONE, TWO! ONE, TWO!
NOW SHAKE, SHAKE YOUR TUSHIE!
むしゃ
MUSHA (MUNCH)
むしゃ
MUSHA
NOW FREYA CHOCOLAT WILL COME AND GREET EACH OF OUR GUESTS! BE NICE TO HER, EVERY-ONE!
WOULD YOU LIKE A PICTURE WITH HER?
THANK YOU VERY MUCH!
UNBRANDED
UNBRANDED
HUH? ARE YOU AN IDIOT?
THE ARTIST GOT CARSICK AND BARFED AFTER, BUT WE GOT THROUGH THE MOVE SAFELY.

PAGE 5
Here, Komi wants to give Tomoki **chocolate** (*chokoreeto*) for Valentine's Day per modern Japanese tradition. But Tomoko mishears her stuttered "*ch...ko*" as *chinko* (slang for "penis").

PAGE 9
The book Tomoko wants to check out is volume 7.5 of the light novel series *My Teen Romantic Comedy SNAFU* (*Yahari Ore no Seishun Rabu Kome wa Machigatteiru*) by Wataru Watari.

PAGE 13
"**...actually saying it...means war!**" is a reference to the manga and anime series *Kaiji* and is from a scene where the title character's supervisor at the convenience store suspects him of stealing money.

PAGE 18
Komi tossing the box is a reference to the light novel series *Ro-Kyu-Bu!* about a grade school girls' basketball club. The series has been adapted into manga, anime, and visual novels.

PAGE 21
The book Komi is reading, *Vura*, is a parody title of the 2008 romantic comedy light novel *Aura* by Romeo Tanaka, author of the series *Humanity Has Declined* and various adult novel games.

PAGE 21
The library rep recommendations shelf includes *Danganronpa/Zero*, the first (but not only) light novel spin-off of the *Danganronpa* series of school survival video games.

PAGE 21
Tomoko is claiming to have developed an interest in **literary fiction**. The titles and authors mentioned are plays on a number of respected modern Japanese novels and their creators. *Jichi, You Idiot* by Dango Sakaguchi is a reference to *Hakuchi, The Idiot* by Ango Sakaguchi. Fuyuki Murakami is a play on famed Japanese novelist Haruki Murakami, and the novels mentioned are nods to his actual works — *Norwegian Grove* is a play on *Norwegian Wood*; *Kafkat on the Windowsill* is a reference to *Kafka on the Shore*; *1Q42* is *1Q84*; *The Wind-Up Beach Chronicle* is a reference to *The Wind-Up Bird Chronicle*.

PAGE 24
"**Mortified, mortified!**" is a reference to the semi-autobiographical manga series *Barefoot Gen*, famous for depicting life in Hiroshima before and after the atomic bomb. The line "*Kuyashii nou, kuyashii nou*" uses Hiroshima dialect and is from when Gen is frustrated about his family and friends being mistreated but feels powerless to do anything about it.

PAGE 28
The **funny cat picture** Tomoko is looking at is Human Face Cat.

PAGE 29
Niigata is a prefecture on the main island of Japan, northwest of Tokyo and bordering the Sea of Japan.

PAGE 29
The image of **Tomoko buried in snow** is a reference to the anime film *Dog of Flanders*.

PAGE 30
The **statues** are, in order, the Peace Statue in Nagasaki's Peace Park that was placed at ground zero of the atomic bomb blast; a statue of William S. Clark in Sapporo, an American famous in Japan for establishing Sapporo Agricultural College in the late 1870s and for his parting words, "Boys, be ambitious!"; the Great Buddha (Daibutsu) statue at Toudai-ji temple in Nara, the world's largest bronze Daibutsu statue.

PAGE 29-31
Kumamoto, Nagasaki, Fukuoka are three prefectures on Japan's large southwestern island of Kyushu.

PAGE 32
Y●●zan Kaibara is a reference to Yuuzan Kaibara, the smug father and antagonist from the gourmet manga series *Oishinbo*.

PAGE 32
The **Kyoto video** Tomoko was watching bears a resemblance to a collection of commercials from the Japan Rail Tokai line campaign "Sou da Kyoto, Ikou." These commercials have been running since 1993, always with a different arrangement of the tune "My Favorite Things" playing in the background.

PAGE 33
Kinkakuji is a Zen Buddhist temple covered in gold leaf, one of the most famous tourist sites in Kyoto.

PAGE 38
Shuuz●u Matsuoka is a retired Japanese male tennis player, currently working as a sports commentator and general TV personality, popular for his energy and enthusiasm. He hosts a yearly tennis camp for children called the "Shuuzou Challenge," which is most likely what Tomoko's thinking of in comparing her teacher to him.

PAGE 41
Kii's Journey is a nod to the light novel series *Kino's Journey* (*Kino no Tabi*) by Keiichi Sigsawa about a young protagonist traveling through various lands with a talking motorcycle.

PAGE 55
Yuri is a genre of Japanese literature, manga, and anime that features romantic relationships between women. The audience can be either male, female, or both depending on the work, and the relationships can range from chaste to very sexual.

TRANSLATION NOTES 2

PAGE 56
In Japanese, **"gunning for me gung ho!"** is *"gangan zuizui guigui,"* which loosely quotes the "Mellow Rap," done by Japanese female snowboard half-pipe representative Melo Imai before leaving for the Winter Olympics in Torino.

PAGE 61
Vocabo is short for Vocarobo, a reference to the Vocaloid line of software for creating songs with synthesized voices.

PAGE 61
The *koe dame* in the name **Koedame-P** means "crappy voice."

PAGE 61
Nigonigo is a reference to the Japanese video streaming site Niconico Douga.

PAGE 61
"Got arrested for hitting on a high school girl" is a reference to Vocaloid producer/composer Panyo's arrest in late December 2013.

PAGE 62
This **scene**, including Tomoko getting barley tea out of the fridge, mimics a scene in episode 6 of the anime series *OreImo* (*My Little Sister Can't Be This Cute*).

PAGE 62
The picture on **VOCAROBO2 Simobukure** is of the most well-known Vocaloid character, Miku Hatsune. *S(h)imobukure* means "fat face."

PAGE 62
Piyapro Studio is a play on Piapro Studio, the actual digital audio workstation software that comes with VOCALOID3 software Hatsune Miku V3.

PAGE 63, 66
Tomoko's "song" in Japanese is on the pattern "o()i," plus a few more syllables: *o-chinchin* ("penis"), *o-Inari-san* (fox deity of the rice harvest), *omisoshiru* ("miso soup"), Ochiai Fukushi (random celebrity whose name fit the pattern).

PAGE 64
Yasushi Akim●to is the creator and producer of current top idol groups, including the AKB48 franchise.

PAGE 64
Sam●ragouchi is Mamoru Samuragouchi, a composer of video game soundtracks, who was considered the digital-age Beethoven for being prolific in spite of deafness. The scandal of him employing another composer to do the writing, as well as not actually being deaf, broke in February 2014.

PAGE 73
Gat●tsu is a reference to Gatotsu, a sword technique used by Hajime Saitou in the samurai manga and anime series *Rurouni Kenshin* by Nobuhiro Watsuki.

PAGE 73
Nagar●boshi is a reference to Nagareboshi ("shooting star"), a sword technique used by Grandmaster Iwamoto in the samurai manga and anime series *Shigurui: Death Frenzy*, written by Takayuki Yamaguchi and based on a novel by Norio Nanjo.

PAGE 74
Zeroshiki is an ironic reference to the most powerful of the Gatotsu sword techniques in Nobuhiro Watsuki's manga series *Rurouni Kenshin*.

PAGE 75
Kaikai Club, Soizeria, Uma Uma all refer to nationwide chains in Japan: Kaikatsu Club is a chain of comics/Internet cafés; Saizeriya is an Italian restaurant chain; Doma-Doma is a chain of *izakaya*, or bars that also serve a variety of light meals.

PAGE 76
Tomoko is reading volume five of **One-Punch Man**, written by One and illustrated by Yuusuke Murata.

PAGE 76
"Learn some shame, hedonists!" (*"haji o shire, zokubutsu ga"*) is a quote from Haman Karn, leader of the Axis Zeon faction in the anime series *Mobile Suit Gundam Zeta*.

PAGE 77
Tomoko is reading the January 2014 issue of Kodansha's shoujo **Monthly Comic ARIA** manga anthology, featuring *Attack on Titan*'s Levi on the cover and his own spin-off series *Attack on Titan: No Regrets*.

PAGE 89
Yuumoko Trick is a reference to the yuri anime and manga series *Sakura Trick*.

PAGE 92
Clubmega is a reference to the Club Sega chain of video arcades.

PAGE 93
30% potential is a reference to Younger Toguro in the manga and anime series *Yu Yu Hakusho*, who could fight at varying power percentages, with his physical appearance becoming more extreme the higher the percentage.

Page 94
Ninja Layer is a reference to *Ninja Slayer*, a novel that was published in pieces in Japanese on Twitter, allegedly as a "translation" of a work by two Americans (who appear to be nonexistent and just part of the backstory). The novel was subsequently given an official print release in 2012 and has spawned a manga series and an upcoming anime series.

PAGE 99

The Tanabata festival is a star festival celebrated on July 7 in Japan as the one day a year when the celestial weaver Orihime (star Vega) and the cowherd Hikoboshi (star Altair) can cross the Milky Way that separates them before returning to their hard and skillful work for the rest of the year. Part of the festival celebration is the tradition of writing wishes on colorful slips of paper and tying them to stalks of bamboo; befitting the origin story, the wishes are often related to the development of skills and success, as well as romance.

PAGE 101

After that, they have wild and crazy s●x is a reference to a Japanese image joke meme, using the same line as a caption.

PAGE 102

I'm gonna be King of the Pirates! is a quote by Monkey D. Luffy, the main character of the manga and anime series *One Piece*.

PAGE 102

In Japanese, **"I weally wanna girlfwend this year! (weenie voice)"** was a request for a girlfriend with the sentence ending in "-ngo." This is a meme joke that started in 2008 after Domingo Guzman, a relief pitcher for the Golden Eagles Japanese baseball team, was sent to the mound in the ninth inning with two outs, then lost the game due to a sayonara home run.

PAGE 105

The original Japanese for **lady lace** is a pun on the word *orimono*, which usually means "textile" but can also be slang for "vaginal discharge."

PAGE 108

"I'm sure this must be punishment" is a paraphrased quote from the anime series *Puella Magi Madoka Magica* as she's being imprisoned by a witch.

PAGE 108

Tomoko's slip is a parody of the song "secret base ~*kimi ga kureta mono~*" by the group ZONE that was the main opening song for the anime series *Anohana: The Flower We Saw That Day*. The original second line means, "I'll trust that I'll get to see you again in August ten years from now."

PAGE 114

Yuu's "tweet" is a reference to a copypasta meme from the Japanese message board 2channel.

PAGE 116

"I'm sorry. I've lost" ("*Gomen nasai. Makemashita.*") was uttered by Hirofumi Watanabe when he was arrested in December 2013 for a long campaign of sending threatening letters to people and events related to the manga and anime series *Kuroko's Basketball*.

PAGE 121

Komi is referring to the local baseball team, the **Chiba Lotte Marines**, based in the city of Chiba and owned by the candy maker and multinational conglomerate Lotte Co., Ltd. It's more common in Japan to refer to baseball teams by their sponsor company than by their home city (for example, the Yomiuri Giants instead of the Tokyo Giants).

PAGE 126

LaLaport is one of the largest shopping malls in Japan, located in Funabashi, Chiba Prefecture, near Tokyo proper.

PAGE 127

Sylvanian Families is a line of anthropomorphic animal figurines created by the Japanese company Epoch, which are known worldwide and have also spawned video games and animated series, as well as this family dining restaurant. Freya Chocolat is the English name for the character Chocolat Usagi-chan in one of the animated series. Currently, Sylvanian Families is available in the United States under the name Calico Critters.

UNICORN
(Latin: *unicornis*)
A legendary horse-like
creature with a single horn
growing from its forehead.

Likes virgins.

Hates sluts.

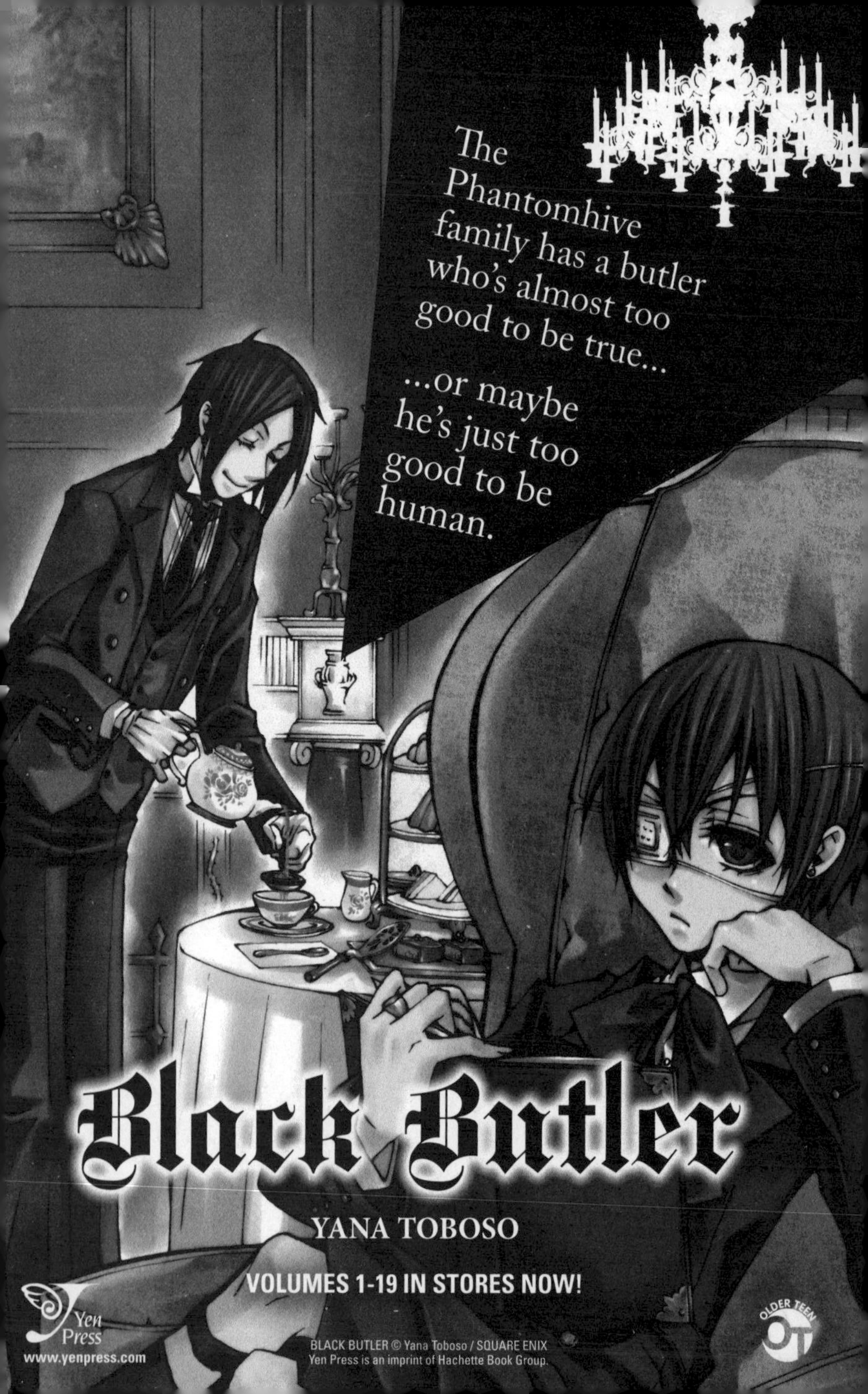
The Phantomhive family has a butler who's almost too good to be true...
...or maybe he's just too good to be human.
Black Butler
YANA TOBOSO
VOLUMES 1-19 IN STORES NOW!
Yen Press
www.yenpress.com
BLACK BUTLER © Yana Toboso / SQUARE ENIX
Yen Press is an imprint of Hachette Book Group.
OLDER TEEN
OT

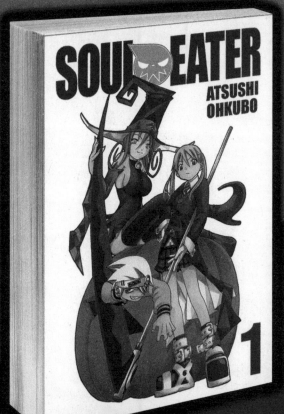

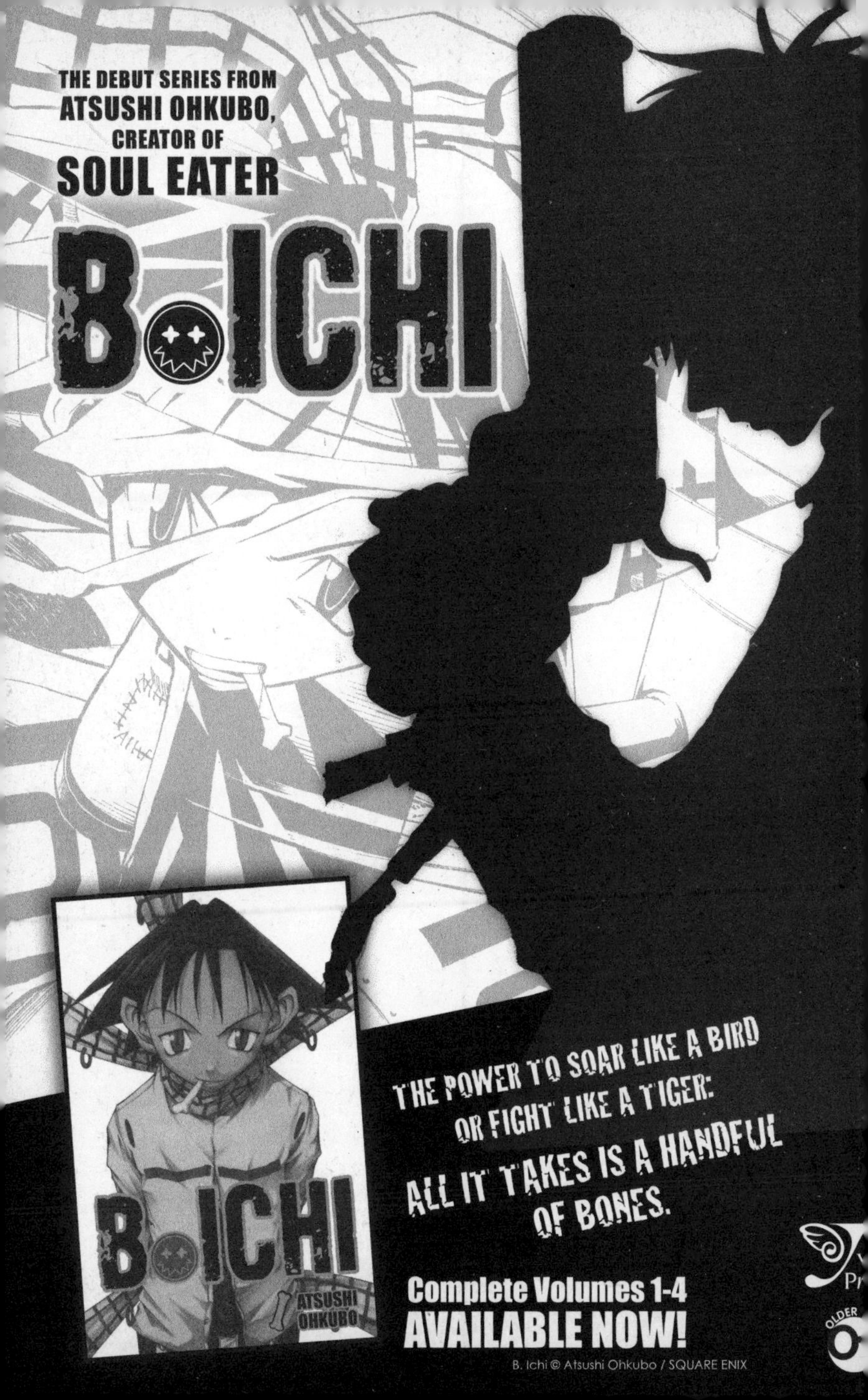
THE DEBUT SERIES FROM
ATSUSHI OHKUBO,
CREATOR OF
SOUL EATER
B. ICHI
THE POWER TO SOAR LIKE A BIRD
OR FIGHT LIKE A TIGER:
ALL IT TAKES IS A HANDFUL
OF BONES.
B. ICHI
ATSUSHI OHKUBO
Complete Volumes 1-4
AVAILABLE NOW!
B. Ichi © Atsushi Ohkubo / SQUARE ENIX

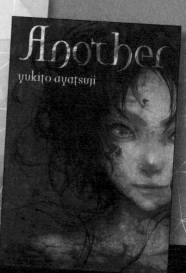

NO MATTER HOW I LOOK AT IT, IT'S YOU GUYS' FAULT I'M NOT POPULAR! ⑥

NICO TANIGAWA

Translation/Adaptation: Krista Shipley, Karie Shipley
Lettering: Lys Blakeslee

This book is a work of fiction. Names, characters, places, and incidents are the product of the author's imagination or are used fictitiously. Any resemblance to actual events, locales, or persons, living or dead, is coincidental.

WATASHI GA MOTENAI NOWA DOU KANGAETEMO OMAERA GA WARUI! Volume 6 © 2014 Nico Tanigawa / SQUARE ENIX CO., LTD. First published in Japan in 2014 by SQUARE ENIX CO., LTD. English translation rights arranged with SQUARE ENIX CO., LTD. and Hachette Book Group through Tuttle-Mori Agency, Inc.

Translation © 2015 by SQUARE ENIX CO., LTD.

Yen Press
Hachette Book Group
1290 Avenue of the Americas
New York, NY 10104

www.HachetteBookGroup.com
www.YenPress.com

Yen Press is an imprint of Hachette Book Group, Inc. The Yen Press name and logo are trademarks of Hachette Book Group, Inc.

First Yen Press Edition: January 2015

ISBN: 978-0-316-25941-5

10 9 8 7 6 5 4 3 2 1

BVG

Printed in the United States of America